THE DEFIANT

THE DEFIANT

PROTEST MOVEMENTS IN POST-LIBERAL AMERICA

DAWSON BARRETT

NEW YORK UNIVERSITY PRESS

New York

NEW YORK UNIVERSITY PRESS
New York
www.nyupress.org

An earlier draft of chapter 2 was previously published in *American Studies* 52, no. 2 (2013): 23–42, University of Kansas; reprinted by permission. An abbreviated version of chapter 3 appears in *Shopping for Change: Consumer Activism and the Possibilities of Purchasing Power*, ed. Joseph Tohill and Louis Hyman (Toronto: Between the Lines; Ithaca, NY: Cornell University Press / ILR Press, 2017), 221–229; reprinted by permission.

Library of Congress Cataloging-in-Publication Data
Names: Barrett, Dawson, author.
Title: The defiant : protest movements in post-liberal America / Dawson Barrett.
Description: New York : New York University Press, 2018. | Includes bibliographical references and index.
Identifiers: LCCN 2017044873 | ISBN 9781479808656 (cloth : alk. paper)
Subjects: LCSH: Protest movements—United States—History. | United States—Social conditions—1980- | Social justice—United States—History.
Classification: LCC HN59.2 .B36 2018 | DDC 303.48/40973—dc23
LC record available at https://lccn.loc.gov/2017044873

New York University Press books are printed on acid-free paper, and their binding materials are chosen for strength and durability. We strive to use environmentally responsible suppliers and materials to the greatest extent possible in publishing our books.
Manufactured in the United States of America
10 9 8 7 6 5 4 3 2 1
Also available as an ebook

For the people of *this* generation,

looking uncomfortably to the world they inherit

CONTENTS

PROLOGUE

WISCONSIN, 2011

Under neoliberalism everything either is for sale or is plundered
for profit. Public lands are looted by logging companies and
corporate ranchers; politicians willingly hand the public's
airwaves over to powerful broadcasters and large corporate
interests without a dime going into the public trust. . . . As markets
are touted as the driving force of everyday life, big government
is disparaged as either incompetent or threatening to individual
freedom, suggesting that power should reside in markets and
corporations rather than in governments (except for their support
for corporate interests and national security) and citizens.
—Henry Giroux, "The Terror of Neoliberalism"

Family farmers, like the labor movement, value economic
democracy. . . . For more than a hundred years, we have been
fighting together, we have been picketing together, we've been
dumping milk, we've been sitting in, [and] we've been blocking
traffic. And we're going to take this thing back. . . . It's a farmers'
issue because public workers are our friends, and our neighbors,
and our family members—and we stand in solidarity with them.
—Tony Schultz, Wisconsin farmer, March 12, 2011

FOR SEVERAL WEEKS IN FEBRUARY AND MARCH 2011, TENS
of thousands of people—more than one hundred thousand on
peak days—marched through the streets of Madison, Wisconsin,
to protest Act 10, the state's new "Budget Repair" bill. Governor
Scott Walker and a Republican-majority state legislature had been
swept into office during the 2010 midterm elections a few months
earlier, and Walker hoped to make a move that would catapult him

onto the national political scene. Despite the governor's threats to mobilize the National Guard, Wisconsin protesters—labor activists, teachers, students, farmers, taxi drivers, firefighters, and off-duty police officers, among others—maintained an around-the-clock occupation of the capitol building. Concerned Wisconsinites also offered an exhausting seventeen hours of official public testimony and blockaded the offices of state representatives with symbolic "sit-ins," to keep them from voting. On February 16, 40 percent of Madison's public school teachers called in sick, forcing the district to cancel classes. The next day, students at Milwaukee's Rufus King High School walked out of class and marched four miles to join college students in one of the several-dozen protests that popped up in cities and towns all over the state. Wisconsin's fourteen Democratic state senators then fled across the state line to Illinois in order to deny a quorum, while sympathetic demonstrations were held in every state in the country.[1]

The "Wisconsin uprising," widely cited as Madison's largest protest wave since the Vietnam War, ultimately could not stop Act 10 from passing. It did, however, draw national scrutiny to the new governor's proposals. Citing the ongoing economic recession, Walker and his allies had presented the bill as a necessary fix for a $100 million shortfall in the state's budget. The same logic, however, also guided their roughly equivalent tax cut for corporations the previous month. Act 10's many inflammatory "fixes" included increased barriers to maintaining labor unions and the effective elimination of collective bargaining rights for thousands of state workers. Walker also sought to cut more than $1 billion from the state's K–12 and university education systems, to offer handouts to energy companies through "no-bid" contracts, to decrease accountability for corporate negligence through tort reform and the repeal of the state's Equal Pay Act, and to loosen regulations on the state's telecommunications and high-interest-loan industries.[2]

As this program advanced in Wisconsin, legislatures in several other states—Ohio, Indiana, and New Jersey, among others—introduced similar bills to undercut workers' rights. Additional proposals from Wisconsin lawmakers also mirrored aggressive anti-immigration legislation adopted in Arizona and Alabama, as well as the "Stand Your Ground" laws used to justify homicide in Florida and elsewhere. These parallels were not coincidences. Pushing "copycat" laws simultaneously in states all over the country, think tanks, such as the American Legislative Exchange Council (ALEC) and Americans for Prosperity, and their financial backers, including billionaires David and Charles Koch and the Wisconsin-based Lynde and Harry Bradley Foundation, were advancing a very specific agenda.[3]

These policies exemplified neoliberalism, an economic and political philosophy with a confusing name but a clear goal—to maximize the wealth and power of the elite. Neither liberal nor new in the parlance of any but its most devoted followers, neoliberalism actually harks back to an earlier historical moment, before the Great Depression and the US government's willingness to intervene in the economy for the public good. It reduces capitalism to a raw and predatory form by reducing taxes for the wealthy, cutting government services for the poor, eliminating regulatory protections (such as labor and environmental laws), and redistributing public resources to corporations through privatization.

This Wild West, no-holds-barred vision for society has led some people to label the neoliberal end goal as a sort of "cowboy capitalism"—rugged, opportunistic, and, presumably, armed.[4] Others have suggested the terms "savage capitalism," "mafia capitalism," and "Jurassic Park capitalism" to capture neoliberalism's ruthless, rapacious nature. Another contender, "casino capitalism," also seems appropriate, as neoliberal policies create an often chaotic series of winners and losers, while the house—the people who

make the rules—always takes the biggest cut.[5] Despite popular political rhetoric, neoliberalism does not, in fact, seek small government or an across-the-board reduction of government rules. Nor
does it reward individual merit or competition. Since the 1970s,
neoliberal policies have repurposed the US government as a tool
for Big Business and transferred into private hands the massive
public wealth that accumulated in the welfare state of the mid-
twentieth century. As sociologist Loïc Wacquant argues, neoliberalism does not seek deregulation but rather *"re-regulates* ... the
economy in favour of corporations."[6]

By the time Wisconsin residents occupied their capitol building in 2011, the neoliberal project had been under way for several
decades. ALEC began allowing US corporations and their lobbyists to write legislation in the early 1970s. By 1987, the organization
boasted a membership of more than two thousand state legislators
who were ready to add their names and change state laws—an enlightening point in the debate over "states' rights." Americans for
Prosperity, founded in 2004 to funnel corporate money into politics, was a major player in the pivotal 2010 midterm elections, but
it was just one of the dozens of neoliberal organizations funded by
the Koch brothers. In the 1970s, the Koches established the Cato
Institute, an influential think tank, and in 1980, David Koch ran
for vice president on a Libertarian Party platform that sought the
elimination of Social Security and minimum-wage laws.[7]

By 2011, aggressive neoliberal economic policies—from both
major political parties—had achieved many of their backers' goals.
Most clearly, they succeeded in making the rich much, much
richer. Individually, the wealthiest 1 percent of Americans, on average, saw their incomes double or triple since the early 1970s,
while a typical worker actually made less in 2011 than in 1968 (ad-
justed for inflation). As a group, the richest 1 percent of Americans
roughly doubled both their share of the nation's income (to 20
percent) and their share of the nation's wealth (to 40 percent).[8]

The 2011 protests in Madison and elsewhere may have paralleled Sixties-era demonstrations in their size and in their zeal, but they occurred in vastly different contexts. The marches and rallies in the Wisconsin cold were just the latest clash of the Post-Liberal Era. They were a valiant, but failed, attempt to defend the labor rights and public-education victories that had been won by previous generations. In the decades since the 1970s, neoliberal policy shifts have reshaped the United States, fundamentally altering relationships between the American people, business interests, and the US government. Neoliberalism's "casino capitalism" has stacked the political deck in favor of powerful private interests. At every step, however, protesters and other activists have opposed neoliberal logic and demanded the rights of people over the right to profits.

INTRODUCTION

THE AMERICAN PROTEST TRADITION

If we appear to seek the unattainable, as it has been said,
let it be known that we do so to avoid the unimaginable.
—Tom Hayden, Students for a Democratic Society, 1962

As I ADD THE FINISHING TOUCHES TO THIS INTRODUCTION, nearly six years removed from the Wisconsin labor protests, police forces representing at least seventy-five agencies from ten different states have converged on the Standing Rock Sioux reservation in North Dakota, equipped with riot gear and armored vehicles. They are not there to join indigenous Americans as they defend the water supply of current and future generations. The police are there to stand with private security forces and ensure the building of a $3.8 billion oil pipeline. They have fired tear gas, concussion grenades, water cannons, and rubber bullets at the Water Protectors. They have arrested more than four hundred people, including journalists and a documentary filmmaker, threatening the latter with up to forty-five years in prison. How this conflict is ultimately resolved—and it may be by the time you read this book—will depend largely on whether the Standing Rock Sioux and their allies can attract enough public support to isolate Energy Transfer Partners, the company building the pipeline, from its financial backers and government supporters. In short, the deciding factor will be whether they can pressure the people in power. Even with support from more than two hundred indigenous nations and thousands of US military veterans, as well as a brief reprieve from the outgoing Obama administration, this will not be an easy task. The current historical moment is one in which the power of US corporations is immense, and the Dakota Access Pipeline's many investors—Goldman Sachs, Wells Fargo, JPMorgan Chase, and President Donald Trump, among them—are well connected at every level of government.[1]

Over the past five decades, US corporate interests, and through them American elites, have seen both their economic power and their influence in government increase dramatically. In the words of economist Richard Wolff, "Years of ideological preaching about the superiority of private, deregulated, market-driven capitalism served to enable and mask one of the largest and fastest upward redistributions of income in modern history."[2] Corporations' lobbying power, ability to direct public narratives, freedom to finance political campaigns, and direct access to the legislative process have allowed them to shape much of the country's foreign and domestic policies. Unsurprisingly, the tax obligations of the wealthy have been greatly reduced (in the 1950s, top earners paid a tax rate of over 90 percent; today it is less than 40 percent), as have restrictions on the ways that businesses can extract profit and pass "external" costs along to the public.[3]

Meanwhile, the US government has acted as a corporate proxy, providing trillions of dollars in revenue from the taxpayers and facilitating access to resources and cheap labor through trade agreements and military force. This process has had devastating, and well-documented, effects on the economic prospects of the American middle class, working classes, and poor. Numerous economic graphs of the US in the twentieth century—the income and wealth of the bottom 90 percent, the middle class's share of the nation's wealth, membership in labor unions, and the income and wealth of the richest 1 percent—show similarly wide but clear bell curves (or reverse bell curves, in the case of the wealthy) with a rise through the 1940s and 1950s and a decline since the 1980s and 1990s. Unquestionably, the period in the middle was the heyday for American workers, and it came at the expense of the people at the very top, though they remained incredibly wealthy throughout. The political shake-up of the post-1960s period has since widened the gap in wealth between the rich and everyone else. Most germane to this book, it has also reshaped the abilities of everyday Americans to influence their government and to pressure the private sector through protest.

In the classic text *Poor People's Movements*, Frances Fox Piven and Richard Cloward present political power at its most basic level. "Those who control the means of physical coercion, and those who control the means of producing wealth, have power over those who do not."[4] In the US, power is contested in a number of different spheres, among them the courts, the media, electoral politics, the marketplace, and the streets. These venues are all dominated by the powerful—the elites. They have the most money. They have the most lawyers. They own the most television and radio stations—as well as social media outlets. They are the biggest donors to both political parties. And they lobby for laws that further tilt the balance in their favor, by discouraging voter turnout, easing media mergers, criminalizing various methods of protest, and, above all, further increasing their wealth.

Protest movements, in all of these arenas, are challenges to the powerful by people without other means. They are bottom-up phenomena. When the people at the bottom of society seek change, they must ultimately clash with those at the top: private interests (the wealthy elite, Big Business, the ownership class) and those who control armies and police forces (essentially, the government). These are rarely separate categories. In recent history, as corporations have grown larger and more powerful, the line between the private sector and representatives of the state has become even less clearly defined. In addition to a revolving door between US regulatory agencies and the industries that they exist to monitor, consider, for example, Peter Chowla's findings that at the beginning of the twenty-first century, eleven of the twenty largest annual revenues in the world belonged to national governments, while nine belonged to multinational corporations. Big Business is very big indeed.[5]

But though unable to match the powers of funds or force that exist at the top, protest movements have some other advantages, among them the potential for strength in numbers and the ability to withhold the cooperation on which elites routinely depend. Workers, for example, can shut down businesses—and entire economies—by simply refusing to work and going on strike. Disobedience by students, pedestrians, journalists, shoppers, bicyclists, prisoners, drivers, and others can have similar effects, though not without repercussions.

When protest movements are successful, they disrupt. They upend the status quo, divide coalitions of the powerful, and compel reforms. Before becoming a war for independence, the American Revolution was a protest movement with hopes and possibilities for freedom that were much wider ranging than those typically associated with the Founders. Through decades of meetings, marches, boycotts, rallies, speeches, and pamphlets, the movement split the loyalties of colonial elites, before eventually provoking a military occupation. The protest traditions of revolutionary America, enshrined in the First Amendment with "the right of the people peaceably to assemble," were incredibly raucous and unruly. They included publicly shaming members of the upper class in person, burning and decapitating them in effigy, and destroying property—tea, most famously, but also ships and the homes of government officials.[6]

Decades later, the divisions between the Northern and Southern states that led to the US Civil War were inflamed by antislavery activists who organized groups, held meetings, published newspapers, gave speeches, and formed political opposition parties—in addition to smuggling escaped slaves to freedom and, occasionally, taking up arms against slaveholders. Their moral demand, for an end to American slavery, was culturally shocking and, importantly, had major economic implications for the nation's wealthy elites. Abolitionists' meeting halls were burned to the ground. Their speeches and writings drew violence and death threats. Pro-slavery mobs broke Frederick Douglass's hand, dragged William Lloyd Garrison through the streets, and murdered ministers Elijah Lovejoy and Anthony Bewley. And when the Southern states seceded, they listed alongside their continued devotion to white supremacy and slavery a series of grievances that included abolitionists' use of "the ballot box" and "seditious pamphlets and papers" to spread the antislavery cause.[7]

Protest and resistance to a range of oppressions were constants in the post–Civil War US, as well. American Indian nations defended their homes from a military invasion in the West. Generations of African Americans resisted the violence and humiliation of systematic "Jim Crow" racism. In the face of beatings and imprisonment, American women picketed the White House to demand voting rights. American workers, many of them recent immigrants, engaged in strikes and armed battles with employers in mines, fields, and factories all over the country. These acts of defiance cost many people their lives, and tangible victories were few and far between. The clearest and most widespread successes culminated in the protest waves of the 1930s and 1960s, which together created the most economically egalitarian moment in US history.[8]

During the Great Depression of the 1930s, factory workers, the unemployed, World War I veterans, farmers, and others engaged in thousands upon thousands of strikes, protests, and other revolts. They picketed and marched. They blocked roads. They walked off their jobs. They occupied factories, and they shut down ports. And they forced a major shift in federal policy, which materialized in President Franklin D. Roosevelt's New Deal—patchwork economic reforms that included a minimum wage, Social Security benefits for the elderly and the disabled, a ban on child labor, food stamps for the hungry, government jobs programs, the legal right to join a labor union, and a series of new rules limiting the reckless behavior of banks and Wall Street.[9]

Despite significant opposition from business leaders, the liberal policies of the New Deal brought an end to the Long Gilded Age, more than half a century in which workers toiled in an unstable and incredibly dangerous "laissez-faire" economy that killed tens of thousands of people in workplace accidents each year. For decades, business owners had demanded "hands-off" government in terms of regulation, but they were otherwise content to accept government contracts and assistance in opening foreign markets and recruiting migrant workers. They were also quick to demand government intervention against their striking workers. Between 1880 and 1930, for example, courts declared labor strikes illegal forty-three hundred times. At the behest of powerful business owners, police, the National Guard, and the US military were also routinely ordered to arrest, attack, or kill striking workers. The Great Railroad Strike of 1877, for example, was crushed—and one hundred striking workers were killed—by thousands of US troops, the National Guard militia of several states, and a variety of police, "special police," and other vigilante groups organized by city mayors. The famous Pullman Strike of 1894 met a similar fate at the hands of more than ten thousand US soldiers and state militia. During the Ludlow Massacre of 1914, mining-company guards, backed by Colorado militia, "machine-gunned and torched" a tent colony of striking workers' families, killing twenty-one people, including eleven children, in a strike that was also ultimately decided by federal troops. In 1921, ten thousand coal miners in West Virginia faced off in open battle with thousands of coal-company soldiers, before the US Army threatened to drop bombs on the striking workers. Such clashes were ubiquitous.[10]

During the subsequent Liberal Era that spanned roughly the 1930s through the 1970s, work was still dangerous, and the US government remained a chief ally of industry—especially through its aggressive Cold War foreign policy. However, New Deal liberalism also offered basic rights for many American workers and at least the potential for government arbitration.

Broadly speaking, liberal policies aimed to soften capitalism's harshest edges, to promote the creation of a middle class, and to circulate money through employment and mass consumption. Food stamps, for example, fed desperate, hungry Americans, while also supporting grocery-store owners, food transporters, and farmers, who then made their own purchases, continuing the cycle. It was good for business, and millions of Americans shared in the rewards of a booming economy: stable employment, a roof over their heads, security in old age, and schools rather than coal mines for their children. However, the benefits of these policies— the New Deal and, after World War II, college tuition and subsidized home and farm loans through the GI Bill—were primarily reserved for white, heterosexual men. Many of the demands for which generations of workers had fought and died became law, but the depths of American inequality were exposed by new mass movements led by those who were deliberately left out: people of color, women, youth, and LGBT folks, among them.[11]

Wealthy elites, who rightly viewed the New Deal as an infringement on their power, quickly began organizing a countermovement to limit the impacts of the reforms and to prevent any further movement gains. They rolled back labor rights through the 1947 Taft-Hartley Act, for example, and they used the Cold War banner of anticommunism to undercut the efforts of labor unions and civil rights organizations. For nearly half a century, however, the ruling classes—Democrats and Republicans alike— were more or less forced to take for granted basic liberal assumptions. New Deal planks such as Social Security, minimum wage, and child-labor bans were mainstream, at least in national politics. Meanwhile, societal shifts after World War II—a judiciary that was more receptive to the legal arguments of marginalized Americans, a Democratic Party suffering from sharp regional divisions, and a national television audience steeped in Cold War propaganda about the virtues of freedom, democracy, and equality—created new vulnerabilities among the powerful and opened new avenues to movement pressure.

The civil rights movement, which had been building for decades, seized on these opportunities. While the broader black freedom struggle was dynamic—and nurtured a range of philosophies on tactics, strategies, and objectives—the most successful protest thread revolved around courtroom battles and widespread civil disobedience. Civil rights lawyers challenged hundreds of the country's white-supremacist laws, while activists organized boycotts, sit-ins, stand-ins, pickets, marches, and other protest campaigns in essentially every city in the country—North and South. Movement strategists were especially adept at framing protest actions for media consumption in the newly televised world. They organized extensive training in the tactics of nonviolent civil disobedience and nonretaliation, emphasized conventional and formal clothing, and selected predictably reactionary targets. The resulting photographs and newsreel footage clearly displayed images of violent, angry racists attacking peaceful, well-dressed activists who were making objectively reasonable demands. These images highlighted the contradictions between daily realities in the "Jim Crow" US and many Americans' view of their country, building national support for civil rights legislation, as well as international pressure on the US government. The civil rights movement's message resonated with youth in particular, sparking protest movements at high schools and colleges nationwide.[12]

As a younger generation began steering the movement in the early 1960s, inspired students sought organizational training from such groups as the Student Nonviolent Coordinating Committee (SNCC) and then used it to challenge their schools' policies, curricula, and roles in US society. The student movement later galvanized around opposition to the Vietnam War, joining a mass movement that protested the centers of government, boycotted the draft, and tried to disrupt the war industry, including napalm-producer Dow Chemical and weapons developers at the country's research universities. The Sixties period is often described as a "movement of movements," as dozens of other protest movements also emerged to make demands of the powerful, modeling themselves on existing groups or responding to shortcomings within them: Black Power, women's liberation, the environmental movement, Yellow Power, Red Power, the Chicano movement, gay and lesbian liberation, the counterculture (and its political wing), and many, many others. Workers not covered by New Deal labor laws also pushed for improved working conditions during the period through new unions, notably the United Farmworkers (UFW).[13]

Angry mobs and the Ku Klux Klan, as well as police, the National Guard, and the FBI, violently defended the status quo through widespread harassment, beatings, bombings, false imprisonment, and murder of American activists. Nonetheless, by the mid-1970s, the many movements of the Sixties era had helped build on the New Deal's legacy with "Great Society" poverty programs, such as Medicare, Medicaid, and Head Start. They also forced significant cultural shifts—and concrete policy changes—on issues of race, gender, sexuality, and militarism.[14]

The civil rights movement, in addition to its many courtroom victories, prompted the passage of the Civil Rights Act of 1964, which prohibited racial discrimination in public accommodations and employment; the Twenty-Fourth Amendment, which eliminated poll taxes; the Voting Rights Act of 1965, which outlawed voter literacy tests; and the Civil Rights Act of 1968, which prohibited racial discrimination in the sale and rental of housing.

Women's liberation activists founded nearly one thousand rape crisis centers and forced the passage of Title X, which established federal funding for family planning services, and Title IX, which mandated gender equality in public education, including athletics programs. Feminist legal activists also won the *Roe v. Wade* decision in 1973, the passage of "no fault" divorce laws, and the elimination of "marital rape" exemptions in many states.

The environmental movement, the subject of chapter 1 of this book, won the passage of the Wilderness Act of 1964, which protected over nine million acres of federal land, as well as the Urban Mass Transportation Act of 1964, which provided federal matching funds for large-scale rail projects. Environmentalists also forced the establishment of the Environmental Protection Agency, in 1970, and the passage of the Clean Air Act of 1970, the Marine Mammal Protection Act of 1972, the Endangered Species Act of 1973, the Safe Drinking Water Act of 1974, and the Soil and Water Resources Conservation Act of 1977, among other protective regulations.[15]

With mixed results and sometimes contradictory demands, the many protest movements of the 1930s and 1960s eras collectively fought to create a United States with a stable economy, middle-class opportunities and rights for workers, access to public education, democratic protection of the environment, and legal, social, and political equality regardless of race, class, gender, or sexuality. These were not the offerings of liberals. They were the demands made of them. They were the victories of protest movements, based on the historical vulnerabilities of the Liberal Era power structure.

By necessity, many of the reforms of the period materialized as federal laws and government programs. Before the New Deal established national child-labor laws, factory owners had simply fled states such as New York, which banned child labor, for states such as Alabama, which did not. Federal initiatives had also been necessary to trump the white-supremacist laws of cities and states. Under "Jim Crow," as under slavery, rallying cries for "states' rights" were not just political principles; their agenda was nonintervention against white supremacy, specifically.

As the Sixties era came to a close, American elites were determined to unravel the changes of the midcentury—to undercut workers' rights, to work around environmental regulations, to re-segregate neighborhoods and schools, and to eliminate poverty programs. To do so, however, they needed, first and foremost, to undermine the enforcement of federal laws and policies. Their guide was neoliberalism, a new iteration of the laissez-faire ideas that predated, and largely caused, the Great Depression.

POST-LIBERAL AMERICA

Beginning in the 1970s and cemented with the election of Ronald Reagan in 1980, the Post-Liberal Era has seen a deliberate and aggressive rollback of liberal policies and a return to many of the economic dynamics of a century earlier. Some scholars have dubbed this period a "Second Gilded Age," noting the increased influence of corporations in US government and the growing gap between the US's wealthy elite and its poor and working classes. In this new Gilded Age, hedge-fund managers and Silicon Valley tech giants have replaced the railroad tycoons of the late 1800s, while bankers and oil barons have simply consolidated and changed company names. The country's richest people have grown considerably wealthier, while cuts to public services, deindustrialization, personal debt, and declines in union membership have undermined the middle class. The bipartisan "War on Drugs" has made the US prison population the largest in the world and created a multibillion-dollar for-profit prison industry that backs "tough on crime" politicians and recruits businesses to relocate their factories behind prison walls—where minimum-wage laws do not apply. Global temperatures, meanwhile, have been the hottest in modern history. The fossil-fuel industry, which has privately acknowledged the dangers of climate change for decades (and receives billions of dollars in annual taxpayer subsidies), spends millions of dollars each year to convince the American public that climate change does not exist—and to fund politicians who promise inaction.[16]

In the Post-Liberal Era, the term "liberal" is still used in American political discourse as a foil to "conservative," but in reality, neither major political party has championed liberal economic policies in many decades. Each has combined neoliberalism with its own package of social policies, presenting the confusing reality that American "conservatives" may simultaneously support conservative social policies, neoconservative foreign policies, and neoliberal economic policies. However, the mainstream of both parties, beginning with Republicans under Ronald Reagan and then Democrats under Bill Clinton, have unquestionably adopted economic policies firmly rooted in neoliberal assumptions. Their proposals have rarely been identical in scale or malice, but they have taken for granted the same broad goals of lowering taxes for the wealthy, cutting public services for the poor, funneling public funds and resources to corporations through privatization, and eliminating rules and regulations for businesses. The Republicans have typically promoted neoliberalism through a combination of fear of outside threats (notably communists and terrorists), assaults on women's rights and LGBT rights, and blame for the country's economic woes on people who, unlike themselves, have effectively no control over economic policy—whether Reagan's mythical "welfare queens," the schoolteachers of Wisconsin, or refugees and other immigrants. The Democrats, meanwhile, have largely offered the same basic economic package, dressed with modestly progressive social reforms, from Clinton's "Don't Ask, Don't Tell" approach to military service to Barack Obama's health-care initiatives and cautious support for marriage equality. The policies of the two parties are not identical, and even minor differences in policy can have major impacts on people's lives. However, like the laissez-faire doctrines that dominated the turn of the last century and the New Deal liberalism that guided the 1930s through 1970s, neoliberalism is the ruling philosophy of its era, not a partisan division.

This book explores how US economic, cultural, and political elites in the post-Sixties period turned the tide against the movement gains of the previous decades and how these changes reshaped the ability of activists to impact the political process. In short, it bridges the study of resistance and protest—the work of Piven and Cloward, James C. Scott, and others—with the growing scholarship on the political economy of the Post-Liberal Era. To demonstrate these links, I use case studies from a range of protest movements.[17]

Chapters 1 and 2 present the Post-Liberal political landscape of the 1980s at the local level, through the work of environmental activists and punk rockers. Chapter 3 offers a slightly broader lens, examining "free"-trade globalization and the complex structures of multinational corporations through a nationwide boycott by migrant farm workers and their student allies. Chapter 4 expands the focus even wider with some of the many clashes that surrounded the US invasion of Iraq in 2003. Chapter 5 acts as a conclusion and outlines how neoliberal policies created the greatest economic collapse in nearly a century and how policy makers then doubled down, using the crisis to pursue their agenda even more aggressively. Rather than focusing on a group or a movement, chapter 5 approaches the ongoing protest politics of recent years as a "movement of movements" against neoliberalism on many fronts: Occupy Wall Street and #BlackLivesMatter, as well as massive, diverse movements for environmental justice, social justice, immigrant rights, peace, and more.

Through these examples, I hope to tell a broad story about the changes of the past half century and to provide a lens onto how protest movements work—first at the level of local activists and organizations, then on increasingly larger scales. The book offers glimpses into some of the relationships between protest movements and the powerful, but it does not claim to be a complete history of either politics or protest during this long period. My hope, rather, is that it can provide a useful framework for understanding the many significant actions, events, activists, organizations, and movements that it neglects.

This book follows the trajectory of neoliberal capitalism, though it is by no means the only historical thread through this period. I delineate the paradigmatic periods of the Post-Liberal Era roughly according to the policy shifts and dominant struggles under US presidential administrations, those of the 1980s of Ronald Reagan, the 1990s of Bill Clinton, the 2000s of George W. Bush, and the 2010s of Barack Obama. However, the specific years and the names of US presidents (with apologies to George H. W. Bush) are much less important than the distinct steps that each represented in the development of the neoliberal project. The Reagan administration undercut the domestic policy shifts of the 1960s and reshaped mainstream political rhetoric about the role of US government. The Clinton administration, under the guise of progressivism, continued to unravel Liberal Era domestic reforms through austerity and deregulation, while overseeing the rapid deregulation of global investment and manufacturing through "free"-trade programs. The Bush administration furthered the deregulation of the fossil-fuel industry, privatized education and warfare, and funneled public funds to Wall Street banks after they sank the global economy. The Obama administration, the most difficult to assess historically, tried to stabilize neoliberal capitalism, pursing many of these same policies while limiting some of their excesses.

I deliberately focus very little on interparty (or intraparty) struggles or whether specific policies were initiated by the president or Congress. Party politics certainly offer an additional lens onto some of these changes, as would an in-depth focus on shifts in media or in courtroom strategies. In this case, however, they distract from the larger point about the overall effects of the neoliberal shift. I am much more interested in the struggle between the people at the top and the bottom than those on the left and on the right (or the center-right and right, in the case of US party politics). For the sake of simplicity, I also focus primarily on federal policies, though similar dynamics shaped political realities at the state and local levels, as seen for example, in Wisconsin in 2011 and, more recently, at the Standing Rock reservation in North Dakota.

Political power (government) and economic power (the wealthy) overlap considerably in the Post-Liberal period, but they are still vulnerable to different protest tactics, whether elections and recalls or boycotts and strikes. The power of elites also depends on a variety of contextual variables, many of which are historical. In other words, the protest methods that were effective in the 1960s may not have been useful in the 1780s, 1880s, or 1980s.

TO AVOID THE UNIMAGINABLE

This book examines US protest movements in the Post-Liberal Era, a period in which neoliberal government policies have returned the US economy to a raw, brutal, and largely unrestrained form that is similar in many ways to that which predated the New Deal. In this new Gilded Age, however, Big Business's global reach is far greater than it was a century ago, and it is backed by the most powerful government apparatus in world history.

This is a book about a fight, and it is not a fair one. On one side are US elites—those with power and those in power—who have used neoliberalism to increase their wealth, expand their influence, and consolidate political control over the course of the past half century. On the other side are countless groups of activists, associated with a wide variety of communities, causes, and movements, who have attempted to challenge the logic and policies of neoliberal capitalism through protest. Their successes have been both rare and dishearteningly limited—often, the status quo or less severe losses than could have been. Life, however, is lived in the margins of these wins and losses. Even without clear, dramatic victories, these clashes altered history and changed people's lives.

In the 1960s, American college students, inspired by the unfolding civil rights movement, conceded in their call to action that the goal of a truly democratic society seemed impossibly naive but that the alternative, to do nothing, would allow for the unacceptable and "unimaginable" continuation of violent, dehumanizing racism and a Cold War foreign policy that inched ever closer to nuclear war. Whether they could alter the trajectory of history or not, they vowed to join those who were already on the front lines and to force those who were in power to go through them, as well. At the very least, they devoted themselves to preventing the worst-case scenario. The protesters and other activists in this book, like those students and their many predecessors in US history, engaged in a struggle to make their world more just and more humane. They did so knowing that the odds were against them and without the promise of a revolutionary victory to reward their sacrifices.[18]

This book contains many arguments, but its underlying premise is a simple one. The history of the United States is a history of conflict. It is a history of violent oppression and tremendous inequality, of settler colonialism, genocide, theft, rape, slavery, child labor, and war. It is also, however, a history of defiance, dissent, and opposition to the status quo—slavery and child labor, yes, but also the protest movements that confronted, and ultimately helped end, those institutions. American rabble-rousers and troublemakers have routinely championed unpopular positions and picked fights with much more powerful opponents. Their victories have been infrequent and nearly always come at great costs, but protesters have been, and continue to be, a major force for American democracy, from the expansion of voting rights and the end of segregation laws to minimum-wage standards and marriage equality.

The world around us is a legacy of struggles won and lost and routinely fought again: free speech, slavery, voting rights, child labor, and segregation among them. Even if you, the reader, choose not to engage in these conflicts, we all still live in the world that they create. They determine the limitations on our basic legal freedoms and rights. They create our opportunities for education, employment, recreation, and leisure. They dictate our access to health care, food, shelter, clean air, and water. They define our relationships to our government, our jobs, our communities, our friends, and our lovers. In short, they decide the quality of our lives.

1

THE FORESTS FOR THE TREES

NEOLIBERALISM AND THE ENVIRONMENT

We are different from previous generations of conservatives. We
are no longer working to preserve the status quo. We are radicals,
working to overturn the present power structure of this country.
—Paul Weyrich, Heritage Foundation

Whenever we decide to go after a law, a regulation, or an agency,
we must ask ourselves the following question: If we win this battle,
how will it feed on itself and lead to future victories?
—Grover Norquist, Americans for Tax Reform

IN AUGUST 1980, REPUBLICAN NOMINEE RONALD REAGAN
launched his presidential campaign by visiting Philadelphia, Mississippi, a town known only for the brutal 1964 murders of civil
rights activists Michael Schwerner, James Chaney, and Andrew
Goodman. Rather than honor their sacrifices, Reagan expressed
his opposition to the reforms of the 1960s, emphasizing his commitment to "states' rights" and asking southern Democrats to
switch their party loyalties.

While the protest movements of the Liberal Era had been
broadly dedicated to creating middle-class opportunities and opposing discrimination, the forces that opposed them had an altogether different understanding of freedom. Armed with the ideas
of economists Friedrich Hayek, Milton Friedman, and others, they
sought to redistribute public wealth to people at the top. During
the 1960s and 1970s, they began testing these new laissez-faire
policies at the state and local levels and mobilizing to capture na-

tional political power. Their efforts culminated with the election of Ronald Reagan.

The strategies of the burgeoning antiliberal movement were rooted in monopolizing the resources and might of the US government for the rich and the powerful. The Heritage Foundation advised the incoming administration to "use the appointment power wisely. Act promptly to fill vacancies and find persons of high quality and friendly persuasion."[1] Though relatively innocuous on the surface, pundit Grover Norquist offered a blunter version of the objective: "First, we want to remove liberal personnel from the political process. Then we want to capture those positions of power and influence for conservatives. Stalin taught the importance of this principle. . . . He understood that personnel is policy. With this principle in mind, conservatives must do all they can to make sure that they get jobs in Washington."[2] Reagan took the task seriously, appointing corporate heads to labor posts, civil rights opponents to monitor civil rights, polluters to head environmental agencies, and antifeminists to oversee women's rights programs.

By handcuffing the nation's regulatory bodies, Reagan simultaneously stalled, or rendered meaningless, many of the Liberal Era's reforms, while also discouraging new attempts to add to them. Accomplishing this task through legislation—thousands of new laws to undo old laws—would have been both politically difficult and subject to public scrutiny. Saboteur appointments, by contrast, offered an immediate and radical solution. They closed formal political channels to protest movements, leaving them to rely almost exclusively on other methods, such as civil disobedience. However, unlike the sit-ins and marches of the 1960s, which aimed to draw federal intervention against state and local powers, activists in the 1980s were essentially on their own. Their protests were less a means to an end than the end itself.

THE NEOLIBERAL COUNTERMOVEMENT

In the early 1970s, the United States was the most economically equal that it had been in its history, and protest movements' demands for workers' rights, poverty assistance, racial equality, environmental protections, and women's rights had been realized to various extents as US laws or government policies. Over the course of the following decade, American elites pooled their resources and funneled vast sums of corporate money into the political process in hopes of turning back this tide. In 1972, corporate leaders formed the Business Roundtable, a probusiness organization whose members included the CEOs of several dozen of the country's largest companies. They called for a "free market," but rather than competing against one another in the marketplace, America's most powerful corporations worked together, spending millions of dollars on various lobbying efforts. Their early successes included blocking the creation of a federal Consumer Protection Agency and defeating a 1978 labor law reform bill that would have bolstered union organizing. Like the General Managers Association that brought railroad companies together to crush the famous 1894 Pullman Strike, the business leaders of the 1970s saw value in a union for themselves, while opposing them for their workers.[3]

In 1973, politicians and business leaders came together to form the American Legislative Exchange Council (ALEC), allowing corporations to write their own laws, which member politicians dutifully passed in states all over the country. The same year, Paul Weyrich, Edwin Feulner, and billionaire beer mogul Joseph Coors launched the Heritage Foundation, which soon became one of the most influential "free market" think tanks in the country. A few years later, billionaire brothers Charles and David Koch established the Cato Institute, a think tank devoted to dissolving Social Security, among similar goals. In 1979, Coors and others founded the Leadership Institute, a "boot camp for young conservatives," which trained forty thousand activists by 2004. Together with the already established, and very well-funded, US Chamber of Commerce and American Enterprise Institute (AEI), these groups spent billions of dollars to finance elections, referenda, public relations campaigns, and business-friendly studies.[4]

In a 1984 exposé of the institutions of the new American Right, John Saloma reported that AEI's "free market" advocacy drew from an $11.7 million annual budget, retained more than two hundred paid scholars, and provided a constant stream of editorials to over one hundred daily newspapers across the US. The average American newspaper reader could thus routinely encounter corporate advertising disguised as the opinion of a concerned neighbor. The upstart Heritage Foundation, meanwhile, already had a $10 million operating budget by the early 1980s. As the Heritage Foundation's Burton Pines described the relationship between the two organizations, "AEI is like the big gun on an offshore battleship. We are the landing party. If they hadn't softened it up, we wouldn't have landed."[5] Founded in response to the New Deal of the 1930s, AEI spent decades developing laissez-faire talking points and policy plans of limited mainstream viability. When political disillusion and an economic downturn created the opportunity for a pivot in the late 1970s, however, AEI had already laid the groundwork for the neoliberal shift. Pines's analogy to warfare is especially potent in this case, as the "big gun" was largely aimed at workers, the poor, women, and people of color. In the Heritage Foundation's 1980 *Mandate for Leadership*, a self-professed "blueprint for conservative government," the organization clarified its invasion plans point by point, federal agency by federal agency.[6]

These groups—the Business Roundtable, ALEC, the Heritage Foundation, and many others—coalesced around neoliberalism: tax cuts for the wealthy, the deregulation of industry, cuts to public services, and the privatization of public resources. Like the "Social Darwinism" that had legitimized sweatshops, child labor, and eugenics programs a century earlier, neoliberal narratives scapegoated the poor for the decisions of the rich, blaming the movements of the 1930s and 1960s for deindustrialization, inflation, and unemployment in the 1970s. When the heads of profitable companies moved their factories to the US South or out of the country entirely, they blamed union workers for demanding living wages. Likewise, the antifeminist backlash, homophobia, and "colorblind" racism that framed political debate around social issues in 1980s (discussed in chapter 2) were not merely organic cultural responses. They were developed and nurtured by well-funded think tanks, whose members tested them for maximum effect.[7]

By 1980, Big Business's direct influence at the federal level had increased substantially. According to political scientists James S. Hacker and Paul Pierson, "The number of corporations with public affairs offices in Washington grew from 100 in 1968 to over 500 in 1978. In 1971, only 175 firms had registered lobbyists in Washington, but by 1982, nearly 2,500 did. The number of corporate PACs [political action committees] increased from under 300 in 1976 to over 1,200 by the middle of 1980."[8] The impacts of this pressure were already materializing in the deregulatory policies of the Carter administration in the late 1970s. With the 1980 election of Ronald Reagan, however, neoliberalism found its true champion. Reagan not only adopted more than 60 percent of the 1,270 recommendations laid out in the Heritage Foundation's *Mandate for Leadership*; he effectively changed the rules of the political game, for the people at the top and the people at the bottom.[9]

During the Liberal Era, civil rights activists strategically packaged their sit-ins, freedom rides, and marches for media consumption, in order to draw political pressure from sympathetic northerners and, more importantly, to embarrass the US government globally. It was this pressure—not moral concern—that compelled the federal government to intervene. By boldly playing to a different political base and assuming a different international posture, Reagan was able to deflect this vulnerability, however. The location of his campaign speech in Philadelphia, Mississippi, has been dismissed by apologists as an unintentional coincidence, but Reagan aide and conservative strategist Lee Atwater later explained the Republican Party's strategy unambiguously: "You start out in 1954 by saying, 'Nigger, nigger, nigger.' By 1968 you can't say 'nigger'—that hurts you, backfires. So you say stuff like, uh, forced busing, states' rights, and all that stuff, and you're getting so abstract. Now, you're talking about cutting taxes, and all these things you're talking about are totally economic things and a byproduct of them is, blacks get hurt worse than whites. . . . 'We want to cut this,' is much more abstract than even the busing thing, uh, and a hell of a lot more abstract than 'Nigger, nigger.'"[10]

To appeal to anxious and resentful white voters, Reagan promised to undercut civil rights gains, but only using methods that masked racist intentions. On this, he was as good as his word. To head the Equal Employment Opportunity Commission (EEOC), which oversees civil rights discrimination claims, Reagan appointed fierce affirmative action critic Clarence Thomas. Predictably, from 1980 to 1986, the percentage of cases that the EEOC found no cause to pursue effectively doubled, from 28.5 percent to 56.6 percent. Despite criticism of Reagan from his own party, he also maintained a firm commitment to the apartheid regime in South Africa, vetoing bipartisan sanctions. Reagan appointed Antonin Scalia to the US Supreme Court, and he promoted William Rehnquist to chief justice. Rehnquist had been a defender of "separate but equal" segregation and had decided against women, the elderly, the disabled, and racial minorities in eighty-two out of eighty-three relevant cases he heard. Scalia, meanwhile, was a bold voice against the rights of women, people of color, and LGBT Americans for decades.[11]

The Reagan administration's approach to women's rights followed a similar pattern. At the urging of the Heritage Foundation, Reagan targeted the Women's Educational Equity Act (WEEA), a program intended to promote equal education rights for girls. Reagan proposed a 25 percent budget cut his first year and complete defunding the next, though Congress eventually limited the cuts to around 40 percent. In response, Reagan undermined the WEEA by appointing new field agents with ties to Phyllis Schlafly's antifeminist organization the Eagle Forum. Under the Carter administration, women had constituted 15 percent of federal judicial appointments; under Reagan, they made up just 8 percent. Reagan eliminated the Coalition on Women's Appointments, the Working Group on Women, and the recently established Office of Domestic Violence. He was also the first US president to take a public position against the Equal Rights Amendment since its congressional approval in 1972, and it failed during his first term.[12]

Reagan also rolled back workers' rights. In addition to his famous dismissal of striking air traffic controllers, Reagan's National Labor Relations Board (NLRB) reversed 40 percent of the 1970s decisions that had sided with workers. His labor secretary, Raymond Donovan, proposed weakening child-labor restrictions by opening up dangerous jobs to fourteen- and fifteen-year-olds, raising the number of hours children could work each week and exempting them from minimum-wage restrictions. To head the Occupational Safety and Health Administration (OSHA), Reagan appointed millionaire construction tycoon Thorne Auchter, whose own company had been cited with forty-eight OSHA violations.[13]

With many of the institutional gains of Liberal Era movements in check, Reagan slashed away at social services, especially those serving the most vulnerable Americans. One notorious attempt at savings included classifying ketchup and pickle relish as vegetable servings in the free food programs of twenty-six million schoolchildren. Reagan's contribution to the "War on Drugs" and the nation's growing prison population included increasing the FBI's antidrug budget from $8 million to $95 million (from 1980 to 1984), while gutting funding for the National Institute on Drug Abuse, from $274 million to $57 million, during the same period (from 1981 to 1984). From 1981 to 1983, the government dropped three hundred thousand Americans from disability rolls. The federal government also cut housing spending from $30 billion in 1981 to $8 billion in 1986, during a decade in which as many as 1.2 million Americans became homeless each year. By the end of Reagan's second term, he had overseen a quadrupling of the nation's homeless population.[14]

Reagan's cuts were targeted. They did not create a small government, just a different one. While scaling back programs for public housing, women's education, and combating domestic violence, Reagan approved the largest peacetime military spending in history—roughly a trillion dollars in his first four years—and a massive tax cut, from 70 percent to 28 percent, for the wealthiest Americans. After-tax profits of US corporations rose during the decade from $82.3 billion to $229 billion, but minimum wage remained at $3.35 per hour, a decrease, given inflation. Despite the popular narrative about Reagan's "economic miracle," many Americans experienced the period as a disaster. In 1982 alone, 1.25 million industrial workers were laid off, and the unemployment rate reached 11 percent. Unemployment dropped to about half of that by the end of Reagan's second term—where it was still higher than it had regularly been throughout the 1950s and 1960s.[15]

Reagan's governing approach was soberingly straightforward. As Paul Weyrich had promised, the "conservative" goal was "to overturn the . . . power structure of this country."[16] When politically feasible, Reagan eliminated or defunded the federal agencies and programs with which he disagreed. When he could not control their funding, he sabotaged their agendas by appointing leaders who were their agencies' fiercest critics.

Though this approach of eliminating, defunding, and appointing saboteurs to undermine government had earlier roots and was notably used by Richard Nixon to debilitate the Office of Economic Opportunity (OEO), I call it the Reagan Method. The Reagan administration embraced the strategy wholeheartedly, and it was as much the basis for the "Reagan Revolution" as anything else. In addition to accomplishing Reagan's own policy goals, sabotaging federal programs also undercut the political power of his opponents. Even if protest movements (or Democrats) could compel new legislation, those laws would simply be ignored. Effectively, Reagan left his opposition with two options. It could remove him by electoral means, or it could use disruptive protest to confront his policies at their local points of impact.[17]

For a variety of reasons, the former proved impossible. In addition to the success of the Republican Party's "southern strategy," Reagan himself was incredibly popular among white voters, independent of his policies. Opinion polls throughout the 1980s showed, for example, that nearly 60 percent of Americans thought the government spent too little to protect the environment (compared to only 6 to 12 percent who thought spending was too high), but these views had minimal impact on voting patterns. Some of this discontinuity can be explained by a 1982 study that found that while 32 percent of US voters were primarily influenced by a candidate's position on abortion rights, less than half as many were as driven by positions on pollution (15 percent) or affirmative action programs (14 percent). Public opinion was not the only barrier in electoral politics, however. Outcomes at the polls were also skewed by the elimination of increasingly large numbers of minority voters through systematic mass incarceration and by the neutralizing of minority votes through redistricting.[18]

With little hope for lobbying efforts or electoral influence, many 1980s activists opted for confrontation through direct action. During the Liberal Era, labor and civil rights activists had often used disruptive protest to gain public sympathy and attract outside intervention, pitting state and federal officials against each other or by prompting government to regulate businesses. Activists opposing Reagan's policies, however, could expect no such relief. Essentially, they had to rely on the disruption itself, while their opponents in government and business, of course, had the backing of police forces. Meanwhile, businesses also developed a number of clever and chilling methods to discourage protest, such as the strategic lawsuit against public participation (SLAPP), which threatened to charge activists for the costs associated with their campaigns—the hiring of security forces or the loss of profits from bad press—a potentially devastating proposition for people advocating, say, a boycott of a major company.[19]

THE MODERN ENVIRONMENTAL MOVEMENT

The shift from national politics to intense, local clashes was perhaps clearest in the area of environmental policy. As many as twenty million people participated in the first Earth Day in 1970, and membership in mainstream environmental groups had grown exponentially in a very short period. The Audubon Society, for example, nearly doubled its membership between 1962 and 1970, growing from 41,000 to 81,500. The National Wildlife Federation grew from 271,900 in 1966 to 540,000 in 1970, while the Sierra Club's membership ballooned from a modest 20,000 in 1959 to 113,000 in 1970. Importantly, these organizations had been able to translate this popular support into political gains, making them much more eager to work hand in hand with major polluters, even recruiting them to participate in Earth Day activities.[20]

Though there were certainly disagreements over policy (and tensions within the environmental movement itself), objective concern for the environment was neither controversial nor particularly partisan through the 1970s. Administrations from John F. Kennedy's through Jimmy Carter's were at least open to the growing environmental lobby, and Republican Richard Nixon, an otherwise criminally violent opponent of protest movements, had overseen the creation of the Environmental Protection Agency (EPA) in 1970 and signed into law legislation that included the Endangered Species Act and regulations for clean air and drinking water. Ronald Reagan, however, shattered this consensus, and not just by removing Carter's solar panels from the White House.[21]

Paralleling Reagan's appointments on civil rights, women's rights, and workers' rights, he called on industrialists to lead and gut federal environmental agencies. To head the EPA, Reagan appointed Anne Gorsuch, a lawyer whose clients included mining and agricultural interests. Gorsuch gave polluters a free pass by eliminating the agency's Office of Enforcement. Of the fifteen people she named to EPA positions, eleven had ties to the industries they were hired to regulate. As secretary of interior, Reagan appointed James Watt, who, along with Joseph Coors, had founded the Mountain States Legal Foundation, an organization that helped corporations fight environmental regulations. To head the government's surface-mining regulatory agency, Reagan selected Robert Harris, who had previously been that agency's chief opponent and the instigator of a lawsuit against it.[22]

Reagan's business-friendly appointees quickly abandoned any pursuit of corporate polluters and even recommended that their own agencies be defunded. The budget for the EPA was cut by 30 percent and the Council on Environmental Quality's by half, and in 1982, Reagan insisted that the United States be the only country not to sign a UN statement declaring a respect for nature. Instead, the Reagan administration moved to "privatize" public land, offering its use to lumber, mining, and agricultural interests. In 1982, Watt announced the administration's intention to sell thirty-seven million acres, and by September 1983, Watt had released 1.7 million acres of wilderness from federal protection—without the required congressional approval. The administration also proposed to double timber production from national forests within the decade. The "privatized" deforestation of public land effectively served as a public subsidy for lumber corporations. A study of national forests in Colorado found that timber purchases returned only thirty-five cents for every taxpayer dollar spent on production and translated to consumer savings amounting to "a discount of about $100 on the cost of a $75,000 wood frame house."[23]

For nearly two decades, environmental organizations had learned a specific formula for success. Rather than focus on grassroots protest, they "professionalized" their efforts by setting up Washington, DC, offices and raising funds for lobbying efforts. The governing assumptions of the Liberal Era gave these organizations access to policy makers, even those who opposed them. Under Reagan, however, this strategy became a dead end, as environmentalists' pleas were drowned out by the sheer volume of corporate lobbyists—and any new legislation would simply go unenforced.

In the face of hopelessness on the national political stage, activists in many movements bypassed government altogether and focused their efforts locally. The religiously rooted Sanctuary movement openly violated federal immigration law by offering asylum to refugees of Reagan's brutal military interventions in El Salvador, Guatemala, Nicaragua, and elsewhere. Antinuclear organizations such as the Clamshell Alliance broke into testing sites and protested the building of new nuclear plants. The Sea Shepherd Conservation Society sabotaged illegal whale hunts on the open seas. ACT UP members disrupted the New York Stock Exchange in hopes of sinking the stock price of a pharmaceutical company. Food Not Bombs gave away free food to antinuclear protesters and the homeless—and met severe police repression for doing so, prompting the United Nations to open an investigation into human rights violations.[24]

EARTH FIRST! AND DIRECT ACTION

Earth First!, founded in 1980, protected American wilderness using direct-action tactics, such as tree-sits, road blockades, and the sabotaging of logging equipment. Their methods were direct in the sense that they literally stopped activities such as the clear-cutting of old-growth forests, at least temporarily. Mirroring the posture of the Reagan administration, the group adopted the slogan "No Compromise in Defense of Mother Earth." It offered a last line of defense, a desperate attempt to turn back its opponents when lawsuits, picket lines, and formal political channels failed. Earth First!'s activism was militant, but the group had an irreverent, often silly, sense of humor that helped offset the traumatic and unsettling implications of its work. Activists knew that if they failed, their losses would be permanent. If ancient forests were destroyed or animals were driven to extinction, they would be gone forever. Earth First! members understood what they were up against and that their defenses were unlikely to hold, but they accepted the burden anyway and willingly put their bodies on the line.

Under Reagan's appointees, federal environmental agencies in the 1980s were openly hostile to the concerns of activists and acted as corporate proxies. Perhaps because these dynamics so clearly paralleled those of pre–New Deal America, Earth First!'s methods and literature drew heavily from the labor movement of the Gilded Age. For example, the group adopted the tactic of "spiking" trees (hammering thick nails into them to discourage cutting), which had been used by striking timber workers many decades earlier.

But while Earth First!'s campaigns often targeted giant lumber corporations and their government allies, those groups excelled at pitting them against workers in a zero-sum game of jobs versus forests. In an attempt counter this narrative, Earth First! activists in Northern California organized their group as a joint chapter of the Industrial Workers of the World (IWW), a radical labor union with roots in the early twentieth century.[25]

Earth First! also drew on 1960s protest traditions, most clearly through an emphasis on nonviolent civil disobedience. Tree-sits, in which activists climbed into trees (often for months at a time) to prevent cutting, and road blockades, in which activists often locked their arms and necks to heavy equipment, were essentially sit-ins. Decades earlier, the civil rights movement had used civil disobedience to challenge white supremacists' claims to segregated spaces, such as schools, lunch counters, buses, and city streets. And while the segregated lunch counters of Woolworth's department stores were clearly racialized spaces, they were also economic spaces. Activists challenged not only who would be allowed to sit together but also whether the rights of businesses to deny service trumped the rights of people to be served. For Earth First!, the conflict zones were old-growth forests, and the group similarly rejected their opponents' ownership claims. With its own unique spin, Earth First! asked the fundamental question of the Post-Liberal Era: should the rights of businesses (say, to poison water supplies or clear-cut forests) in their pursuit of profit outweigh the rights of people (to clean air and water) or the rights of animals (to exist)?

For challenging the free rein of business, Earth First! was routinely targeted by private security, police, and the FBI—the latter using tactics strikingly similar to the Counter-Intelligence Program (COINTELPRO) it used to spy on, harass, frame, and murder activists during the 1960s. Public outcry about COINTELPRO and the Watergate scandal in the mid-1970s had compelled Congress to investigate the actions of the FBI, CIA, and National Security Agency (NSA). Among other misdeeds, the Church and Pike committee investigations uncovered massive CIA and FBI mail-opening programs, FBI death threats against Martin Luther King Jr., and a CIA database of one and a half million potentially "subversive" Americans. The Ford administration, however, including Chief of Staff Donald Rumsfeld and CIA Director George H. W. Bush, stonewalled investigators. The Carter administration later implemented tighter controls on national security agencies by executive order, but these regulations were then loosened under Reagan.[26]

By the late 1980s, FBI infiltrators and informers were rampant within Earth First!, numbering as many as fifty. In 1989, following more than two years of prodding by undercover agents, Earth First! founder Dave Foreman and four other environmental activists were arrested on charges of conspiring to sabotage Arizona power lines. FBI agents admitted in their own tape-recorded conversations that Foreman was not "an actual perpetrator" but that his imprisonment would "send a message."[27] The following year, after the group received dozens of death threats for its campaigns in Northern California, a car carrying Earth First! activists Judi Bari and Darryl Cherney exploded, shattering Bari's pelvis. Oakland police and FBI investigators accused Bari and Cherney of making the bomb themselves, linking Earth First! with terrorism in national news coverage. Twelve years later, however, a federal jury exonerated Bari and Cherney and ruled that federal agents and Oakland police officers had violated their civil rights. Incidentally, the special agent in charge of the San Francisco FBI office at the time of the bombing was Richard W. Held, who had played a key role in COINTELPRO operations that framed members of the Black Panther Party two decades earlier.[28]

STRUCTURE AND CAMPAIGNS

Partially because activists were fearful of police provocateurs and informants, Earth First! was highly decentralized—more of a network than a formal organization. In 1982, the group's national directory included fifty-one contacts in twenty-eight states. By the end of 1988, that list had expanded to seventy-five local contacts and thirteen national working groups, as well as sister organizations in thirteen other countries. Local affiliates communicated through updates in the *Earth First! Journal* and a variety of traveling "roadshows." Activists also met annually at the Round River Rendezvous, a weeklong retreat that often culminated with protest actions in support of the regional hosts' campaigns.[29]

Earth First!'s projects were varied. Chapters primarily focused on issues of local importance, but they also cooperated on national and regional campaigns. From 1984 to 1987, the group led a national boycott of Burger King, whose cattle imports were fed on clear-cut rain forests. Earth First! activists also allied themselves with the efforts of indigenous activists, the antinuclear movement, and the Sea Shepherd Conservation Society, which was later featured on the television program *Whale Wars*. Many of the group's opponents were corporations, such as timber giant Maxxam, but its campaigns frequently targeted the US Forest Service and the US Bureau of Land Management, which activists viewed as extensions of corporate power. Indeed, while Ronald Reagan vilified welfare recipients to justify cutting poverty programs, his administration offered public land to corporate interests below market value and allowed ranchers to use public land for cattle grazing. This was not merely bad environmental policy; that would imply that ecology was of any concern. It was economic policy—the transfer of public holdings to corporations through "privatization"—and the hypocrisy of these corporate welfare programs was not lost on environmentalists.[30]

Earth First!'s most famous campaigns involved protecting the US's few remaining old-growth forests from the encroachment of real estate developers, mining companies, and timber interests. Prominent stands included the defense of the Kalmiopsis Wilderness area and Cathedral Forest in Oregon, areas of Glacier National Park and Yellowstone National Park in Montana, the Grand Canyon in Arizona, the Okanogan National Forest in northern Washington, the Jemez Mountains in New Mexico, and the redwood forests of Northern California.

Because these efforts were defensive, they often lasted for years, with alternating periods of intense action, lull, and stalemate. Campaigns also routinely changed form and venue, as clear-cutting and building logging roads were weather dependent, forcing annual winter breaks for loggers and activists alike. Earth First! teams might spend summers blocking roads and smuggling supplies to tree-sitters and winters raising funds, reflecting on failures, and strategizing for the next round. One particularly illustrative Earth First! campaign was the nearly twenty-year struggle to prevent the University of Arizona from building a telescope complex on the ecologically sensitive 10,700-foot peak of Mount Graham, in Arizona's Coronado National Forest.

"THE MOUNT GRAHAM ROLLER-COASTER"

In July 1994, after a decade-long series of protests, arrests, temporary victories, and subsequent setbacks, environmental activists won an injunction against the University of Arizona that demanded compliance with the Endangered Species Act and the National Environmental Policy Act (NEPA). If the school wanted to finish construction of its $100 million telescope, it would have to do so in accordance with federal environmental law. University officials already knew that their development plans could not meet those standards, however, and their own scientists had advised a less vulnerable location. But the school pushed on, and in 1996, President Bill Clinton signed into law a $160 billion omnibus spending bill that included a rider, an unrelated add-on, by Congressman Jim Kolbe of Arizona. The rider exempted the University of Arizona from following federal law, allowing it to build its telescopes without concern for their environmental impact.[31]

For more than ten years, Earth First! activists had used a combination of pickets, legal challenges, direct-action disruptions, and pressure campaigns against financial backers in order to prevent the university's Steward Observatory from building its telescope complex at Mount Graham. Earth First!'s coalition included American Indian activists, college students at dozens of schools across the US, and several other environmental groups, notably including the Sierra Club. In the end, however, the university and its financial partners, including the Catholic Church, were able to outspend the Mount Graham coalition and outmaneuver it through connections with legislators.

Earth First!'s campaign against the Mount Graham observatory began in the fall of 1985 with a demonstration at a public meeting regarding the university's proposal. Then, in October, activists dressed as bears, a raccoon, a mountain lion, and a spotted owl marched on the forest supervisor's office to deliver a list of the animals' demands. As the university's plan proceeded, a coalition of more than thirty organizations began publicizing the significance and fragility of the mountain's ecosystem.[32]

A spruce-fir forest in the middle of a desert, Mount Graham is a "sky island," a mountain with an ecological makeup that is radically different from the surrounding lowlands. As a result of this isolation, the area was home to fifteen unique species of insects, "eight plants found nowhere else, two unique snails, Peregrine Falcons (an Endangered Species), Spotted Owls,"[33] and the Mount Graham red squirrel, an endangered species with an estimated population at the time of between 150 and 300. Biologist Peter

Warshall, one of over two hundred members of Scientists for the Preservation of Mt. Graham, likened the area's uniqueness to only a small handful of other places in the world, such as the Galapagos Islands, the Celbes of Southeast Asia, and the highlands of East Africa. In a 1990 *Washington Post* article, Arizona Game and Fish Department biologist Tom Waddell described Mount Graham as "an isolated museum of what was here 11,000 years ago."[34] For these reasons, as well as the range's spiritual significance for the San Carlos Apache Nation, Mount Graham was a controversial location for the telescope complex, and the school itself had also identified nearly forty other locations that could meet its needs.[35]

Administrators pressed on nonetheless, recruiting a range of investors and hiring the high-profile Washington lobbying firm Patton, Boggs, and Blow to plead their case on Capitol Hill. In 1988, attempts by Senators John McCain and Dennis DeConcini of Arizona to create an "astrophysical preserve" for the telescopes failed. After the congressional recess, however, the university's $1 million lobbying investment paid off when McCain, DeConcini, and Congressman Jim Kolbe attached a rider to that year's Arizona-Idaho Conservation Act, allowing it to bypass much of the Endangered Species Act and the National Environmental Policy Act. While other environmental activists launched a legal challenge, Arizona Earth First! members Nancy Morton, Nancy Zierenberg, and Lynn Bohi occupied the Tucson office of Congressman Mo Udall of Arizona, a self-professed conservationist (and University of Arizona alumnus), who had refused to intervene against the rider.[36]

In February 1990, members of Earth First! and Greenpeace targeted one of the telescope's principal backers, the Smithsonian Institute. Protesters hung a twenty-five-foot banner on the front of the Museum of Natural History, displayed squirrel-sized coffins on the National Mall, and carried signs that read, "Extinction on Mount Graham Courtesy of the Smithsonian." They also targeted a national conference on environmental law, whose attendees returned from lunch to find Earth First! pamphlets on Mount Graham at their place settings. All references to the Smithsonian had been circled in red. Unaccustomed to public protest, the museum withdrew from the Mount Graham project altogether the next year, choosing instead to invest in a telescope based in Hawaii.[37]

While Earth First! activists were pressuring the Smithsonian, a Sierra Club lawsuit uncovered a pattern of government malfeasance. The telescope complex's exemptions from environmental law were contingent on an official "biological opinion" from the US Fish and Wildlife Service (USFWS), which oversaw the Endangered Species Program. But while the opinion's authors, including biologist Sam Spiller, had concluded that the project would in fact threaten the area's wildlife, Regional Director Michael Spear pressured them to give their approval.[38]

This embarrassing revelation led the USFWS to order a new biological opinion, but it did not convince the Forest Service to revoke the university's permit. A subsequent investigation by the congressional General Accounting Office (GAO) determined that development "posed an unacceptable risk to the red squirrel's survival,"[39] a conclusion amplified by new data showing that the squirrel population had dropped from 215 in 1988 to as few as 132 by May 1990. This finding led to a thirty-day delay for the project, but the committee in charge of reviewing biological data was headed by Michael Spear, who had sabotaged the first assessment. The GAO investigation also unearthed allegations that Senator John McCain had pressured Coronado National Forest Service supervisor Jim Abbott to ensure the project's success or else have "the shortest tenure of any Forest Service Supervisor on record."[40]

But while the GAO investigation prompted widespread outcry in Congress (with McCain, DeConcini, and Congressman Jon Kyl of Arizona awkwardly joining the chorus), other federal officials showed less concern. George H. W. Bush had expressed a desire to be known as the "environmental president," but his interior secretary, Manuel Lujan Jr., announced in a May 1990 interview with the *Denver Post* that the Endangered Species Act (ESA) was "too tough." As "the best example," Lujan cited the Mount Graham red squirrel, and he questioned why "we have to save every subspecies": "nobody's told me the difference between a red squirrel, a black one or a brown one." In a subsequent *New York Times* editorial, Donald Falk, executive director for the Center for Plant Conservation, described Lujan's statement as showing "an alarming ignorance of basic biology" for the "highest public official entrusted with the stewardship of our natural resources." President Bush distanced himself from Lujan's comments, but he threatened to block the ESA's renewal just two years later.[41]

That September, with the review process complete and a temporary injunction lifted, the Ninth Circuit Court of Appeals allowed construction to begin anew. With legal options exhausted, Earth First! turned to more direct methods: disruptive protest and sabotage. On October 2, logging and construction crews arrived to find two forest gates chained shut, and the crews had to use blowtorches to open them. The next gate was blocked by a protester, who was attached to it with a bicycle lock (which required a slow, careful removal). After clearing this hurdle, the convoy encountered an additional seven roadblocks before finally reaching the building site. There, they found even more Earth First! activists chained to trees. By the time they were all cleared, work had been delayed by eight hours. The next day, a "funeral march" through the forest and a temporary tree-sit prevented cutting for two hours. The third day, yet another march, followed by civil disobedience protests, resulted in a three-and-a-half-hour delay and twenty-three arrests.[42]

In the weeks that followed, activists mounted another gate blockade and blocked roads with logs almost daily, but they could not stop the clearing of two of the three designated telescope areas.

The third cut, however, was delayed by a weeklong tree-sit, which compelled the school officials to opt for an alternative location with less environmental impact. It was a small victory but a victory nonetheless. In November 1990, activists closed the Mount Graham preservation camp for winter, dejected that their efforts were "the equivalent of hubcap theft in the face of a project which threatens a species extinction."[43]

In 1991, Mount Graham defenders focused their efforts on the telescopes' sponsors outside Arizona. In addition to the withdrawal of the Smithsonian Institute, activists also forced the collapse of Ohio State University's support for the project. A year of student protests at Ohio State had forced the Astronomy Department to hire its own PR firm, and two days after a mock funeral for Mount Graham on campus, the school's Board of Trustees eliminated the telescope from its agenda—leaving the Astronomy program to find its own funding. Building on this victory, protesters in Ohio disrupted a campus visit by University of Arizona President Manual Pacheco with a banner drop, informational fliers on car windshields, and an airplane banner reading, "OSU, U of A save Apache rights and Mt. Graham." A few weeks later, multiple banner drops and ten thousand fliers greeted the arrival of the University of Arizona football team as it kicked off its season, with a 38–14 loss in Columbus. After activists, including "Ruth the Red Squirrel," began talking to media at the nationally televised game, OSU officials announced that the school would not participate in the Mount Graham project.[44]

With funding from the Smithsonian and Ohio State cut off, activists shifted their focus to another major co-sponsor, the Catholic Church. In 1992, the Vatican Observatory finally addressed Apache opposition to the Mount Graham project, which included two unanimous Tribal Council resolutions in 1990 as well as a 1991 resolution endorsed by fifteen American Indian nations and eleven US environmental groups. In the response, Father George

Coyne, the Vatican astronomer at the University of Arizona, noted that while Apache oral traditions linked the Apache to Mount Graham much earlier, "there are no clear written records of any group of Apaches using Mt. Graham until the mid-1600s."[45] In effect, Coyne argued that violating even four hundred years of tradition was insignificant compared to the interests of the Catholic Church. Coyne later said of the native view, "[It is] a kind of religiosity to which I cannot subscribe, and which must be suppressed with all the force we can muster."[46]

While Father Coyne held the paternalistic and racist view that Apache claims were little more than environmentalists' attempts to "manipulate the American Indians,"[47] Father Charles Polzer, another Jesuit priest and Arizona faculty member, identified a different source of opposition to the telescopes. According to Polzer, the effort to protect Mount Graham was a conspiracy of the "Jewish lawyers of the ACLU to undermine and destroy the Catholic Church."[48] With the Vatican unmoved by Apache concerns, movement allies planned solidarity actions, including an October 1992 protest at the Vatican embassy in London by Earth First! and a group calling itself "Catholics Against Vatican Exploitation of Apache Traditional Sites."[49]

In 1993 and 1994, Earth First! and its allies escalated their campaign. During the summer of 1993, the group held its annual Round River Rendezvous at Mount Graham. Following the retreat, activists occupied the office of the University of Arizona president and were forcefully removed. That same summer, acknowledging the public relations blunder of using the telescope project to honor another defiler of indigenous land, the university changed the name of the third proposed telescope from the "Columbus" to the more generic, less offensive "Large Binocular Telescope" (LBT).[50]

While continuing to condemn the original name, native activists refused to offer the school an opportunity to restore its image.

Ola Cassadore Davis of the Apache Survival Coalition responded bluntly, "They can name it Sally or John or whatever name they want, but we still don't want it. That mountain is our church, it's a temple, so they should leave it alone, leave it the way it is."[51]

In September, Apache activists joined Earth First! in a protest action at the dedication of the first two telescopes. The disruptions included bicycle-lock blockades, a tripod-sit, and a loud drum circle by the Arizona American Indian Movement, leading to ten arrests and delaying the dedication ceremony for three hours. A month earlier, Colorado and Arizona Earth First! activists had converged on the Vatican-sponsored World Youth Day in Denver, which closed with an airplane flying over the crowd pulling a banner reading, "The Pope Sins on Mount Graham— Earth First!" The Catholic Church's seeming omnipresence made it powerful, but it also provided protesters with many opportunities for confrontation.[52]

By 1994, the campaign to stop the Large Binocular Telescope reached its peak, as the project's North American backers began withdrawing one after the other. In January, student activist Naomi Mudge addressed the University of Arizona faculty senate in order to debunk public statements by the school's vice president. The same month, the University of Toronto, the telescope's only Canadian backer, dropped out, following a demonstration against the school's astronomy department. In February, an Earth First! climber occupied, and hung banners from, the University of Arizona's clock tower for nearly a week. Though police blew whistles and focused spotlights on the squatter to prevent him from sleeping at night, they stopped short of granting University of Arizona business major (and apparent racist) Greg Chapin's request "to see him beat, . . . to see Rodney King all over."[53] In response to the occupation, the university threatened to file a SLAPP suit to reimburse the school for police expenses as well as the cost of installing surveillance cameras on the tower.[54]

In March, Michigan State University responded to student protests by removing its name from consideration for the telescope. In April, Earth First!, the Student Environmental Action Coalition (SEAC), the Apache Survival Coalition, and other groups conducted an international "Day of Action." Activists in more than forty cities participated, including occupations of Forest Service offices in Vermont, Minnesota, Georgia, and Oregon, as well as actions against the archdiocese in San Francisco, California, and the Research Corporation, another telescope partner, in Tucson, Arizona. Fifty European astronomers also signed a petition against the LBT. In response to an on-campus demonstration related to the day of action, officials at the University of Pittsburgh, the last American school still considering the Mount Graham project, also withdrew. Activist pressure on Pitt's administration had been building for years, including a visit by San Carlos Apache member Raleigh Thompson in March 1993 and a student occupation of the chancellor's office that December.[55]

On the heels of this string of victories, and after nearly ten years of legal appeals, the Ninth Circuit Court of Appeals finally issued a permanent injunction against the building of the LBT, requiring the University of Arizona to comply with both the Endangered Species Act and the National Environmental Policy Act. A year later, the court officially denied the school's appeal, seemingly dooming the expansion of the complex for the foreseeable future. As Mark Hughes of the Sierra Club Legal Defense Fund had predicted, "as soon as someone really studies the impacts of the observatory on the squirrel—and no one has done this—the project will be dead."[56] Indeed, the Mount Graham project could not proceed within the confines of the law.[57]

Earth First!'s pressure campaign was working, but with so much money on the line, University of Arizona officials and their business partners refused to accept defeat. In December 1995, President Clinton vetoed an appropriations bill full of environmental exemptions, including waivers for Alaskan old-growth forests, roadless areas in Montana, and Mount Graham—a provision added by Arizona congressman Jon Kyl. Six months later, however, the university finally succeeded in freeing itself from the responsibilities of US law. In May, Clinton signed Congress's omnibus budget bill, which included a new rider exempting the project from environmental considerations. The next month, the court implemented the rider and lifted its ban, allowing construction to proceed unhindered.[58]

With the legal hurdles removed, Ohio State University rejoined the project in February 1997. Two years later, Notre Dame University signed on. In 2002, the University of Virginia and the University of Minnesota joined the project as well, despite intense protests from students, faculty, and indigenous groups. Virginia's participation was particularly biting, as the Virginia Council on Indians, representing all eight of the state's tribes, had joined the Apache plea against the telescope. The faculty committee in charge of the decision recommended participation, with the condescending and contradictory caveats that the school encourage the University of Arizona to form a committee to improve relations with American Indians and that its own school also attempt to improve relations with American Indian students and faculty. At a cost of over $120 million, the Large Binocular Telescope was dedicated in 2004 and became fully operational in 2008.[59]

★ ★ ★

The exhausting, twenty-year defense of Mount Graham was just one of dozens of campaigns by Earth First! activists during the 1980s and 1990s, and many of them were engaged simultaneously. This feat is especially impressive given the physically and emotionally exhausting nature of their activism and the constant stream of death threats, beatings, and arrests that they faced. Though the organization's activities were widespread, Earth First!

made up only a small portion of the environmental movement of the period. While prominent national organizations continued to lobby politicians—with little hope for success—Earth First! members used their bodies to blunt the efforts of polluters and clear-cutters on the front lines. Their tactics, including nonviolent civil disobedience and sabotage, were inherently defensive, however, and could only impede, not permanently stop, their opponents.

The Mount Graham campaign—a seemingly minor, local conflict between environmentalists and a university—required activists to organize an international pressure campaign against the Catholic Church, the Smithsonian, a dozen universities, multiple federal agencies, and several members of Congress. Earth First! built coalitions with indigenous rights groups, college students, scientists, and others and targeted the University of Arizona and its financial backers with a combination of legal challenges, public shaming, and direct-action disruptions. It was smart, strategic protest, and it was able to slow construction dramatically. However, it ultimately failed.

Activists, by putting their bodies in the way, preserved the forests of Mount Graham through the destructive years of the Reagan administration, the Bush administration, and into the Clinton administration. They effectively opened a decade-long window for an environmentally friendly regime to emerge, but it never did. Earth First!'s loss in the Mount Graham campaign was a failure of progressives in the broader political arena, not just of the activists on the ground. Over the course of the 1980s, leaders in the Democratic Party increasingly embraced neoliberalism, trading the party's Liberal Era base for corporate donors. Environmental lobbyists were able to compel Bill Clinton to reject the blatant assault on the 1995 Interior Department appropriations bill, but his economic priority was deregulation. For Earth First!'s broader efforts to succeed, neoliberalism would have had to be a Republican position that was turned back following the Reagan and first Bush years. Instead, it became a bipartisan philosophy. Environmentalists, as well as labor unions and women's and civil rights activists, were left with an obvious party to vote against but without a clear choice to support. As the Mount Graham case illustrates, the success of protest movements cannot rely on either direct action or participation in electoral politics—it requires pressure on the powerful through both.

Many of the direct-action groups of the 1980s are still active, including Earth First!, the Sea Shepherd Conservation Society, and Earth First! offshoot the Rainforest Action Network (RAN). Their most significant legacy may be at the tactical level, though, where they served as a bridge between 1960s guerrilla theater groups, such as the Yippies and the Diggers, and the carnival protesters of the 1990s. The Yippies had been experts at using humor and myth-making for political ends, reportedly dumping money onto the trading floor of the New York Stock Exchange (to watch traders trip over one another in pursuit) and applying for a government permit to levitate the Pentagon and purge it of its Vietnam War demons. During the conspiracy trial of the Chicago 8, Abbie Hoffman and Jerry Rubin appeared in court dressed as judges, Chicago police officers, and American Revolutionaries. Earth First! activists similarly protested in animal costumes and made public appearances as Smokey the Bear, at which he denounced the US Forest Service.

The forest-centered tactics that Earth First! developed, including tree-sits, tripod-sits, and burying oneself waist deep during a road blockade, had largely originated in the Australian environmental movement and reappeared in different contexts in subsequent decades. In the early 1990s, Reclaim the Streets, which was originally an Earth First! UK spin-off, organized illegal dance parties in busy intersections, and activists suspended on tripods were a frequent staple. Earth First!'s taste for disruption and oc-

cupying space was also paralleled in the protests of the AIDS Coalition to Unleash Power (ACT UP) and Critical Mass. ACT UP
activists interrupted the New York Stock Exchange in 1989 and
the *CBS Evening News* in 1991, while Critical Mass blocked traffic
with large-scale bicycle parades. Many of Earth First!'s blockading
tactics were also used during the protests that shut down the 1999
meeting of the World Trade Organization in Seattle.[60]

Groups such as Earth First!, ACT UP, Food Not Bombs, and
others took bold, dangerous actions to defend the environment,
steer government and drug-company responses to the AIDS crisis,
and feed the hungry. They responded to a period of political hopelessness with local engagement. However, the long-term inability
of protest movements to impact national elections—and, specifically, to counter corporate influence at the federal level—proved
disastrous. The protest movements that had been so successful during the Liberal Era—movements for workers' rights, civil
rights, women's rights, the environment, and others—could not
stem the tide of the "Reagan Revolution." They could not provide
a serious challenge to neoliberal hegemony at the federal level, and
their grassroots power hit a wall. Meanwhile, however, pockets of
resistance developed in some unorthodox, if not entirely unex-
pected, places.[61]

2

REBEL SPACES

YOUTH, ART, AND COUNTERCULTURES

Somewhere between the distanced slogans and abstract calls to
arms, we . . . discovered through Gilman a way to give our politics
some application in our actual lives.
—Mike K., 924 Gilman Street

One of the ideas behind ABC is breaking down the barriers between
bands and people and making everyone equal. There is no Us and
Them.
—Chris Boarts Larson, ABC No Rio

EARTH FIRST! RESPONDED TO THE POLITICAL CLIMATE OF
the 1980s by blockading roads and sabotaging logging equipment
to slow the encroachment of timber, mining, and other corporate
interests onto public land. In the nation's rapidly deindustrializ-
ing urban areas, new youth countercultures, such as punk rock,
hip-hop, and graffiti, confronted the period's political shifts with
rather different forms of protest.

While Earth First!'s activism was intended to halt new acts of
privatization and deregulation, these youth movements emerged
from urban contexts already impacted by a decade or more of declining economic opportunities, cuts to public services, and the
elimination—and criminalization—of public spaces. Their protests, too, often targeted neoliberal policies at their points of impact, though not always with a clear understanding of the source
or even of the political implications of their actions. Within these
broad arts movements, though, there were clear examples of direct

opposition to neoliberalism and to the conservative social agenda that accompanied it.

THE CRIMINALIZATION OF YOUTH CULTURE

The modern graffiti movement began as an accessible and crudely democratic art form. While experienced artists might graduate to more complex tools, amateur tagging initially required little more than a permanent marker—enough to write, "I was here." The popularity of street art has since spread along a number of diverse trajectories, but it initially grew out of inner cities in the late 1960s and 1970s—areas that had been devastated by a combination of economic strangulation and so-called urban-renewal and slum-clearance policies. During this period, the city of Cleveland closed some $50 million in recreational facilities, while New York City cut $40 million from its public parks. The era's budget cuts also limited access to public schoolyards during after-school hours, a problem compounded by a lack of employment opportunities for American teens—young people of color, in particular. For African American youth in the 1980s, unemployment hovered at around 40 percent.[1]

In New York City, which faced bankruptcy while watching much of its infrastructure fall into disrepair, graffiti writers became convenient scapegoats for the city's politicians. The city government used its budget shortfalls to justify slashing social programs (and to demand $150 million in loans from public school teachers), but it found nearly $400 million to combat graffiti. City leaders justified these expenditures by publicly likening graffiti to rape and terrorism, rather than petty vandalism. Graffiti art was very much an outgrowth of Post-Liberal America. As budgets for public art and after-school programs were cut, graffiti writers targeted and "reclaimed" abandoned or increasingly privatized urban spaces. But while their protests were often "prepolitical," the repercussions were not dissimilar from the official responses to Earth First! In the process of a decades-long campaign, New York City and transit police arrested and beat up countless graffiti artists, including twenty-five-year-old writer Michael Stewart, whom they beat to death in 1983. The city also poisoned more than two hundred city workers, killing one, by exposing them to "the Buff," a chemical compound intended to keep subway cars graffiti free.[2]

Other aspects of hip-hop culture as it emerged in the 1970s and 1980s were similarly structured and met similar receptions. Like graffiti art, rap music required minimal investment in equipment; rappers deliberately recycled the underlying beats of already-recorded songs and distributed music on bootleg cassette tapes. It was an art form accessible to youth of limited means. As Tricia Rose notes in *Black Noise*, the famous break-dancer Crazy Legs took up dancing in part "because his single mother couldn't afford Little League baseball fees."[3] Break-dancers, DJs, and rappers also often used atypical venues for their performances, taking over public spaces such as intersections, abandoned warehouses, and vacant lots. Break-dancers were arrested for attracting undesirable crowds of loiterers, and rap artists such as Ice T and N.W.A. were publicly condemned by the FBI, police, members of Congress, and both the president and vice president of the United States for lyrics that (profanely) confronted racial profiling, police brutality, and the "War on Drugs."[4]

DO-IT-YOURSELF PUNK

The punk-rock movement also emerged from this cultural moment, and many of its core impulses paralleled those of graffiti and hip-hop. Like hip-hop, punk rock developed in many different directions, but it was generally guided by a "do-it-yourself" (DIY) ethos that encouraged participants to move beyond the role of consumers and instead become actively involved, by distributing self-produced magazines ("zines"), organizing shows (often in alternative venues, such as union halls and the basements of houses), or playing music (a frequently cited excerpt from an early punk zine, for example, contains a diagram of three guitar chords and features the caption, "Now Form a Band").[5]

One outgrowth of the movement's participatory emphasis was the reclamation and reappropriation of space, whether the basements of rented homes or squatted warehouses. In the least structured forms of these "free spaces"—areas separate from the watchful eyes of the state or profit-seeking vultures—they allowed youth to exert control over their immediate environments. Like the empty lots occupied by DJs and the city walls temporarily claimed by graffiti writers, much of the punk world was ephemeral—on borrowed time and in borrowed spaces. However, the movement also produced a number of more formal counterinstitutions, including music venues, media, and record labels. Punk rock took for granted that participants could shape the world around them and that they could do so according to their principles, not their profitability. The movement's structures operated as cultural and economic alternatives to the corporate entertainment industry and, more specifically, as sites of resistance to the privatizing agenda of neoliberalism. Punks rejected the notion that all interactions should be guided by economic self-interest, and, like Earth First!, they tried to carve out spaces outside the market.

This type of activism had precedents in the movements of the 1960s, which founded cooperative bookstores, coffee shops, and organic grocery stores all over the US. These spaces were typically organized according to basic democratic principles: consensus-based decision making, voluntary participation, and (relatively) horizontal leadership structures. Like Earth First!'s blockades, these institutions took a direct-action approach to politics—"a congruence of means and ends."[6] Rather than protesting to recruit outside assistance or gain access to dominant institutions, organizers instead built their own alternatives.[7]

Among many such examples were two collectively run, all-ages punk-rock venues: Berkeley, California's 924 Gilman Street and New York City's ABC No Rio. During the 1980s and 1990s, these spaces nurtured a culture of resistance that opposed sexism, racism, and homophobia and rejected the financialization of human relationships. Through both their structural organization and their interactions with neighbors, these clubs also gave their members opportunities to develop their political beliefs and, importantly, to learn the skills needed to apply them. 924 Gilman and ABC No Rio encouraged active democratic participation, and, as a result, they cultivated skilled, empowered activists.[8]

CLAIMING A SPACE

The introduction of punk-rock shows at the ABC No Rio art gallery, in 1989, and the establishment of 924 Gilman Street, in 1986, were very much of their specific political and cultural moment. As neoliberal organizations such as ALEC, the Heritage Foundation, and the Business Roundtable pursued their economic agenda during the 1970s, they made common cause in establishing a new Republican Party base with a growing movement of social conservatives, including Jerry Falwell, Anita Bryant, and Phyllis Schlafly. In 1972, the antifeminist Schlafly, who once equated sex-education classes with "in-home sales parties for abortions," founded the group STOP ERA (which later became the Eagle Forum).[9] Perhaps no other individual deserves more credit for derailing the Equal Rights Amendment, though she certainly represented the male-supremacist beliefs of millions of American men and women. Anita Bryant of Save Our Children, meanwhile, spent the late 1970s promoting discriminatory antigay laws in Florida, California, Minnesota, Kansas, and elsewhere and using her fame to publicly legitimize homophobic bigotry. Bryant worried, "If gays are granted rights, next we'll have to give rights to prostitutes and to people who sleep with St. Bernards."[10] During the same period, Gilburn Durand, who had previously worked with the conservative John Birch Society, launched "Operation Avalanche," a campaign to organize Catholic clergy to "mobilize the [country's] 43 million Catholics into an army of pro-life political activists."[11]

Cultural conservatives' reach was substantial. Falwell alone was broadcast on 300 radio stations and 373 television channels, and his Moral Majority claimed a membership of four million people by 1981. And though Christian conservatism was not new, the anxiety that guided this particular push was clearly a reaction to Sixties-era cultural shifts around gender, sex, and sexuality. Rev. Falwell was driven by the twin fears of homosexuality and feminism, the latter of which he described as a "satanic attack on the home."[12] Abortion soon became the main plank in the movement against women's rights, but Falwell was clear about his broader agenda, professing, "With all my heart, I want to bury the Equal Rights Amendment once and for all in a deep, dark grave."[13] Other Christian conservatives expressed similar sentiments. The conservative group Christian Voice argued, "America's rapid decline as a world power [was] a direct result" of activism by feminists, who were "moral perverts" and "enemies of every decent society," while one evangelical minister counseled that "wife beating is on the rise because men are no longer leaders in their homes. I tell women they must go back home and be more submissive."[14]

Many American punk-rock bands, such as the Dead Kennedys and Reagan Youth, were openly hostile to the Reagan administration and its policies; but punk rock as a whole was politically ambiguous, and it often veered toward nihilism. By the mid-1980s, American punk shows had become increasingly apolitical and violent spaces. This trend was exacerbated by the lax security standards of traditional music venues, where owners sought to maximize admission revenue at all-ages shows to make up for the loss in alcohol sales. Club bouncers were also unpredictable, as likely to respond to minor conflicts with force as to ignore actual fighting. The founding members of 924 Gilman and ABC No Rio had to confront all of these issues, not only the reliance on privately owned venues but also destructive elements within their own punk communities. They did so by building volunteer-based, nonprofit clubs and taking unequivocal responsibility for their patrons' security.[15]

The clubs were both structured according to the same basic two-part mission: to provide a safe atmosphere by confronting violence and oppressive behavior and to involve each member of the punk community directly, through a process of consensus-based decision making. To accomplish the first task, each collective adopted explicit policies against fighting, drugs and alcohol, and the oppressive trio of racism, sexism, and homophobia. These policies were clearly printed on their fliers, and they applied to the bands that they booked as well as audiences at their shows.

While openly stating these principles ensured that each club generally attracted a less aggressive audience, collective members also experimented with a number of tactics for enforcing them. For example, during various periods in each club's history, collective members formed impromptu crowd-monitoring teams to identify potentially violent behavior, surround the offenders, and break into silly dances (such as conga lines) to deescalate the situation. At Gilman, bands stopped playing if fights broke out, so that the entire audience could address the problem together. According to volunteer Kamala Parks, "The fighters would be brought out into the street, and . . . the show wouldn't go on unless something was resolved."[16] In one notable case, the singer of a performing band responded to an altercation by leaping into the crowd, microphone in hand, to interview the antagonists. After hearing the absurdity of their grievances through the sound system, the two parties quickly made amends. However, such lighthearted antics were not sufficient for every threat.[17]

924 Gilman's association with antiracist bands, fund-raising events, and the well-known, outspokenly antiracist zine *Maximum RocknRoll* made it a favorite target for Bay Area neo-Nazi skinhead gangs. After experimenting with hiring off-duty police officers and professional security services, Gilman eventually trained security personnel from among its own ranks, placing responsibility for safety on its own shoulders. According to Gilman member Martin Sprouse, skinhead attacks often led to "huge confrontations" that involved "the entire crowd blocking the front door, keeping the bad guys out."[18] Parks recalls an incident in which "a gang of about twenty skinheads showed up, and . . . a huge fight, complete with baseball bats, chains, and chairs, erupted in front of Gilman."[19] In these cases, words alone were not enough; the collective had to back up its principles physically, with united action.[20]

The outspoken policies against homophobia at the clubs were protest positions, even within punk (and they were, of course, at odds with the platforms of both major political parties). Most bands and individuals were specifically drawn to Gilman and ABC No Rio because they supported their principles, but those who felt excluded periodically lashed out, as in the case of a particularly inflammatory November 1990 letter to the editors of *Maximum RocknRoll*. In response to vaguely feminist comments by ABC No Rio–associated bands, the author of the letter writes, "I'll tell you what's wrong with girls. . . . They're . . . weak and it's easy to kick their ass. . . . I've talked to people who go to ABC NO RIO's [sic] and it seems a new trend to be anti-homophobic because some faggot runs the club, yes faggot. I was brought up to refer to those people as such, and I'm not going to change my whole vocabulary for the sake of some stupid trend."[21]

In another incident, a band that wanted to play at ABC No Rio submitted a demo tape that featured a song titled "The Faggot Stomp." When confronted by Mike Bromberg, who booked the first ABC No Rio punk shows and was openly gay, band members apologized and said that they no longer espoused such beliefs. Satisfied with their response, Bromberg eventually booked them for a show.[22]

Enforcing a policy against sexism was also difficult, and offenders often included collective members themselves. Gilman member Michael D., for example, says that while he never had to "think twice" about confronting racism, he "went through a real mind shift on [sexism] because of Gilman."[23] Although much of the responsibility for challenging sexist behavior ultimately fell to the women of the club, naming sex-based oppression as a collective problem helped create a negotiable, if not entirely "free," space. Volunteer Lauren L., for example, says about Gilman, "I'm comfortable enough there to speak up when guys say stupid shit to me or other women. I don't have to accept that kind of stuff. I know that the other people there will back me up."[24]

In addition to speaking out, women at Gilman used a variety of creative methods to confront chauvinist attitudes. At one point, women hung giant banners in the club that read, "'She plays really good for a girl' (think about what you just said)" and "'Hey, Baby, hold my jacket so I can go in the pit' FUCK YOU!"[25] Gilman women also organized events that celebrated women in punk, hosted touring punk-feminist Riot Grrrl bands, coordinated a regularly meeting women's caucus, and, perhaps most importantly, started bands of their own. Because of the collective's egalitarian structure, women also performed jobs typically dominated by men, serving as club security guards, sound engineers, and booking agents. Gilman did not deliver a utopian model for gender equality, but the club did provide a supportive environment where women could assert their own agency. Volunteer Athena K. credits her experiences at Gilman for giving her "a sense of self-respect about being biracial and . . . a young woman," and several other women offer similar accounts of empowerment.[26]

924 Gilman and ABC No Rio each operated on a system of modified consensus. Day-to-day decisions were made by elected

officers; but the clubs' major decisions required unanimous approval at monthly meetings, and every member's vote was equal. As ABC No Rio member Tucker explains,

> Anyone is welcome to come to our meetings and have input on what we do, though only collective members have voting rights (which are obtained by volunteering regularly). Also, in an effort to increase the openness of the collective and what we're doing, each of the bookers hold booking hours which are open to anyone to attend. . . . If we have a problem with any person or band then we give them the opportunity to speak at a collective meeting before any decisions are made about them (bannings, etc.). . . . Any decision we make is open for discussion and not made by some ultimate authority.[27]

924 Gilman employed similar practices, but the collective also required that patrons pay an annual membership fee with admission to its events. Doing so made all audience members accountable to the club's policies and gave them an equal stake in the club's future. Volunteer Mike Goodbar explains the significance of the access that Gilman provided its members: "At meetings, 14-year-olds have an opportunity to deal with issues sometimes as complex as those faced by 46-year-olds involved with big business corporations. In the regular world a person would have to have . . . access to the right job or [a privileged] situation that would provide the same experiences that Gilman does to anyone who's interested."[28]

The Gilman collective also experimented with a number of innovative methods to increase participation in the democratic process. Early in the club's history, for example, the collective installed a suggestion box and read its contents aloud over the microphone during shows. It also tried a short-lived policy of leaving the microphone on in between bands, allowing audience members the opportunity to question performers about their lyrical content. Gilman's inner walls likewise served as a canvas for free expression and ongoing dialogue—they were covered in graffiti. Though not all of these policies were successful, they illustrated the collective's desire to involve as many people as possible in the maintenance of the club.[29]

Despite the clarity of the clubs' goals, however, both ABC No Rio and 924 Gilman experienced pitfalls and growing pains as they attempted to establish functioning democracies. During Gilman's early years, Tim Yohannon of *Maximum RocknRoll* often held informal veto power over the collective's decisions, due to the magazine's large financial investment. Yohannon eventually became frustrated with what he interpreted as a lack of initiative among the membership and withdrew from the project. The remaining members opted to continue running the club, however, and Yohannon offered them the building's lease and sound system. During this transition, the collective decided to officially incorporate the venue as a nonprofit, which limited its financial risk but also created an undesired de facto hierarchy by requiring the appointment of officers who were legal adults.[30]

ABC No Rio faced similar challenges. Although the art gallery itself had been run collectively since 1980, the initial punk shows in the late 1980s and early 1990s were organized in a less formal manner that was typical of DIY punk. Individuals such as Mike Bromberg booked the shows, but band members and friends contributed by taking money at the door, preventing fights, and cleaning up afterward. Within a few years, the ABC No Rio punks began organizing their efforts in a much more structured fashion, which subsequently allowed them to take a greater stake in the maintenance of the building. However, this transition presented the group with several obstacles. Initial efforts to democratize booking practices, for example, resulted in a free-for-all that failed to ensure that every show had the sufficient bands, volunteers, and promotion. Eventually, the group learned from these mistakes and developed practices that were both effective and in line with its democratic values.[31]

The collectives at 924 Gilman and ABC No Rio each benefited from the initial involvement of members with more extensive organizational backgrounds, but most of those who got involved had no previous experience with activism. However, because the clubs allowed room for democratic experimentation that empowered members and taught them how to resolve conflict collectively (and sometimes creatively), Gilman and ABC No Rio were prepared when each faced external crises.

CONFLICTS AND CAMPAIGNS

During the 1990s, altercations with neighbors and government officials nearly forced 924 Gilman to close on three separate occasions. The first major conflict began in 1991, when the collective requested a change to its city permit. At the behest of Tim Yohannon, the club's original 1986 charter had contained a clause that prohibited advertising for Gilman events. Yohannon had hoped that the punk community would support the club regardless of which bands were playing, but the policy had never been successful. As part of the permit-modification process, the Berkeley Zoning Board sought input from local police, who reported that Gilman's control over its patrons was inadequate, leading to underage drinking, loitering, and vandalism. After reviewing these complaints, the board not only rejected the collective's request but also threatened to revoke the permit altogether. The board eventually granted the club six months in which to make the necessary improvements before facing a final judgment.[32]

If the Gilman punks had previously taken their status in their community for granted, the permit crisis awakened them to their responsibilities. In response to the board's ruling, the collective quickly launched a petition drive and began acquiring letters of support from former workers, patrons' parents, and other members of the Berkeley community. Volunteers also went door-to-door to solicit suggestions and support from the club's neighbors. Throughout the process, Gilman members worked closely with the police department and the city government. In January 1992, representatives of the club met with local police through the city's dispute-resolution service in order to build a more constructive working relationship. When the venue's permit again appeared on the Zoning Board's agenda, more than one hundred Gilman supporters attended the meeting. The overwhelming support for the club pressed the board to grant the requested permit changes, with stipulations that the collective provide additional outdoor trash cans and continue to improve its internal security.[33]

Gilman's second major crisis began in 1995, when the Pyramid Brewing Company announced its intention to open a brewpub directly across the street. In addition to the inherent problems with locating a drinking establishment near an all-ages venue, collective members were also worried that the arrival of an upscale business would drive up property costs and eventually force them out of the neighborhood. To voice these concerns, Gilman representatives attended Pyramid's preliminary permit hearing, and three collective members even visited the brewing company's Seattle headquarters, at the company's behest. The collective also issued a series of successful press announcements, conducted an outreach campaign with other neighbors, and filed a formal petition with the Berkeley Zoning Board.[34]

When the brewpub's permit came before the board, dozens of Gilman supporters spoke on the club's behalf, and one zoning officer later described the presentation as "one of the most professional" he had seen.[35] Though the board approved the permit, it also addressed many of the collective's concerns by requiring Pyramid to pay for a new traffic light, hire security guards to contain bar patrons, and meet regularly with Gilman members to resolve disputes. Gilman's interaction with Pyramid, while serious in its potential ramifications, was not entirely antagonistic. Pyramid responded to the collective's objections with seemingly genuine concern, and a representative of the brewpub even wrote a letter of support for Gilman during its next major conflict.[36]

Gilman's third altercation of the decade was its most hostile. In October 1998, DiCon Fiber Optics, a neighboring business, filed a grievance with the city that the club's patrons were responsible for an increasing amount of vandalism, graffiti, and litter. The company's complaints, which included the sensational claim that Gilman patrons had attacked the company's trees with machetes, were probably overblown. Gilman cleanup crews already tended to neighborhood trash and vandalism, and, according to Gilman volunteer John H., "Eighth Street was a sort of no-man's-land on which many users dumped trash. Gilman [unfairly] received the blame for much of it."[37] Nonetheless, the company's threat to relocate its four hundred high-paying jobs was enough to persuade the city to intervene. In December, Berkeley police set up video and still-camera surveillance on the club in order to catch vandals in the act, though they were apparently unsuccessful.[38]

During the ensuing months, Gilman members canvassed the neighborhood for support and gathered several thousand signatures on an online petition. DiCon initially refused the club's offer to pursue mediation. However, at the city's behest, representatives from both sides met with police and city planning officials to draft a memorandum of understanding. The collective agreed to increase its attention to neighborhood graffiti, but DiCon stopped meeting with the club's representatives and moved out of the neighborhood soon afterward. As in Gilman's two previous conflicts, it was able to work through formal government channels from a position of relative strength, but this was only because of the collective's ability to gain the support of its neighbors, rather than alienating them. Like Earth First! in its Mount Graham campaign, the Gilman group needed allies, as the default loyalties of city officials and the police were to local businesses.[39]

ABC No Rio also faced major crises during this period, but their circumstances ultimately required a more aggressive response. The ABC No Rio art gallery had been enmeshed in the housing politics of New York's Lower East Side since its 1980 founding. In fact, its very lease was a concession from the city following a dispute over an illegal protest art exhibit that focused on gentrification in the neighborhood. The punk contingent that took over the space a decade later inherited an institutional history of conflict with the city government and solidarity with the neighborhood's homeless and squatter populations—relationships that continued to shape the gallery's development.[40]

In the summer of 1988, the city attempted to enforce a curfew on nearby Tompkins Square Park, which had become a residence for the neighborhood's homeless community. Over the next several months, a series of protests were held to contest the city's actions, which also included the eviction of squatters in nearby buildings. Police responded to the protests with force, resulting in arrests and injuries—and over one hundred complaints of police brutality from one incident alone. The city pressed on, however, and by June 1991, the two hundred homeless residents of the park had been evicted; and the area was indefinitely cordoned off for renovations. Though ABC No Rio was not directly involved in this dispute, the gallery did host benefits for local evictees and screened raw footage from the Tompkins Square riots. Meanwhile, the collective's own relationship with the city government continued to be as adversarial as ever. The city was a negligent, and often hostile, landlord, and the collective responded by filing several lawsuits and engaging in a five-year rent strike that was resolved, only unofficially, in 1993. Two years later, the neighborhood's housing conflict again intensified, this time with more intense effects for ABC No Rio.[41]

In May 1995, hundreds of New York City riot police, complete with an armored vehicle, arrived in the Lower East Side to evict squatters from buildings on East Thirteenth Street. The thirty-one squatters inside were expecting the eviction and had barricaded the doors and stairways of their buildings. Although the squatters were forced out within a few hours, several reoccupied one of the buildings on the Fourth of July, while police forces were engaged with crowds at a nearby fireworks display. Police again cleared the squat and arrested nearly twenty people. The circumstances of these evictions were particularly controversial, as the Supreme Court of the State of New York had previously ruled in the squatters' favor.[42]

In this context of overt hostility, overwhelming police force, and bad-faith negotiations, the ABC No Rio collective became embroiled in its own eviction battle. In October 1994, the city stopped accepting its rent checks, and over the next several months, officials moved to evict it and formally "dispose" of the building. Despite the collective's many offers to purchase the building, the city instead made arrangements to sell it to a nonprofit housing organization, Asian Americans for Equality (AAFE). Hesitant to battle another advocacy organization, ABC No Rio members attempted to negotiate for partial use of the space. AAFE's proposal would have required that ABC No Rio pay double the market rate for rent, however, and the two parties were unable to resolve a temporary relocation for the gallery during proposed renovations.[43]

Talks between the groups quickly broke down, and city officials moved to bypass normal public hearings by declaring the space an "Urban Development Action Area Project" (UDAAP). ABC No Rio responded by taking its case to the media, publicly vowing to fight for the gallery through "the courts, . . . outreach, protest, . . . public support, and . . . physical defense of the building."[44] Squatters, meanwhile, moved in to provide a last line of defense against eviction.[45]

In November 1995, ABC No Rio representatives testified at a hearing of the city's Permits, Dispositions, and Concessions Subcommittee. They explained the collective's significance to New York's alternative arts scene, their attempts to feed the neighborhood's hungry each week through Food Not Bombs, and their efforts to host children's arts classes. They also recounted their long history with the city, including the many offers to purchase the building. The council nonetheless voted unanimously to expedite the sale of the building to AAFE. From late 1995 through 1996, the collective worked to publicize its struggle and prevent its ousting through legal channels. In April 1996, it won an important, though temporary, victory when eviction proceedings were dismissed—for the third time. In preparation for yet another eviction hearing in October, ABC No Rio, along with several other threatened arts organizations, held a fund-raising rally at the Metropolitan Museum of Art.[46]

By December 1996, ABC No Rio's situation had become desperate. That month, a judge suspended eviction proceedings, but only until city officials restored utilities to the building, which they had illegally disconnected. The stay was expected to last only for a few months, so the collective began 1997 by escalating its tactics. In January, collective members organized two public actions that targeted AAFE. In the first, ABC No Rio sympathizers plastered the group's headquarters with posters reading, "Greed," "Profiteering," and "Corruption." Two dozen protesters rang bells and played drums, while others loudly decried the group's role in eviction proceedings. Later that month, in an action reminiscent of Earth First! or ACT UP, collective members chained themselves to desks and windows at the AAFE office and demanded that the eviction process be stopped. Five of the protesters were arrested. The collective then shifted its focus to the housing department, with a sit-in at the agency's office. Following the demonstration, outgoing commissioner Lilliam Barrios-Paoli invited ABC No Rio representatives to a meeting, at which she offered to sell the building to them for one dollar. In exchange, the gallery was required to expel its squatters and acquire $100,000 for renovations. The collective accepted the offer and began developing formal plans for building restoration and fund-raising.[47]

Over the next several years, city officials repeatedly changed the amount of money that they expected the group to raise. By October 2004, ABC No Rio had secured nearly $300,000 (primarily through small donations), and the long process of transferring ownership of the building began. In June 2006, the sale was finalized, after more than twenty years of fighting the city over the building. However, the collective soon realized that simple renovations would be insufficient for the dilapidated space, and it instead began pursuing a more ambitious, $2 million "tear down and rebuild" plan. Three years later, almost to the day, the group announced an interesting twist to its historically volatile relationship with the city government. In June 2009, city officials granted $1,650,000 in municipal funding for its rebuilding project.[48]

ABC No Rio's decisions to work with the city and to relocate squatters were not without detractors. However, according to ABC No Rio director Steven Englander, the collective's decisions were reached democratically, and squatters had been recruited for the explicit purpose of fighting the eviction. The decision not to "go out on principle as martyrs" was not a difficult one. Says Englander, "thousands and thousands of people have benefited from [ABC No Rio's survival]. . . . Eight people lost where they were living, me being one of them."[49]

During the eviction battle, the ABC No Rio collective used a variety of tactics to maintain control of the building. Through official channels, the gallery engaged local officials and fought its eviction, ultimately extending its month-to-month lease for over two years. As the conflict escalated, collective members engaged in civil disobedience, in the form of sit-ins, the physical occupation of their building, and attempts to jam the city's fax machines with messages reading, "Save ABC No Rio."[50] Ultimately, the group's greatest asset was its ability to gather public support through extensive, positive press coverage in both alternative and mainstream media. ABC No Rio members, like their counterparts at 924 Gilman, refused to be isolated in their struggles, and they used every tool available to them—not just those that they deemed "punk."

★ ★ ★

In a decade in which government officials were slashing away at public services and selling off public possessions, young people at 924 Gilman Street and ABC No Rio volunteered their time to create social spaces devoted to diversity and art, not financial profit. While the Reagan administration condemned the Equal Rights Amendment and mocked the AIDS crisis, punk-rock youth called out homophobia and sexism in their own ranks. As political pundits tried to reframe antiracism as "political correctness" run amok (following a decade in which membership in the Ku Klux Klan nearly tripled), punks at 924 Gilman proudly fought off neo-Nazi skinheads. And as New York City officials slashed poverty programs and attacked the homeless population, punks at ABC No Rio picked a fight with the city's housing department—and won.[51]

Today, 924 Gilman and ABC No Rio are the most well-known youth-run, all-ages punk-rock venues in the US, due to both their longevity and their progeny. Gilman helped launch the careers of bands such as Operation Ivy, Jawbreaker, Samiam, and Green Day, while ABC No Rio was a home base for Born Against, Ted Leo, and the zine *Slug & Lettuce*. They are not otherwise unique within punk rock, however. Similarly structured venues have been organized with varying degrees of success throughout the US, including the Vera Project in Seattle, 1919 Hemphill in Fort Worth, Solidarity Books in Indianapolis, the BRYCC House in Louisville, and the Mr. Roboto Project outside Pittsburgh. Many of them

have hosted hip-hop events, as well. Additional punk-rock counterinstitutions have also included cooperative record labels and
zines, most notably *Maximum RocknRoll* and *Profane Existence*.
Members of all of these groups confronted organizational challenges similar to those faced by the Gilman and ABC No Rio collectives, but even less structured DIY punk ventures necessitated
the development of basic organizing skills, such as designing and
distributing fliers, monitoring crowds, and negotiating with police
and neighbors.[52]

Perhaps because these skills have been so essential to the survival of the punk movement, it has played a significant role in the
broader global fight to maintain autonomous cultural spaces. Just
as ABC No Rio's eviction battle represented only one portion of a
much-larger struggle over housing and public space in New York
City, the conflicts faced by both groups were also part of broader
trends in the Post-Liberal Era: gentrification, dramatic increases
in housing costs, and the criminalization of homelessness, among
them. Police surveillance of 924 Gilman Street in the late 1990s
was relatively innocuous, but dozens of other alternative arts
spaces experienced similar, and often more repressive, challenges
from state and private interests. Indianapolis's Solidarity Books
was closed in 2003 for a fire-code violation, following weeks of
surveillance and a joint raid by the local police, the bomb squad,
and the Bureau of Alcohol, Tobacco, Firearms, and Explosives.
Richmond, California's Burnt Ramen and Buffalo, New York's Hey
Dude! venues suffered similar fates the same year. Outside the US,
police have clashed with youth over a host of arts spaces, including
the Ungdomshuset in Copenhagen, Denmark; Metelkova in Lju-
bljana, Slovenia; the Fabryka squat in Warsaw, Poland; and Köpi in
Berlin, Germany—all of which also served as punk-rock venues.[53]

In chapter 1, Earth First! activists challenged the rights of business interests to harvest and "develop" natural spaces, and they
were met with surveillance, imprisonment, and violence for doing

so. DIY punk, too, revolved around contested spaces, clashed with the private sector, and faced repression. Punk rock is at its core a form of direct action. For more than forty years, it has been a struggle for the freedom to construct, rather than consume, culture. This is one of the reasons that it has been a frequent site of conflict with authority—with governments and private-sector interests, not just parents.

3

LINKS IN THE CHAIN

WORKERS' RIGHTS NETWORKS AND GLOBALIZATION

I believe we have made a decision now that will permit us to create an economic order in the world that will promote more growth, more equality, better preservation of the environment, and a greater possibility of world peace. . . . Today, as I sign the North American Free Trade Agreement into law . . . I believe we have found our footing. And I ask all of you . . . to recognize that there is no turning back from the world of today and tomorrow.
—President Bill Clinton

Behind the shiny, happy images promoted by the fast-food industry with its never-ending commercials on TV . . . there are farm workers who contribute their sweat and blood so that enormous corporations can profit, all the while living in sub-poverty misery, without benefits, without the right to overtime or protection when we organize. Others are working by force, against their will, terrorized by violent employers, under the watch of armed guards, held in modern-day slavery. The right to a just wage, the right to work free of forced labor, the right to organize—three of the rights in the United Nations' Universal Declaration of Human Rights—are routinely violated when it comes to farm workers in the United States.
—Lucas Benitez, Coalition of Immokalee Workers

IF THE ELECTION OF RONALD REAGAN MARKED THE DAWN of the Post-Liberal Era, the election of Bill Clinton twelve years later established a bipartisan neoliberal consensus. Clinton undercut poverty-assistance programs, aggressively expanded the nation's prison population, and signed major legislation to deregulate mass media and investment banks. Perhaps the Clinton administration's most substantial contribution to the neoliberal project, however, was the expansion of neoliberalism globally, through "free"-trade initiatives. In 1993, after more than six years of negotiations spanning three US administrations, Clinton signed the North American Free Trade Agreement (NAFTA) into law. The treaty's many corporate supporters included the Business Roundtable, the National Association of Manufacturers, the US Chamber of Commerce, and the Heritage Foundation. Mexican envoy Hermann von Bertrab received additional letters of support for NAFTA from the American Farm Bureau Federation, the Chemical Manufacturers Association, and the Charles and David Koch–funded Citizens for a Sound Economy—which later became Americans for Prosperity, a major player in Tea Party politics. NAFTA received bipartisan support in both congressional houses, and opposition, at least in the US, was primarily limited to labor unions and environmental groups.[1]

By creating a "free-trade zone" spanning the US, Mexico, and Canada, NAFTA deregulated the movement of manufacturing, investment capital, and goods, allowing multinational corporations the freedom to more easily relocate their factories in search of the cheapest labor and the fewest environmental and safety restrictions. The same freedom of movement was not offered to people, however, as the Clinton administration tightened security along the US-Mexico border during the same period. Thousands of people have since died attempting to enter the US, and the criminalization of migrant populations has further exacerbated the exploitation of undocumented workers. In the fifteen years following the implementation of NAFTA, law enforcement in Florida alone freed more than one thousand enslaved farmworkers who had been "held in chains, pistol whipped, locked at night into shacks in chain-link enclosures patrolled by armed guards," and threatened with beatings or death if they tried to escape. This modern American slavery was facilitated by a combination of dehumanizing neoliberal economic policies—enforced both globally and in the US—and the restructuring of corporations to decrease their social and legal accountability. This chapter examines these dynamics through a boycott campaign by farmworkers in Immokalee, Florida, and their network of activist allies—namely, the Student-Farmworker Alliance.[2]

NEOLIBERAL GLOBALIZATION

In the aftermath of World War II, the Allied powers began constructing a new global governing system to guide international relationships. In addition to political organizations, such as the United Nations (UN), the system also included financial institutions, such as the World Bank and the International Monetary Fund (IMF), which went into effect in 1945, and the General Agreement on Treaties and Tariffs (GATT) two years later. As the Cold War escalated, global elites formed additional working groups, including the North Atlantic Treaty Organization (NATO), in 1949, and the Group of Six (G6), in 1975.

Paralleling shifts in domestic policy during the 1970s and 1980s, US-led global organizations, including the World Bank and the IMF, began demanding from poorer nations a range of neoliberal concessions—the privatization of state-owned resources, the removal of protective tariffs, and the widespread gutting of social services and safety nets—as preconditions for developmental loans or the renegotiation of payment plans. According to one analysis, because of the incredibly high interest on these credits, "from 1982 to 1998, indebted countries paid four times their original debts, and at the same time their debt increased four times."[3] BBC News reached a similar conclusion, noting that the nations of Africa, for example, had paid back more than their original debts by 2002 but still owed about half the original sum, around $300 billion. Even after repaying the initial loans, these indebted countries remained perpetually vulnerable to neoliberalism through coercion. In effect, the IMF and World Bank gave Western elites both a mechanism and leverage to financially colonize—or recolonize, in many cases—much of the developing world. According to former World Bank chief economist and senior vice president Joseph Stiglitz, "When the IMF arrives in a country, they are interested in only one thing. How do we make sure the banks and financial institutions are paid? . . . It is the IMF that keeps the [financial] speculators in business. They're not interested in development or what helps a country get out of poverty."[4] During the last quarter of the twentieth century, this speculation became even more predatory. While the world's poorest countries were $25 billion in debt in 1970, that number ballooned to $523 billion by 2002.[5]

In the late 1980s, the Soviet Union began to unravel, creating a global power vacuum. The Cold War had been an ideological and economic standoff, and leaders—on both sides—used the conflict to justify many millions of deaths in proxy wars, as well as widespread human rights abuses, both domestically and abroad. It had also been a literal "world war," involving wars, coups, and other conflicts in countries all over the planet. For many US businesses, the Cold War was a financial windfall, as the arms race (and the backing of proxy armies) funneled massive public funds to manufacturers, while US-backed regimes from Iran to Guatemala to Indonesia streamlined corporate access to cheap resources and labor. As the conflict concluded, one of the ideas offered as a replacement was unregulated, or "free," trade.

Just as US elites in the public and private sectors had formed ALEC and the Business Roundtable to pursue a neoliberal domestic agenda in the 1970s, a parallel effort at the global level drove the formation of the World Trade Organization (WTO), which replaced the GATT in 1995, and NAFTA, which went into effect on January 1, 1994. NAFTA eliminated barriers to corporate expansion in Canada, Mexico, and the United States, while the WTO pursued similar ends on an international scale, facilitating the free movement of investment capital and the relocation of factories. This emerging global economic power structure (the World Bank, IMF, NAFTA, WTO, and others) expanded corporate power immensely, compelling neoliberal debt concessions from less powerful nations and allowing multinational companies to bypass national, state, and local laws—with the help of government officials. In effect, it allowed business interests to pursue their own imperialistic agendas virtually unchecked by, and with assistance from, national governments. Unsurprisingly, when business interests clashed across borders, the clearest winners were those with the backing of the most powerful governments.

THE IMPACTS OF "FREE" TRADE

For consumers, the most tangible effects of "free" trade take the form of cheap goods: T-shirts, shoes, produce, cell phones, and the like. Business interests, however, see "free" trade in terms of investment and profit. NAFTA, for example, encouraged investment (the relocation of factories) by providing corporations with contractual guarantees that they would enjoy specific rights and privileges in all three countries—and it worked. Accelerating processes that had been under way since the 1970s, NAFTA helped increase foreign investment in Mexico from $3.46 billion in 1993 to $24.73 billion in 2001. The returns for US businesses were substantial, as well. Aided by bubbles in the housing and "dot-com" markets, the combined results of Clinton-era policies allowed US corporate profits to rise by some 88 percent during the 1990s, while CEO pay rose a staggering 463 percent during the same period.[6]

The benefits of the booming economy were not shared evenly, however. In NAFTA's first decade, the US lost one-sixth of its manufacturing jobs, adding to the millions that were lost in the 1970s and 1980s. While mechanization—a favorite talking point of NAF-

TA's supporters—played a significant role in this shift, roughly one million of the three million manufacturing jobs lost during this period can been traced directly to the agreement. American workers without college degrees (roughly 75 percent of the workforce) were forced to compete directly with their lower-wage counterparts in Mexico and suffered a 12 percent wage decline. Thirty-eight thousand small farms in the US also went bankrupt, though giant agribusiness corporations, such as Cargill and Con-Agra, saw sharp increases in their profits.[7]

NAFTA helped US companies flood Mexican markets with artificially cheap, government-subsidized US corn. More than one million Mexican farmers were put out of work, and income for Mexican farmers declined by 70 percent. The minimum wage in Mexico also dropped 20 percent, impacting forty million workers. Many of those who were displaced sought work in the *maquiladoras*, megafactories along the US-Mexico border. For companies such as Hasbro, Fisher Price, and General Motors, these areas, along with other "free-trade zones" around the world, provided a sort of neoliberal endgame—factory towns with essentially no labor laws, environmental regulations, or human rights protections. A constant influx of desperate Mexican workers, 70 percent of them young women between the ages of sixteen and twenty-four, encountered dangerous conditions and poverty wages (a minimum wage of $3.40 per day, compared to $5.15 per hour in the US). Outside of the factories, this lawlessness had other effects. In Ciudad Juarez, just across the border from El Paso, Texas, the bodies of hundreds of women have been found raped, dismembered, and mutilated since the early 1990s. Hundreds more women have disappeared.[8]

But while NAFTA eased the cross-border movement of capital, destabilizing economic and social life in Mexico, new US border policies restricted the movement of human beings. The budget for the US Immigration and Naturalization Service (INS) tripled between 1993 and 2002, and the number of border patrol agents doubled, making the INS the second-largest federal law enforcement agency at the time, behind the FBI. Between 1994 and 2001, at least seventeen hundred people died attempting to cross the Mexican border into the US. According to migration scholar Wayne Cornelius, the death toll "rose in tandem with the intensification of border enforcement," as increased patrols forced desperate migrants to face ever more dangerous border crossings. In 2008, the UN estimated that as many as 70 percent of women trying to cross the border illegally were raped by "coyotes" or US border agents. NAFTA and other "free"-trade policies were a boon for manufacturers, especially those from wealthy nations. However, they devastated blue-collar workers in the US, as the manufacturing jobs that were lost were often union jobs that paid middle-class wages. "Free" trade, like the US's Cold War interventions, also created huge numbers of political and economic refugees from countries all over the world.[9]

CHALLENGES OF GLOBALIZATION

In addition to the impacts on the populations of the US, Mexico, and Canada, NAFTA also represented an assault on the very foundations of their democracies. During the 1980s, the Reagan administration had slashed federal budgets and appointed saboteurs to head federal agencies, in order to ensure that legislation protecting the environment, workers, and marginalized groups would not be implemented. These actions severely limited the avenues of change for protest movements, at least at the national level. However, activists still had some limited successes defending Liberal Era reforms and, especially, making changes at the local and state levels. NAFTA undercut many of those efforts by giving corporations the ability to supersede local initiatives.

Among the contractual obligations that NAFTA offered multinational corporations was a secretive appeals process called

"Chapter 11," which allowed them to seek exemptions from national, state, and local laws. The extent of these challenges remains deliberately unclear, but publicly known cases include Canadian corporations suing the state of California over its mining regulations and its ban on the gasoline additive, and suspected carcinogen, MTBE; US corporations suing the Canadian government for banning another gasoline additive, MMT, which is a suspected neurotoxin; US companies opposing Canada's ban on exporting toxic waste; and the US-based company Metelclad suing the Mexican city of Guadalcázar for blocking its efforts to open a toxic-waste site. In short, Chapter 11 expanded neoliberal deregulation across borders by undermining the laws and democratic wills of local populations.[10]

The WTO provided a similar mechanism for corporations to sidestep the laws of nations—and ruled in favor of corporations in 100 percent of known appeals. Among the laws that the WTO allowed businesses to bypass were a US law that banned a tuna-fishing net responsible for killing hundreds of thousands of dolphins each year, a Massachusetts law that denied state contracts to companies doing business with the military dictatorship in Burma, gasoline standards in the US Clean Air Act, a provision of the Endangered Species Act that required shrimp nets to include a device to allow endangered sea turtles to escape, and a European Union ban on beef from hormone-injected US cattle.[11]

As intended, "free"-trade initiatives such as NAFTA and the WTO rapidly expanded the global movement of raw materials, consumer goods, capital investments, factories, and workers. To maximize profits, companies moved their manufacturing facilities to the areas with the lowest wages and fewest government regulations. Wealthy nations around the world, meanwhile, imported poor laborers to do domestic, agricultural, and construction work. This was not an inevitable, natural, or market-based process, however. The global race to the bottom was facilitated by World Bank /

IMF loans, which demanded the erosion of workers' rights, social services, and environmental protections at the same time that NAFTA and other "free"-trade arrangements allowed cheap imports to undercut local industries and displace workers. Neoliberal globalization was steered by the people who profited from it.[12]

While expediting the exploitation of the already oppressed, neoliberal globalization also complicated global power structures in ways that made organized opposition more difficult. While economic power was concentrated in fewer and fewer hands, the vulnerabilities of elites were decentralized. In this unregulated global economy, no individual in the supply chain had to claim responsibility for "sweatshop" working conditions or child labor in contracted, "outsourced," factories—or for the extensive environmental damage that the factories caused. Independent factory owners could rightfully claim that they would not receive contracts if they, say, raised wages, while parent corporations could argue that their contracts were based on prices, not their repercussions. Consumers, meanwhile, made their purchasing decisions on the basis of the limits of their own personal budgets.

Adding to the difficulty of organizing across borders, this lack of accountability created a tangible problem for protest movements. Whom should they try to pressure? Whom could they lobby to make change? In organizations such as the WTO, the decision makers were relatively anonymous, and the distinction between state and corporate actors was not entirely clear. Unpopular decisions—or even blatant human rights violations—were difficult to trace to any particular politician or company. Furthermore, the mobility of the global assembly line allowed officials at multinational corporations to move their operations quickly if they felt pressured to improve working conditions. During the Long Gilded Age, American antisweatshop activists had faced a similar dilemma, as manufacturers moved to states with lax labor standards. Ultimately, their solution was to establish national labor standards through the New Deal. However, there is no world government to adopt safety guidelines, minimum-wage standards, or child-labor bans, and the international organizations that exist are devoted to the opposite goal.[13]

THE GLOBAL JUSTICE MOVEMENT

The evolution of global corporate power in the 1990s provoked a parallel shift in the organizational strategies of activists. One particularly influential example was the Zapatista uprising in Chiapas, Mexico. In response to NAFTA, indigenous rebels took up arms and declared their independence from the Mexican state. Though outmatched militarily, the Zapatistas (EZLN) were able to gather support throughout Mexico and in countries all over the world, providing enough pressure to convince the Mexican army to refrain from an all-out assault. Margaret Keck and Kathryn Sikkink call this solidarity strategy the "boomerang pattern." By sending *out* information, the Zapatistas, in this case, were able to apply pressure on their opposition *from behind*. Public outcry and media attention directed at the Mexican government made it reluctant to use force.[14]

As sympathizers around the world offered their assistance, the EZLN also rejected any notion of leadership in a worldwide revolutionary movement. Instead, the group called for a "movement of movements" that could work together, as equals. The EZLN's open embrace of democratic principles, independence, and broad coalition building resonated with activists across movements and across borders.[15]

One example of this influence was a series of protests that ultimately forced the WTO to cancel its 1999 meeting. Under the organizational guidance of the Direct Action Network (DAN), environmental activists, students, fair-trade advocates, labor activists, indigenous rights activists, anarchists, and others converged on Seattle, Washington, to challenge the WTO's authority to make global political decisions. While often considered separate movements, these groups worked together to block intersections, prevent delegates from reaching meetings, and occupy the city's streets with marches and rallies. Rather than being directed by a few leaders, the Seattle protests were organized in a way that respected participants' autonomy and allowed for a diversity of tactics (within a general agreement of nonviolence). Much of the coordination was done via the Internet, and many of the methods used to shut down the convention borrowed heavily from the work of groups such as Earth First!, Reclaim the Streets, and ACT UP a decade earlier. Like those earlier activists, DAN and others also attempted to create a lighthearted atmosphere, providing compelling visuals through the use of puppets and other theatrics. As a result, in addition to riot police and tear gas, images of the "Battle in Seattle" also featured protesters in turtle costumes. Subsequent meetings of global decision makers—the WTO, the World Bank / IMF, and the G20, among others—were also greeted with massive, disruptive protests.[16]

While the EZLN seceded from the "free"-trade economy, and the Seattle protesters disrupted the institutions that maintained it, another group, United Students Against Sweatshops (USAS), answered the globalization dilemma that I outlined earlier: in a complex and decentralized supply chain, who can be held accountable for sweatshop conditions? Formed in 1998 as a student offshoot of the labor union UNITE (which traces its own history back to the antisweatshop movement of the early 1900s), USAS attempted to confront sweatshop working conditions by targeting bulk purchasers, specifically the activists' own universities.

Through investments in athletics, logos, and related public imagery, these schools used their "brand" names to sell collegiate apparel, to barter lucrative athletic contracts with such companies as Nike and Reebok, and to encourage donations from corporations and wealthy alumni. By the late 1990s, the estimated value of the collegiate apparel industry was $2.5 billion.[17]

The power of these schools' brands was also a vulnerability, though, as student activists could ruin their value by associating them with sweatshops and human rights violations. Through pickets, rallies, marches, sit-ins in administrators' offices, disruptions at sporting events, and media campaigns, USAS activists focused public attention on the working conditions that produced university apparel. While some university administrators threatened to expel protesters, many felt compelled to negotiate with students by establishing labor standards for school apparel, rather than risk additional bad publicity. By 2012, USAS had convinced over 180 colleges and universities to affiliate with the Worker Rights Consortium, an organization that monitors clothing factories.[18]

Networks of USAS activists also played significant roles in other global justice struggles, including the Seattle WTO protests and the campaigns of the Coalition of Immokalee Workers (CIW), a group of Florida farmworkers. In March 2005, the CIW and its allies ended a four-year national boycott of Yum! Brands (the parent company of Taco Bell, Kentucky Fried Chicken, A&W, Pizza Hut, and Long John Silver's). In exchange, Yum!, the largest restaurant corporation in the world, granted the workers a roughly 75 percent raise and agreed to work with them directly to combat slavery in Florida fields. Throughout the campaign, which specifically targeted Taco Bell, the CIW adapted many of the organizing methods popularized by activists in Chiapas and Seattle, specifically the use of broad, horizontal coalitions.

THE COALITION OF IMMOKALEE WORKERS

The David and Goliath nature of a group of twenty-five hundred seasonally rotating workers—primarily Mexican and Guatemalan immigrants with no formally recognized bargaining rights—making demands of such a powerful corporation as Yum!, particularly following decades of devastating defeats for organized labor, has earned the CIW international acclaim. Very little about the group's approach was new or unique, however. The CIW's insistence on a democratic and cooperative structure drew heavily from the examples of the Zapatistas and paralleled a broader movement of worker centers in the US during the same period. The group's use of hunger strikes and city-to-city marches, as well as its boycott strategy, harked back to the campaigns of American farmworkers decades earlier. Even its alliances with student organizations built on more than fifty years of solidarity work on US college campuses, including the USAS campaigns of the late 1990s.[19]

The CIW began organizing in 1993 in an agriculture industry that was rampant with brutal working conditions, low wages, physical abuse, and coercion. Many migrant farmworkers were refugees from countries destabilized by US military and economic interventions in the 1980s and 1990s, and a combination of legal precariousness, language barriers, and a culture of fear made workers hesitant to push back against employers' abuses. Before the CIW launched its "Fair Food" campaign in 2001, it had built its base by focusing primarily on immediate targets and easing workers' fears. The group confronted violent crew bosses and launched undercover investigations that led to the prosecution of five Florida slavery rings. The CIW also organized a 230-mile march from Ft. Meyers to Orlando and a monthlong hunger strike by six of its members. By the end of the 1990s, the group had forced their employer, the Six L's Packing Company, to raise long-falling wages back to pre-1980s levels. In addition to these tangible gains, the CIW also developed important alliances with more privileged groups, including religious congregations, student activists, and labor unions.[20]

These relationships were vital to the CIW's campaign against Taco Bell. For just as the Zapatistas were unable to confront the

Mexican army directly, the CIW exhausted its ability to make direct demands of Six L's. Instead, the group developed a strategy to pressure the company from another angle, by targeting one of its main purchasers.[21]

This approach, known as a secondary boycott because it targets someone other than an immediate employer, had successful historical precedents among American farmworkers, most notably the National Farm Workers Association (NFWA, which became the United Farm Workers) in the 1960s and 1970s and the Farm Labor Organizing Committee (FLOC) a decade later. In order to pressure vineyard owner Schenley Industries, the NFWA organized a boycott that spread to include Cutty Sark liquor, Chiquita bananas, and Safeway grocery. Schenley ultimately agreed to recognize the union, and several other grape growers and wine makers followed suit. Similarly, FLOC launched a successful campaign against Vlasic pickle cucumber growers through their parent company, Campbell's Soup, and the victory gave it leverage to force an additional agreement with the H. J. Heinz Company. Incidentally, secondary labor boycotts were effectively made illegal by the New Deal, but its reforms had left out farmworkers.[22]

The CIW built on these models and adapted them to its organizing philosophy. Most notably, the group insisted on its own independence—and thus rejected offers to become a subsidiary of either the UFW or FLOC—as well as that of its allies. So while CIW members focused their efforts on organizing fellow workers, coordinating annual awareness tours, protesting at Yum! headquarters, and drawing attention from national media outlets, allied groups pursued boycott strategies that played to their own strengths.

Sympathetic unions, for example, framed the CIW struggle as a labor grievance. They encouraged their members to participate in the boycott and provided the CIW with logistical assistance. Allied church groups, meanwhile, built their campaigns around the moral issue of modern-day slavery. They spread the boycott from congregation to congregation and solicited public endorsements from powerful national religious organizations. Student activists, recognizing their status as Taco Bell's target market, launched a campaign called "Boot the Bell," which sought to expel the restaurant from high school and college campuses. By confronting and pressuring Yum! Brands from many directions at once, the CIW and its allies kept the company under constant pressure. Yum! could not respond to the variety of attacks with just one public relations campaign. However, addressing each of them individually proved both time-consuming and costly. As the campaign reached its peak, it pressured Taco Bell to face a dilemma: either negotiate with the farm workers or risk irreparable damage to its brand image.[23]

BOOTING THE BELL

Student solidarity movements have a long history in the US. In the early 1900s, students at women's colleges joined the antisweatshop movement, writing editorials for their school newspapers and walking picket lines with striking workers. Decades later, civil rights groups such as the Student Nonviolent Coordinating Committee (SNCC) and the Congress of Racial Equality (CORE) built strategic alliances with university students, who led fund-raising drives and recruited volunteers for their often-dangerous campaigns, including the 1961 Freedom Rides and the 1964 Mississippi Freedom Summer. Much of the northern student movement of the 1960s grew directly out of these relationships, including Students for a Democratic Society (SDS), the Berkeley Free Speech Movement, and the Columbia University strike in 1968. In subsequent decades, student protesters compelled dozens of major universities to divest funds from apartheid South Africa—and to sever ties with the University of Arizona's Mount Graham telescope project.

The CIW's allied student wing, the Student/Farmworker Alliance (SFA), was most directly influenced by USAS, which had excelled at finding pressure points in university bureaucracies. The SFA adopted a similar organizational structure, and its member groups also followed USAS's model for confronting university administrators. During the "Boot the Bell" campaign, activists also built on antisweatshop victories directly, using their schools' membership in the Worker Rights Consortium as a reference point for university labor standards.

When Yum! Brands reached agreement with the Coalition of Immokalee Workers in March 2005, student groups at twenty-two schools, including UCLA, Portland State University, and the University of Chicago, had succeeded at either cutting or preventing contracts with Taco Bell. Campaigns were active at roughly three hundred colleges and fifty high schools, and, importantly, that number had been steadily growing. Two of the "Boot the Bell" campaigns were organized by students at the University of Texas and the University of Notre Dame. Their stories demonstrate the complex, bureaucratic structures of both universities and corporations during this period. Like Earth First! in chapter 1, these students had to engage simultaneously in local and national struggles with a range of powerful opponents.[24]

The University of Texas (UT) campaign against Taco Bell began in 2001. In December, members of the campus Green Party picketed and distributed literature about the CIW in front of the campus restaurant, in conjunction with actions in thirty other states. The following October, Green Party members held another demonstration—complete with tomato costumes—that also coincided with similar activities elsewhere. Over the course of the next year, students began meeting with representatives of Aramark, the company contracted by UT to oversee all campus food outlets. By November 2003, the student coalition had broadened to include not only the campus Green Party but also global justice groups such as Acción Zapatista and Resist FTAA! When CIW members visited the UT campus on their national tour, students held another rally and introduced a resolution to the student government that, if passed, would have encouraged the administration to cut ties with Taco Bell. The legislation failed without debate, however, and activists saw their student government representatives "working on papers [and] picking their finger nails" during its presentation.[25] UT activists were able to attract publicity, but they quickly reached dead ends both with their student council and with the company that controlled the school's restaurants.[26]

The following school year, the "Boot the Bell" campaign at UT reached its peak. Under the leadership of the Student Labor Action Project (SLAP), the student coalition grew to include thirty-five other groups. Inspired by a recent victory against Taco Bell at UCLA, student activists presented the Texas Union Board of Directors, the administrative body responsible for contracting with Aramark, with a petition of over one thousand signatures. Unmoved, board chairwoman Nada Antoun responded that removing Taco Bell would be a "disservice to the students" who were "strapped due to tuition increases" and needed access to cheap food.[27] CIW farmworkers again visited the campus, and activists began flooding the school newspaper with letters supporting the campaign. Austin-area ministers also submitted a letter, noting religious groups' participation in the boycott and quoting former UN high commissioner for human rights Mary Robinson's condemnation of Taco Bell's role in "profiting by exploitation."[28]

The pressure from this negative publicity drew out some additional power brokers. In response to the students, Dirk Dozier and Don Barton, respectively, CEO and vice president of human resources for Austaco, the company that directly owned the UT Taco Bell and several others in the area, began their own media campaign. In February, as the Union Board was gearing up to vote on the issue, Dozier published an opinion piece in the school newspaper defending Six L's as "a very good organization," condemning student and community activists, and asking, "Where is the concern for the tax-paying, wage-earning US citizens—employees of our company—who potentially will lose their jobs for the sake of Florida Immokalee farm workers?" But while Dozier, like Antoun, saw the benefits in exploiting farmworkers, he did not explain why a one-cent-per-pound raise for tomato pickers would cause other workers to lose their jobs. Barton, meanwhile, maintained that by representing only sixty-eight of the six thousand Taco Bell restaurants in the US, Austaco was in no position to influence the company. More importantly, Barton argued, the UT Taco Bell franchise did not buy tomatoes from Six L's and thus was "far removed from what [the CIW was] trying to do." Student activists responded that they had never used Six L's in their literature—as the CIW campaign aimed to reshape the entire tomato market—and that the franchise nonetheless benefited from its connection to Taco Bell, a company whose success had come on the backs of CIW laborers. Barton admitted that representing and benefiting from the parent company was, of course, "why you become a franchise," and he further acknowledged that he could offer no information on the conditions of the workers who picked his franchises' tomatoes. However, Austaco's statements were enough to muddy the moral argument against the company. The Union Board moved to vote on Taco Bell's future at the end of February.[29]

Before the vote, SLAP published additional opinion pieces in the newspaper, and a local church held a public forum on the topic. During discussions at the Union Board meeting, protesters held up thirty-six signs, each with the name of a supporting student organization. The board voted unanimously to keep Taco Bell but stipulated that Six L's would be banned from operating at UT—a nonissue, since Six L's already did not. The board ended the Texas students' campaign anticlimactically, but a bigger victory arrived a week later, when Yum! Brands reached an agreement with the CIW. SLAP and its allies ultimately could not sway either its administration or its own government representatives. However, the students' actions exposed some of the bigger issues confronted by the campaign.[30]

Despite Taco Bell's name recognition and seemingly singular identity, the structure of the company was actually quite complicated. Its distribution and licensing network included many other powerful corporations, such as Aramark and Austaco. Similarly, the hierarchy of the university also included a variety of powerful decision-making bodies, including the student government, the Union Board, and others. The problems that the University of Texas students faced were not all structural, however. Their campaign also revealed the nature of their opponents' positions. Taco Bell apologists initially claimed either ignorance of farmworkers' struggles or impotence to affect the situation. When pushed, however, they effectively admitted that their own financial gain outweighed the human costs. Union Board chair Nada Antoun conceded that the exploitation of farmworkers benefited students, who themselves were being squeezed by the rising costs of college tuition. A similar argument accompanies "free" trade more broadly, as cheap consumer goods become an increasing necessity in an economy that replaces union manufacturing jobs with low-wage retail work. Austaco representatives added a xenophobic emphasis in this case, maintaining that the conditions of workers who were not "tax-paying, wage-earning US citizens" did not concern their company and should not concern anyone else.

The "Boot the Bell" campaign at the University of Notre Dame forced a similarly raw response from Taco Bell headquarters. The campaign at Notre Dame, like its Texas counterpart, started in 2001. It reached its peak during the 2003–2004 school year. That September, members of the Progressive Student Alliance (PSA) met with Notre Dame General Counsel Carol Kaesebier to discuss the university's affiliation with Taco Bell through a local franchisee's sponsorship of the football postgame show. In March, after traveling to Kentucky for a protest at Yum! headquarters and visiting Immokalee over spring break, two PSA members, Melody Gonzales and Tony Rivas, participated in a Cesar Chavez Day forum, at which they discussed both their involvement in the campaign and their own parents' experiences as migrant farm laborers. Rivas also began a weeklong hunger strike as a lead-up to a protest of Taco Bell.[31]

The student campaign at Notre Dame relied on articulating contradictions between the school's mission and its relationship to Taco Bell. Importantly, PSA members were able to identify an additional leverage point with the university: Board of Trustees member Matt Gallo was the director of Gallo of Sonoma Winery, a company accused of unfair labor practices by the United Farm Workers. By targeting Gallo, as well, student activists presented a pattern of worker exploitation at the university that allowed them to embarrass school officials at very high levels and counter administrators' attempts to dismiss their petitions.[32]

The publicity of Rivas's hunger strike and the subsequent protest, which were part of a national week of student actions, prompted official responses from both Notre Dame officials and Taco Bell. University spokesperson Matthew Storin told the school newspaper that the fact that Rivas learned about migrant labor issues in a university seminar "should count as University awareness on some level."[33] Speaking on behalf of Taco Bell, Laurie Schalow claimed that the free market was to blame for low produce prices, not the company. In effect, if the market dictated poverty wages, slavery, and the use of birth-defect-causing pesticides, who was Taco Bell to do otherwise? Schalow also noted that Taco Bell's Supplier Code of Conduct specified a nine-dollar-per-hour minimum wage, though student activists quickly pointed out that tomato pickers were paid by the bucket, not the hour. Undeterred, PSA members began a letter-writing campaign to the university's president, Father Edward Malloy, and launched a forty-person hunger strike. After two weeks of sending letters, dozens of PSA members went to Malloy's office to hand deliver more and to ask the administration for a public statement on the university's relationship to Taco Bell. Though the president's assistant told them that it was "not [Malloy's] style" to meet with students, Father Peter Jarret, counselor to the president, agreed to discuss the PSA's conditions for ending the hunger strike.[34]

The administration offered to investigate the students' concerns, but only after it received an official response from Taco Bell. PSA members, identifying the university's delay tactics, expanded the hunger strike to include 126 students, wrote editorials that connected their campaign to the school's membership in the USAS-supported Worker Rights Consortium, and accused the university of involvement in "a financial chain that exploits workers."[35] As the hunger strike escalated, Notre Dame officials demanded an immediate response from Taco Bell representatives, who had been using delay tactics of their own. A week later, Notre Dame announced that it would postpone negotiations for the renewal of its Taco Bell contract until the company provided its official explanation. Though President Malloy publicly thanked the students for bringing the issue to his attention, he stipulated, "It remains to be seen whether all their concerns were justified."[36] Anxious to maintain a business-friendly appearance—particularly on issues related to the school's football program—he promised that the university would not rush to judge Taco Bell before hearing the company's side of the argument.[37]

In August 2004, the deadline for renewing the annual sponsorship contract passed quietly without the university receiving a response from Taco Bell. As PSA declared victory, university spokesperson Matt Storin, cautious not to reveal that students had pressured the administration into making a decision, thanked students for bringing up the issue "in a very responsible and studied way."[38]

★ ★ ★

The Notre Dame campaign to boot Taco Bell succeeded for several reasons. Chief among them were the students' abilities to highlight contradictions between the school's mission and its actions, to connect that relationship to other labor issues involving the school, and, perhaps most importantly, to threaten the image of the football team. The Texas campaign, meanwhile, failed because students were unable to identify or apply pressure on the necessary decision-making bodies. Student activists remained public and active for the full four-year campaign, but their attempts to influence various governing bodies never produced the desired results. On the larger scale of the national campaign, however, the "pressure from all sides" strategy of the CIW's conflict with Yum! allowed farmworkers to benefit even from unsuccessful local campaigns by their allies. The University of Texas's Taco Bell remained open, but public statements by its various owners and stakeholders made clear the pressure they felt from the students' protests.

These campaigns demonstrate the difficulties that activists face in confronting opponents who not only are powerful but are also protected by elaborate bureaucracies, whether those of universities or multinational corporations. Just as other activists had during the defense of Mount Graham and in USAS's antisweatshop campaigns, the "Boot the Bell" organizers were tasked with determining who the key decision makers were and then developing strategies to reach and pressure them. For the students, this process was complicated by the corporatization of US campuses, including both an increased corporate presence through sponsorships and subcontracted services and the expansion of bureaucratic models of organization. Outside the university, the CIW faced a similarly complex production chain that included an elaborate web of farms, distributors, and subcontractors, as well as Taco Bell's own labyrinth of franchisees and subcontractors. To identify and exploit the right pressure points, the CIW and its allies looked to historical and contemporary examples, from the United Farm Workers to the Zapatistas. The CIW's efforts eventually forced Yum! to negotiate, and the CIW has since reached agreements with several other companies, as well, including McDonald's, Burger King, Whole Foods, Subway, Trader Joe's, and Chipotle—and has ongoing campaigns against Wendy's and Publix grocery. The group's goal is not just to raise wages for its members but to alter the market and reshape the entire agriculture industry.

The Coalition of Immokalee Workers and the Student-Farmworker Alliance, along with the Zapatistas, United Students Against Sweatshops, Direct Action Network, and other global justice organizations, offered an important next step beyond the single-issue defensive direct action of 1980s-era groups. The global justice movement's emphasis on broad, global coalitions of environmental, labor, and human rights activists is absolutely crucial in the era of NAFTA and the WTO. The farmworkers of Immokalee were able to pick a fight with a much more powerful opponent—and win—because, in addition to their own often-dangerous organizing, they developed relationships with a variety of allies, whom they encouraged to pressure Yum! from many directions. And as the CIW's campaigns illustrate, even the most powerful institutions have vulnerabilities.

From the beatings and chains in Florida fields to tear gas in the streets of Seattle, backlash and repression were constants, but the global justice movement of the 1990s generally operated within a cultural context in which mainstream Americans were receptive—or at least not openly hostile—to moral arguments against human rights violations. Even "free" trade was typically framed as a benefit for the world's poor. Upon signing NAFTA, which undermined many of the labor and environmental protections of the Liberal Era and created an economic refugee crisis, President Clinton drew on the language of liberalism, announcing that NAFTA would lead to "more growth, more equality, better preservation of the environment, and a greater possibility of world peace."[39] This context allowed activists to apply pressure by threatening to tarnish companies' (and schools') brand names by linking them to sweatshops, child labor, and slavery.

By contrast, the peace movement that opposed the "War on Terror" of the early 2000s faced a hostile political culture of panic, fear, and demands for unquestioning obedience. Its opponents rejected established human rights conventions, openly embraced torture, and accused protesters of treason, naivety, and providing aid for terrorists. Antiwar protesters' appeals to humanity fell flat.

4

INVASION AND OCCUPATION

FIGHTING THE "WAR ON TERROR"

I can't tell you if the use of force in Iraq today would last five days, or five weeks, or five months, but it certainly isn't going to last any longer than that.
—Secretary of Defense Donald Rumsfeld

That's why the thugs in Iraq still resist us, because they can't stand the thought of free societies. They understand what freedom means. See, free nations are peaceful nations. Free nations don't attack each other. Free nations don't develop weapons of mass destruction.
—President George W. Bush

IN SEPTEMBER 2000, THE PROJECT FOR THE NEW AMERICAN Century (PNAC) released a report titled *Rebuilding America's Defenses: Strategy, Forces, and Resources for a New Century*. In it, the think tank called for a broad retooling of the US military and even identified potential targets, including Iran, Iraq, and North Korea—the countries President George W. Bush later called the "Axis of Evil" in his 2002 State of the Union Address. Unfortunately, PNAC lamented, the massive funding increase that would be required to pursue such expansion was unlikely to be provided "absent some catastrophic and catalyzing event—like a new Pearl Harbor."[1] One year later, just such an event occurred. The September 11 tragedy took nearly three thousand lives. It also offered the Bush administration a nearly limitless budget for war and surveillance—and very little political opposition. Following an invasion of Afghanistan in October 2001, the Bush administration, which included prominent PNAC members Donald Rumsfeld, I. Lewis "Scooter" Libby, and Paul Wolfowitz, shifted its focus to attacking Iraq. PNAC members had been advocating the overthrow of Iraqi President Saddam Hussein since the late 1990s, and they used the 9/11 attacks to renew their call, even without a connection between Hussein and the hijackers.[2]

Estimated costs of the "War on Terror" vary, but the US military's own conclusion is that at least sixty-six thousand Iraqi civilians were killed under the US occupation. The invasion of Iraq also displaced over two million Iraqis inside their country, while another two million sought refuge in Syria and Jordan. It is likely that US interventions in Iraq, Afghanistan, and Pakistan collectively cost one million civilians their lives, perhaps two hundred thousand of whom died violently. Additionally, more than six thousand US soldiers were killed, and approximately fifty thousand were physically wounded. Roughly one-third of US military veterans also suffer from psychological injuries, including post-traumatic stress disorder (PTSD) and severe depression.[3]

The "War on Terror" cost US taxpayers more than $1 trillion, and its final price tag may be as high as $6 trillion. Much of that public money, however, went not to Iraq, Afghanistan, or to US soldiers but rather into the coffers of US corporations. This chapter examines a massive expansion of neoliberalism into the spheres of global warfare and domestic surveillance, as well as the emergence of one of the largest protest movements in world history.[4]

NEOLIBERALISM IN THE TWENTY-FIRST CENTURY

George W. Bush became the forty-third president of the United States in 2001, despite receiving half a million fewer votes than his opponent. Though lacking a mandate from American voters, and having campaigned as a "compassionate conservative," Bush aggressively pursued the neoliberal project, slashing taxes and government services, privatizing public assets, and deregulating industry.

In Bush's first year in office, he signed the Economic Growth and Tax Relief Reconciliation Act, cutting roughly $1 trillion in tax revenue over the following decade. Two years later, he signed the Jobs and Growth Tax Relief Reconciliation Act, cutting an additional $800 billion over ten years. As the first of these "Bush tax cuts" was being debated in April 2001, the Heritage Foundation published a report arguing that "even with increased spending," tax cuts would "effectively pay off the federal debt" in the following decade.[5] In other words, massive tax cuts would so stimulate the economy that many trillions of dollars in additional government revenue could be expected. Instead, however, the combination of tax cuts and increased spending actually doubled the debt during the period. And despite the names that the cuts were given, their benefits primarily went to the wealthiest Americans (according to one analysis, 53 percent of the savings went to the wealthiest 10 percent of Americans), while Bush's job-creation numbers were the worst of any US president since World War II.[6]

The tax cuts were an example of "starving the beast," a strategy of deliberately limiting revenue in order to justify subsequent cuts to public services. Indeed, Bush admitted in 2001 that he hoped his tax cuts would be a "fiscal straitjacket for Congress."[7] The administration ultimately did not commit itself to the same asylum, however, instead greatly expanding government expenses in specific areas, often with benefits for the same people who most profited from the tax cuts.[8]

The Bush administration also pursued an expansive agenda of deregulation and privatization. Bush's landmark education bill, No Child Left Behind (NCLB), funneled federal dollars from public schools into the hands of testing and tutoring corporations. The administration's energy policy, meanwhile, was directed by Vice President Dick Cheney in a series of private meetings with lobbyists and other representatives of US coal, mining, and oil companies. The Energy Task Force's requests eventually became a proposal that Republican Senator John McCain called the "no lobbyist left behind bill."[9] Environmental groups such as Friends of the Earth and the Sierra Club mobilized their members to pressure Congress, and they were able to defeat the bill on multiple occasions during Bush's first term. In 2005, however, the bill passed, allotting $6 billion in public subsidies for oil and gas companies, $9 billion for coal companies, and $12 billion for nuclear power. The bill also gave exemptions to the Clean Water Act and Safe Drinking Water Act for companies engaging in hydraulic fracturing ("fracking"). A primary beneficiary of this exemption was Halliburton, whose former CEO, Dick Cheney, drafted it.[10]

One of the key members of the Energy Task Force was Kenneth Lay, the CEO of energy giant Enron and a major donor to Bush's election campaign. When Enron went bankrupt in December 2001, its crashing stock took with it the savings of many of its workers, as well as the pensions of California and New York state employees. As the seventh-largest US multinational corporation, Enron had been presented as a safe investment. For the previous six years in a row, *Fortune* magazine had declared Enron "America's Most Innovative Company," and indeed it was, though not likely in the way that the *Fortune* writers had assumed.[11]

Much like Yum! Brands and Taco Bell, discussed in chapter 3, Enron's structure was multitiered and complex. While the company claimed over $100 billion in annual revenue, it hid its bad debts in subsidiaries. Enron was also able to use its clout to gain regulatory exemptions from the Clinton-era Securities and Exchange Commission (SEC) in both 1993 and 1997. Ultimately, despite constituting the largest bankruptcy in US history at the time, with $63 billion in assets, Enron's collapse was not treated as a "canary in the coal mine." Corporate consolidation and deregulation continued, and Enron's demise was subsequently eclipsed by the even-greater failures of Worldcom (in 2002), Lehman Brothers (2008), Washington Mutual (2008), General Motors (2009), and CIT Group (2009)— and was nearly rivaled by those of Conseco (2002), Chrysler (2009), and MF Global (2011). Like the laissez-faire markets of the Gilded Age that led to the Great Depression, the deregulated market of the Post-Liberal Era was both profitable and unstable.[12]

In addition to aggressive tax cuts, corporate handouts, deregulation, and direct involvement of the private sector in policy making, the Bush administration also gutted federal agencies from within. Like Ronald Reagan, Bush appointed people who were openly hostile to their agencies' missions or had ties to the industries they were hired to police. As secretary of the interior, Bush appointed Gale Norton, a former protégé of Reagan's interior secretary James Watt. As expected, Norton used her position to cater to corporate interests, approving massive oil and gas development plans in Alaska, Utah, Wyoming, and elsewhere.[13]

As deputy secretary of the interior, Bush appointed J. Steven Griles, another former member of the Reagan administration. As a high-ranking employee at National Environmental Strategies (a lobbying firm for energy interests) and the United Company (a coal and mining corporation), his knowledge of the energy industry was intimate, making him a natural fit for Cheney's Energy Task Force. Among his key contributions to the Bush administration was to remove obstacles to mountaintop removal mining for coal companies. Griles was later forced to resign, however, when it became apparent that he had been meeting with former clients, who paid him over $1 million. Griles was also one of the many Republicans convicted in the scandal involving lobbyist Jack Abramoff. He was eventually sentenced to ten months in prison for offering to use his position to help Abramoff block construction of a casino.[14]

Bush also recruited from prominent neoliberal think tanks. At least twenty American Enterprise Institute (AEI) fellows served in his administration, and AEI also later hired John Bolton, Bush's ambassador to the United Nations. Bolton, who was also affiliated with PNAC, had once suggested that the UN could lose ten stories' worth of its New York offices without making "a bit of difference."[15] The Bush team recruited heavily from the Heritage Foundation, including Secretary of Labor Elaine Chao (wife of Senator Mitch McConnell), Angela Antonelli, Mark Wilson, Kay Coles James, Alvin Felzenberg, and Gale Norton. From the Federalist Society, an organization of conservative lawyers and judges, Bush appointed Attorney General John Ashcroft and US Supreme Court Justices Samuel Alito and John Roberts, among many others. Appointees with connections to the antifeminist Independent Women's Forum included Chao, Diana Furchgott-Roth, Anita Blair, and Jessica Gavora. In addition to developing policy proposals, these think tanks trained and vetted socially conservative, economically neoliberal personnel.[16]

Bush also exercised a veto on his branch's activities. On his inauguration day, he put a freeze on all pending Clinton regulations and clamped down on regulatory approval through his Office of Information and Regulatory Affairs (OIRA). Congress had established the OIRA in 1980 in order to streamline paperwork and regulations, effectively allowing the president to overrule federal agencies' proposals if they were deemed detrimental to business. In the last two years of the Clinton administration, an average of 20.5 proposed regulations were rejected by the OIRA. During Bush's first year, his OIRA rejected 172. That number tapered off in subsequent years, but Bush's OIRA officials reported that they did not become more accommodating. Rather, representatives of federal agencies merely stopped submitting new regulations, realizing that they had little chance of being implemented. Bush's Environmental Protection Agency (EPA) issued just three regulations in the first three years of his term. By comparison, Clinton's first three years produced thirty EPA regulations, and George H. W. Bush's first three years yielded twenty-one.[17]

In addition to neoliberal economic policies, the Bush administration also promoted a number of conservative social policies. Perhaps most famously, Bush oversaw a massive increase in funding for "abstinence-only" sexual education. Building on Reagan-era policies, Bill Clinton had authorized $50 million per year for the religiously inspired curriculum in his push for welfare reform. Bush tripled funding to $176 million per year by 2006. But despite the more than $1 billion of federal funding spent on "abstinence-only" programs since 1982, a 2007 study for the Department of Health and Human Services found no statistical impact on the sexual behavior of American youth. However, the curricula have been shown to include factually inaccurate information about pregnancy, birth control, sexually transmitted infections, and abortion.[18]

In 2001, Bush also established the White House Office of Faith-Based and Community Initiatives (OFBCI) to transfer the government's social service obligations to religious organizations. By 2006, more than $2 billion per year in federal funds were being funneled to such groups. During the 2004 presidential campaign, Bush also publicly advocated a constitutional amendment to ban "same-sex" marriage, though the 1996 Defense of Marriage Act already accomplished some of this discriminatory goal, by establishing that only heterosexual couples could receive federal benefits.[19]

In many areas, the Bush administration did not represent a departure from the policies of its predecessors. Ronald Reagan had appointed industry insiders to undermine regulations and remake the government as a tool for business. Bill Clinton had approved "faith-based" initiatives, funded "abstinence-only" sexual education, and signed the Defense of Marriage Act—in addition to helping Enron hide its fraud and approving the deregulation of the US media and Wall Street banks.

The Bush administration's major neoliberal contribution was the "War on Terror," which aggressively expanded the privatization of military services, forced business-friendly laws onto the Iraqi people, suspended civil liberties in the US, abandoned the accepted rules of armed conflict, and embraced a state of perpetual warfare. In the words of Vice President Dick Cheney, this war "may never end, . . . at least not in our lifetime."[20]

THE IRAQ WAR

As early as January 2001, the Bush cabinet began discussing the invasion of Iraq. Eight months later, the September 11 attacks offered a relatively clear mandate for war on Afghanistan, but Iraq had not been involved. Dick Cheney told *Sixty Minutes* and *Meet the Press* viewers that 9/11 hijacker Mohamed Atta had met with Iraqi officials in Prague, but US intelligence had already determined otherwise. Atta, in fact, was in the US when the Prague meeting allegedly occurred, and investigations have exposed the meeting itself as a likely hoax. Without a link between Saddam Hussein and 9/11, however, the administration was forced to find a different pretext for invasion—the imminent threat of an Iraqi attack.[21]

On the surface, presenting Hussein as a serious danger to the American people was absurd. During the first Iraq War, in 1991, US forces repelled the Iraqi military from Kuwait in a number of weeks. The UN, following the US's "Food for Oil" plan, then controlled Iraq's imports and its oil exports for more than a decade. The US, UK, and France also maintained "no-fly zones" over much of the country. Iraq was contained in nearly every sense. Saddam Hussein also made an awkward villain, as the US had not only played a role in his rise to power but also provided funding, military equipment, and chemical weapons during the brutal 1980–1988 Iran-Iraq War, in which the US supported both sides. Moreover, the US's backing of Hussein had continued after his genocidal Al-Anfal campaign and the Halabja poison gas attacks on the Kurdish populations of northern Iraq—events often pointed to as justification for his ouster.[22]

Furthermore, while the 9/11 hijackers, as nonstate actors, had targeted US civilians, the role of the US military in the world made state-sponsored attacks on the US extremely unlikely. According to the Department of Defense's own 2002 figures, the US operated at least seven hundred military bases in foreign countries, in addition to the thousands of bases on US territory. In the 2006 book *Nemesis*, Chalmers Johnson noted that US forces were active in more than 130 countries. And while Saddam Hussein had indeed been a hostile neighbor and a violent head of state, the US's own Cold War record of bombing and invading other countries, toppling democratically elected governments, and supporting violent dictators was extensive. In addition to arming both the Hussein regime and the Mujahideen fighters in Afghanistan, the US's post–World War II activities included interventions in Albania, Angola, Australia, Bolivia, Brazil, Bulgaria, Cambodia, Chile, China, the Congo, Costa Rica, Cuba, the Dominican Republic, East Timor, Ecuador, El Salvador, Ghana, Greece, Grenada, Guatemala, Haiti, Indonesia, Iran, Italy, Jamaica, Korea, Laos, Libya, Morocco, Nicaragua, Panama, Peru, the Philippines, Syria, Uruguay, Vietnam, and Zaire, among others.[23]

But while 9/11 did not provide the clear case for invading Iraq that the Bush administration desired, the culture of fear surrounding the terror attacks did provide a context in which it could present Iraq, thoroughly devastated by two decades of war and economic sanctions, as a viable threat to the world's only superpower. Claiming that the Hussein regime was developing weapons of mass destruction (WMD) and thus constituted a global terrorist threat, the Bush administration began ramping up support for an invasion under the banner of its "War on Terror."

In August 2002, Cheney announced, "We now know that Saddam has resumed his efforts to acquire nuclear weapons. . . . Simply stated, there is no doubt that Saddam Hussein now has weapons of mass destruction."[24] A few months later, on the eve of the invasion in March 2003, Bush used similar language, assuring Americans, "Intelligence gathered by this and other governments leaves no doubt that the Iraq regime continues to possess and conceal some of the most lethal weapons ever devised."[25] But while Bush and Cheney each communicated absolute certainty with their use of "no doubt," no such weapons programs were discovered. In fact, the only WMD found in Iraq were abandoned and decaying, awkward reminders of Reagan's support for Hussein—which the Bush administration suppressed.[26]

Other federal officials were less concerned with baseless guarantees than with stoking Americans' fears of terrorist attacks. National Security Advisor Condoleezza Rice told CNN that while there would always be uncertainty about Hussein's abilities to develop nuclear weapons, "We don't want the smoking gun to be a mushroom cloud."[27] Secretary of Defense Donald Rumsfeld, meanwhile, advised CBS's *Face the Nation* viewers to "imagine a September 11 with weapons of mass destruction. It's not 3,000 [dead]. It's tens of thousands of innocent men, women and children."[28] For those who were still unconvinced, Cheney, Deputy Secretary of Defense Paul Wolfowitz, and Senator John McCain also made more positive overtures, assuring the American public that "like the people of France in the 1940s," Iraqis would greet US soldiers as liberators. Rumsfeld further claimed that the use of force would last less than five months and cost under $50 billion.[29]

But while the Bush administration's pitch to the public was rooted in misinformation and fear, it presented its "War on Terror" in much more tangible ways to US corporations. According to the Department of Defense, military contracts for 2003 alone totaled over $200 billion, nearly $30 billion more than the year before. Lockheed Martin, which made an estimated $1 million per year in political campaign contributions, received $21.9 billion in defense contracts. Another $17.3 billion went to Boeing, whose chief financial officer was later imprisoned for bribing the US Air Force's chief weapons buyer in exchange for $5 billion in preferential contracts. The Northrop Grumman Corporation, whose former vice president James G. Roche served as Bush's secretary of the Air Force, received $11.1 billion in contracts. Two years later, the company settled a $62 million lawsuit with the US government for overcharging for its services. In addition to these routine defense contracts for the giants of the US military-industrial complex, the "War on Terror" took war profiteering to new levels by offering traditional military tasks to businesses such as Halliburton, Blackwater, CACI International, and Titan.[30]

Halliburton, the top US contractor in Iraq, received $3.9 billion in military contracts in 2003 alone to perform a variety of tasks, such as supplying oil to the military, building barracks, and providing meals. In 2004, the *Wall Street Journal* reported that Halliburton had overcharged taxpayers by more than $16 million by claiming to have served as many as twenty-five thousand more meals per day than it actually had. A subsequent 2004 Pentagon audit found that the company's unsupported charges were as high as $1.8 billion. Halliburton subsidiary Kellogg, Brown, and Root (KBR) was also implicated in the deaths of more than a dozen soldiers who were electrocuted while showering or swimming at KBR-built facilities. In 2009, prompted by allegations that KBR employees gang-raped a co-worker, the US Senate passed the "Franken Amendment." It barred defense contracts for companies, such as KBR/Halliburton, that prevented workers from taking legal action against them for sexual crimes. The amendment was opposed by the US Chamber of Commerce, and US Senator Jeff Sessions described it as a "political attack on Halliburton."[31] All thirty of the senators who voted against it were Republicans. By 2009, KBR's contracts for Afghanistan and Iraq totaled more than $31 billion.[32]

Blackwater, meanwhile, received nearly $1 billion from the US government to maintain a private army of roughly one thousand mercenaries in Iraq. Like Halliburton, Blackwater performed a variety of duties that previously would have been performed by the US military itself, such as guarding key occupation officials. However, Blackwater employees were not held to the same standards of accountability as either US soldiers or civilians, and official US policy—specifically Coalition Provisional Authority Order Number 17—made contractors exempt from Iraqi law. In 2006, a drunken Blackwater operative killed the bodyguard of Iraqi Vice President Adil Abdul-Mahdi; rather than face murder charges, however, he was simply returned to the US. A few months later, Blackwater snipers shot to death three guards at the Iraqi Media Network. Blackwater mercenaries were also linked to the deaths of other Iraqi civilians, including a September 9, 2007, incident in which five Iraqis were killed and the infamous Nisour Square shootings a week later, in which seventeen were killed. In the company's attempt to distance itself from the negative publicity, it changed its name, first to Xe Services, then to Academi. In many ways, Blackwater epitomized neoliberal warfare—taxpayer funded and largely free from government regulation.[33]

CACI International, with over $1 billion in annual revenue, and the Titan Corporation, which took in more than $2 billion per year, offered the privatization of human rights abuses. CACI and Titan provided interrogation and translation services for the US military at Abu Ghraib prison, where detainees were tortured, beaten, and raped. According to US Major General Antonio Taguba, abuses by US soldiers and interrogators included "breaking chemical lights and pouring the phosphoric liquid on detainees; pouring cold water on naked detainees; beating detainees with a broom handle and a chair; threatening male detainees with rape; allowing a military police guard to stitch the wound of a detainee who was injured after being slammed against the wall in his cell;

sodomizing a detainee with a chemical light and perhaps a broom stick; and using military working dogs to frighten and intimidate detainees with threats of attack, and in one instance actually biting a detainee." In 2005, CACI announced plans to abandon interrogation work. The same year, after settling a $28.5 million corruption case for bribing foreign officials, Titan was purchased by L-3 Communications Holdings for just under $2 billion. In 2010, a US federal appeals court, citing the immunity of government contractors, dismissed a 2004 lawsuit against the two companies by Abu Ghraib torture victims.[34]

The naked brutality of the "War on Terror," in which torture was excused as "enhanced interrogation" and prisoners of war lost their basic human rights as "enemy combatants," is inseparable from its neoliberal structure. In 2007, the *Los Angeles Times* reported that while US troops in Iraq totaled 160,000, there were more than 180,000 contractors, not counting security companies such as Blackwater. This privatized warfare, with its massive profits and limited accountability, in many ways mirrored the dynamics of global free-trade zones and Mexican *maquiladoras* under NAFTA. In this sense, the "War on Terror" was the extension of neoliberal globalization by military force. And the neoliberal model was not only integral to the invasion and occupation on the US side; it was also forced on the Iraqi people.[35]

Two months after the US invasion, L. Paul Bremer III, head of the US Coalition Provisional Authority (CPA), announced that Iraq was "open for business."[36] That September, Bremer implemented Order Number 39, which "announced that 200 Iraqi state companies would be privatized; decreed that foreign firms can retain 100 percent ownership of Iraqi banks, mines and factories; and allowed these firms to move 100 percent of their profits out of Iraq."[37] The declaration undermined Iraq's constitution, which outlawed the privatization of state resources and the foreign ownership of Iraqi firms. Other executive edicts from the US "dictator of Iraq"[38] included Order Number 12, which enforced free trade by suspending "all tariffs, customs duties, import taxes, licensing fees and similar surcharges for goods entering or leaving Iraq."[39] Order Number 17, mentioned previously, granted immunity from Iraqi law to coalition military personnel and private contractors. Order Numbers 37 and 49 cut corporate taxes in Iraq. Order Numbers 80, 81, and 83 rewrote Iraq's copyright laws in order to meet the World Trade Organization's standards for protecting corporate property (and as early as 2004, the WTO granted Iraq observer status). Through the CPA, Bremer and the US forced neoliberalism onto Iraq by fiat, with direct benefits for US corporations.[40]

The US invasion of Iraq provided a huge financial windfall for defense contractors such as Lockheed Martin, Halliburton, and Blackwater, and the subsequent occupation was intended to create long-term investment opportunities for US banks and oil companies. Meanwhile, in the US, the fear of terrorism stifled dissent and provided justification for widespread repression and surveillance.

THE WAR, AT HOME

Addressing a joint session of Congress in the days following 9/11, President George W. Bush announced that the nations of the world had to choose a side, warning, "either you are with us, or you are with the terrorists."[41] This rhetorical dichotomy, between absolute obedience to the Bush administration or support for terrorism, proved a powerful and threatening tool, and it was openly applied domestically, as well.

A month after the attacks, at the behest of the Bush administration, Congress passed the Uniting and Strengthening America by Providing Appropriate Tools Required to Intercept and Obstruct Terrorism (USA PATRIOT) Act. Among its more than one thousand provisions, the PATRIOT Act greatly expanded the Justice Department's ability to administer wiretaps and searches, obtain personal records from third parties, freeze financial assets, define what constituted terrorist activity, and monitor immigration. As Morton Halperin, a member of President Richard Nixon's National Security Council, warned, under the PATRIOT Act, "If the [US] government thinks you're under the control of a foreign government, they can wiretap you and never tell you, search your house and never tell you, break into your home, copy your hard drive, and never tell you that they've done it. . . . Historically, the government has often believed that anyone who is protesting government policy is doing it at the behest of a foreign government and opened counterintelligence investigations of them."[42] Within a year, as many as five thousand people in the US had been detained in the investigation of September 11, none of whom were charged in connection with the attacks.[43]

In March 2002, the Bush administration also instituted the Homeland Security Advisory System, a color-coded guide intended to keep Americans informed of the risk of additional terrorist attacks. The five levels, from highest risk to lowest, were severe (red), high (orange), elevated/significant (yellow), guarded/general (blue), and low (green). In the nine years before the system was discontinued in 2011, the threat never dipped below an "elevated, significant risk of terrorist attack." The US government's daily warning to the American people was that the next big terrorist attack was always imminent.[44]

To take advantage of this fear, in 2002, the Bush administration also launched the Terrorism Information and Prevention System (Operation TIPS), a program designed to use citizen volunteers' "unique position to serve as extra eyes and ears for law enforcement." In its pilot stage alone, TIPS was to involve one million "truckers, letter carriers, train conductors, ship captains, utility employees, and other" American citizens as spies and informants.[45] However, as news reports about TIPS circulated, opposition to the program grew. Despite support from Senator Joe

Lieberman, among others, Congress voted to eliminate it. But while TIPS was abandoned, other domestic surveillance programs continued unabated. "Antiterrorism" activities of law enforcement at various levels included the surveillance, infiltration, and disruption of nonviolent activist groups. Echoing the FBI's COINTEL-PRO efforts against 1960s activists and its attacks on Earth First!, publicly known incidents of police forces infiltrating peace organizations under the guise of fighting terrorism occurred in Fresno and Oakland, California; Baltimore, Maryland; Iowa City, Iowa; Olympia, Washington; and Minneapolis, Minnesota. As Halperin predicted, the PATRIOT Act was used not just to "obstruct terrorism" but also to repress political dissent.[46]

Some of the coordination between law enforcement agencies can be explained by the emergence of the Department of Homeland Security (DHS). The Office of Homeland Security was established in the weeks after 9/11. A year later, the DHS merged customs, transportation security, the Secret Service, emergency management, the US Coast Guard, immigration, and border control into one cabinet department, with an annual budget of roughly $30 billion. By 2010, DHS had given state and local police agencies $31 billion in grants, some of which was used to apply new military technologies, such as facial recognition programs, Predator drones, and infrared cameras, to domestic populations. The Department of Defense also contributed to the militarization of domestic police forces, distributing more than $100 million worth of vehicles, aircraft, and weapons in 2006 alone.[47]

The political environment of the "War on Terror"—heightened fear and paranoia, expanded and consolidated police powers, and widespread accusations that any hesitation, let alone opposition, provided aid to terrorists—was incredibly hostile. And yet despite an official campaign of disinformation and the overt threat of government repression, the Bush administration's imperial endeavors encountered widespread public opposition.

THE PEACE MOVEMENT

In the six months before the March 2003 invasion of Iraq, a massive, global peace movement emerged. Worldwide protests on October 26, 2002, involved as many as 250,000 people, including some 80,000 in San Francisco and 100,000 in Washington, DC. Two months later, on December 10, activists organized more than one hundred coordinated vigils, protests, and teach-ins in thirty-seven US states. In January, hundreds of thousands again took to the streets of San Francisco and Washington, DC, the latter in below-freezing temperatures. Months before the war even began, peace protests already rivaled those of the Vietnam War era.[48]

On February 15, an estimated eight to twelve million people—in more than three hundred cities in sixty countries—demonstrated in hopes of preventing the war. They included as many as 250,000 in New York City, more than 750,000 in London, 300,000 throughout France, 500,000 in Berlin, 1.3 million in Barcelona and 600,000 in Madrid, more than 1 million in Rome, and 500,000 in Australia. Protests in Israel, Pakistan, India, Thailand, Japan, Canada, Syria, and South Africa also drew large crowds. Demonstrations of various sizes also occurred in Chicago, Illinois; Colorado Springs, Colorado; and Wausau, Wisconsin—roughly 150 US cities in all. Governments in more than ninety US cities, including Baltimore, Chicago, and Seattle, also passed resolutions against the war.[49]

In March, as war preparations escalated, the protests became even more disruptive. Nearly ten thousand people in fifty cities signed the Iraq Pledge of Resistance, a promise to participate in civil disobedience in the event of a war on Iraq. On March 14, less than a week before the invasion, two hundred protesters blocked access to the Pacific Stock Exchange in San Francisco. Among the eighty demonstrators arrested was retired Air Force lieutenant colonel Warren Langley, a former head of the exchange. Three days later, 250 people marched on the US Capitol building in Washington, DC. Capitol police arrested fifty-four people, including Robert McIlvaine, who carried a sign reading, "Not in my son's name," in honor of his son, Bobby, who was killed in the 9/11 attacks.[50]

On March 20, 2003, as the invasion began, mass civil disobedience shut down intersections, highways, and business districts in San Francisco, Washington, DC, Chicago, New York City, and elsewhere. In San Francisco, in a coordinated action similar to the Seattle WTO protests, roving demonstrators shut down dozens of intersections and repeatedly disrupted Bay Bridge on-ramps. Thousands of people were arrested. In Chicago, protesters were arrested "by the busload" after blocking traffic around Federal Plaza and shutting down north- and southbound lanes of Lake Shore Drive. Over the next few days, additional protests erupted around the country. In Chicopee, Massachusetts, fifty-three people were arrested for blocking the road to Westover Air Reserve Base. In Johnston, Iowa, sixteen people were arrested while occupying the state's National Guard headquarters. Around the world, major protests occurred in South Korea, Brazil, Ireland, Germany, Taiwan, and elsewhere. Protesters in Bahrain threw rocks at the British embassy, while police in New Delhi, India, were forced to defend the US embassy. Several US embassies in Middle Eastern countries were closed entirely, while protesters in France targeted McDonald's fast-food restaurants as symbols of American imperialism.[51]

In the US, protests were primarily coordinated by two activist networks: Act Now to Stop War and End Racism (the ANSWER coalition) and United for Peace and Justice (UFPJ). ANSWER organized the first major marches against the invasion of Iraq. The coalition was initially spearheaded by members of the Marxist-Leninist Workers World Party (WWP), though both the WWP and the war's supporters overestimated their ideological influence on the broader movement. UFPJ, meanwhile, served as the umbrella for large, mainstream organizations, such as the National Council of Churches, Peace Action, the Quaker-affiliated American Friends Service Committee, and Veterans for Peace. Several of the WWP's positions provided easy fodder for red-baiters, who tried to use them to discredit the entire opposition to the war. However, the much more moderate UFPJ was also attacked along the same ideological lines. In reality, ANSWER, UFPJ, and other antiwar coalitions were more significant as vessels than as organizations in themselves. Rather than recruiting new members, they primarily offered a mechanism for existing groups to pool their resources and focus their efforts on mass events. By January 2003, three months after UFPJ's founding, it represented 150 different organizations.[52]

Contrary to recycled Cold War accusations that the peace movement was merely a communist front, groups from across the political spectrum participated in antiwar protests in the months before the invasion. They included progressive stalwarts such as the National Association for the Advancement of Colored People (NAACP), the National Organization for Women (NOW), the American Indian Movement, and the Sierra Club. They also included hundreds of others, many with revealing names, including Gulf War Veterans, Veterans for Common Sense, Veterans Against the Iraq War, September 11 Families for Peaceful Tomorrows, Physicians for Social Responsibility, Mormons for Equality and Social Justice, A Jewish Voice for Peace, the Catholic Worker, Pax Christi, the Catholic Diocese of Community and Justice, the International Women's League for Peace and Freedom, Mothers Against War, Code Pink, Grandparents for Peace, Latinos Together Against the War, Black Voices for Peace, Not in Our Name, the Green Party, People for a Just Peace in the Holy Land, the Gandhi Alliance for Peace, Students Against the War, the Campus Anti-War Network, the Direct Action to Stop the War Project, Positive Force, Moratorium to Stop the War, Standing

United for Peace, Win Without War, the International Socialist Organization, Voices in the Wilderness, and the National Youth and Student Peace Coalition. Opposition to the war also came from MoveOn.org, which doubled its membership in the months before the invasion, and Labor Against the War, which included sixty unions by January 2003.[53]

Despite massive demonstrations—among the largest in world history—the war's supporters were openly dismissive of the peace movement. When asked about the millions who participated in the February 15 protests, President Bush countered, "You know, the size of protests is like deciding, 'well, I'm going to decide policy based upon a focus group.'"[54] Parroting Bush, Australia's Prime Minister John Howard mused, "I don't know that you can measure public opinion just by the number of people who turn up at demonstrations."[55] Perhaps most cynically of all, Britain's Prime Minister Tony Blair told protesters that if there were no war, they would have "blood on their hands" and be responsible for the future crimes of the Hussein regime. Moreover, Blair remarked, no matter how many people marched in London, the number paled in comparison to those killed in the wars Hussein started. Blair did not mention the role of the British government in Iraq's history, in Hussein's reign, or in the past wars he referenced. He also failed to mention any scenarios in which blood would be on his own hands for the war that he helped start.[56]

In February 2003, Secretary of Defense Rumsfeld rejected any links between the Vietnam War and the prospective war in Iraq, calling them "a real stretch. Any comparison to that period and that long, long, long conflict with enormous numbers of young people killed is not relevant."[57] But while Rumsfeld sought to distance Iraq from the negative legacy of Vietnam, other war supporters deliberately equated modern protesters with those of the 1960s era. Members of the group September 11 Families for Peaceful Tomorrows were told to "go back to the Sixties." Tens of thousands of antiwar marchers in Washington, DC, were greeted by counterprotesters, sitting on a balcony, drinking champagne, and displaying a sign, reading, "Hippies Go Home."[58] In New York City, a war supporter attempted to belittle a marching protester by shouting, "Flower child, huh? . . . It didn't work in the '60s. Why do you think it's going to work now?"[59] This line of attack simultaneously rewrote the history of the 1960s—in which a global peace movement opposed a US war that killed several million civilians—while also, presumably, labeling twenty-first-century protesters as naïve. Other responses to the war's opponents were even more hostile.

When country music stars the Dixie Chicks expressed their opposition to the invasion of Iraq in March 2003, conservative pundit Pat Buchanan called them "the Dixie Twits, . . . the dumbest bimbos . . . I have seen."[60] Clear Channel Communications, the mega media conglomerate that formed after Clinton-era deregulation, used its stations to organize a boycott of the group, as well as protests at several of its concerts. Protesters at the poorly attended—but well publicized—demonstrations referred to the group as "Saddam's Angels," among other sexist and jingoistic epithets. The Dixie Chicks also received death threats. Less prominent dissidents faced accusations of cowardice and treason, as well. In 2006, long after Bush had secured a second term, pundit Ann Coulter denounced four women whose husbands were killed in the 9/11 attacks for demanding an investigation into US intelligence failures. Regarding the widows, Coulter claimed she had "never seen people enjoying their husbands' deaths so much."[61] In the context of the "War on Terror," such vitriol was not uncommon.[62]

When Yale history professor Glenda Gilmore published an op-ed against the war in the campus newspaper, she was targeted online by blogger Andrew Sullivan, whose readers bombarded Gilmore with rape and death threats. Nicholas de Genova, a professor at Columbia University, was forced to use a security escort on campus after receiving death threats for participating in a teach-in about the war. At Wheaton College in Massachusetts, students who hung an upside-down "distress" flag at their home had rocks thrown through their windows, received death threats, and had a dead fish nailed to their front door. At Yale, several men wielding a two-by-four attempted to break into a female student's room late at night after she, too, hung an upside-down flag in her window.[63]

On the eve of the invasion, Rupert Murdoch's *New York Post* encouraged the boycott of movies starring "appeasement-loving celebs," such as Susan Sarandon, Martin Sheen, and Danny Glover. These "Saddam lovers," the paper argued, should be punished with box-office flops. On Fox News, also owned by Murdoch, Bill O'Reilly announced that any protests that continued after the invasion would be "un-American." A February editorial in the *New York Daily News*, meanwhile, referred to supporters of UN weapons inspections as "the surrender crowd" and likened the peace marches of October to "an Al Qaeda meeting."[64] An editorial in Pennsylvania's *Lancaster New Era* the next month referred to protesters as the "terrorist tolerance movement" and the "hate-America crowd."[65] Others simply referred to activists as "reds" and "Trotskyists."[66] Signs carried by counterprotesters at demonstrations around the country included "Protester Equals Terrorist," "Anti-War = Pro-Saddam," and "Bomb Iraq."[67] But although pro-war demonstrations received disproportionately significant news coverage, given their tiny numbers, they were not as "grassroots" as they appeared. Some of them—including demonstrations in Fort Wayne, Indiana; Charleston, South Carolina; and Sacramento, California—were actually organized by the Clear Channel radio corporation.[68]

During the 1960s, the American peace movement reached significant numbers only after years of war. In the 2000s, a mass movement emerged less than a year into the occupation of Afghanistan and several months before the invasion of Iraq. However, months of consistent, disruptive protests did not pressure the Bush administration or its allies to abandon their plans. President Bush's statements that protests had no impact on him may have been as much an attempt to disempower the movement as a statement of fact, considering the decision to limit protesters to "free-speech zones" during his 2004 reelection campaign stops. Nonetheless, disinformation about Iraq and the demonization of the peace activists by both the Bush administration and the corporate media limited the antiwar movement's impacts.[69]

As the occupation wore on, mass protests continued, though with less frequency. Civil disobedience continued as well, including numerous sit-ins at government offices and blockades of ports shipping military vehicles, notably in Olympia and Tacoma, Washington. Activists also tried to disrupt other elements of the war machine. In order to combat misinformation about military service and to challenge the administration's capacity for unlimited warfare, activists, including many veterans, disseminated counterrecruitment information, held sit-ins at recruitment offices, and disrupted recruiters at public events. To challenge the deceptions of Fox News and Clear Channel, activist journalists developed alternative media networks and bolstered support for dissident news programs such as *Democracy Now!* To challenge official narratives about the morality of US intervention, peace activists publicized the Bush administration's protorture policies, as well as Iraqi opinion polls that refuted the administration's claims about its democratic aims. They also formed new organizations, including Gold Star Families for Peace, Iraq Veterans Against the War (IVAW), and Code Pink. These groups in particular tried to reclaim from the Bush administration and its prowar cheerleaders their monopoly on patriotism and "Americanness."

GOLD STAR FAMILIES FOR PEACE

Gold Star Families for Peace (GSFP) was founded in early 2005, as an offshoot of the larger group Military Families Speak Out. Its members were families of fallen soldiers, and its name referenced the gold star displayed in their homes. In August 2005, a dozen GSFP members—most famously Cindy Sheehan—set up an encampment outside President Bush's Crawford, Texas, ranch. "Camp Casey," named for Sheehan's son, who was killed in Iraq a year earlier, quickly became a hub for antiwar activists. Over the course of the month, several thousand supporters visited the camp, including actors Martin Sheen and Viggo Mortensen, singer Joan Baez, American Indian activist Russell Means, and the Reverend Al Sharpton. In addition to support from Texas-based churches and peace organizations, Camp Casey received organizational support from Veterans for Peace, IVAW, and Code Pink, among others. Sheehan became a media sensation, in part because journalists were already in the area to cover Bush's five-week vacation. On August 17, more than fifteen hundred candlelight vigils were held around the world in solidarity with the encampment.[70]

But while Camp Casey served as a focal point for the peace movement, it also attracted Bush supporters. Within the first few days, the conservative organization Move America Forward sent a bus of self-proclaimed "flag-waving citizens" to Crawford to counterprotest. In the weeks that followed, tensions steadily escalated. In mid-August, a prowar demonstrator pulled up in a pickup truck, blaring country music, waving an American flag, and displaying a sign reading, "Texas Is Bush Country." A few days later, an angry neighbor fired a shotgun in the air, causing panic among protesters and the Secret Service. Next, a man drove a pickup truck toward the camp, dragging chains and a pipe in order to destroy a display of wooden crosses memorializing the

US war dead. War supporters accused Sheehan of "working for the devil" and carried signs reading, "Cindy Supports Osama," "Bin Laden Says Keep Up the Good Work, Cindy," and "You Are Aiding Terrorism." An open letter in the local newspaper was addressed, "To the woman complaining about her son's death."[71]

As the month went on, and Camp Casey grew, public pressure on Bush mounted. Though he maintained his refusal to meet with Sheehan, on August 24, Bush went on the offensive, meeting privately with the families of nineteen other fallen soldiers—all of them hand-selected war supporters. At the end of the month, the camp closed. Three separate buses, carrying members of GSFP, Military Families Speak Out, IVAW, and Veterans for Peace, then set out on informational speaking tours, before reconnecting in Washington, DC. Sheehan's tour covered fifty-one cities in twenty-eight states.[72]

IRAQ VETERANS AGAINST THE WAR

Like the Gold Star Families, IVAW, too, was an outgrowth of a larger coalition. Launched in 2004 at a Veterans for Peace conference, the group initially focused on supporting other organizations' work, as it had at Camp Casey. IVAW members served as speakers for antiwar protests, gave talks at universities, and made appearances on Fox News' *O'Reilly Factor* and National Public Radio's *Tavis Smiley Show*. In 2007, the group expanded its efforts.[73]

In May and June 2007, IVAW launched "Operation First Casualty" on the streets of New York City, Washington, DC, and Chicago. A reference to the first casualty of war being truth, the demonstrations included reenactments of war scenarios—taking sniper fire, confronting Iraqi protests, arresting suspected insurgents—in full uniform and at full volume but without weapons.

Despite being disruptive and visually stunning political theater, however, Operation First Casualty was largely ignored by corporate media until the US Marine Corps began pursuing (ultimately unsuccessful) charges against participants for wearing its uniforms. In August, members of IVAW protested military recruiters' use of video games at the St. Louis Black Expo, under the banner "War Is Not a Game." In September, IVAW members joined five thousand others in a "die-in" in Washington, DC, as part of a larger one-hundred-thousand-person protest. That same month, IVAW launched "Befriend a Recruiter," a campaign in which veterans and youth with no intention of enlisting booked appointments in order to clog recruiters' calendars.[74]

In March 2008, IVAW marked the fifth anniversary of the Iraq invasion with a four-day event called "Winter Soldier." Based on similar hearings held by Vietnam veterans in 1971, Winter Soldier provided a venue for more than two hundred veterans to share their experiences in the occupations of Iraq and Afghanistan. Some veterans described the constantly shifting rules of engagement. Others testified about aspects of military culture, such as the Marine Corps greeting "kill babies" and the ubiquitous use of racist terms for Iraqis, including "towel head," "camel jockey," "haji," and "sand nigger." Specialist Jeffrey Smith of Florida described seeing a pickup truck full of decapitated bodies, torn apart by US weapons: "These 'insurgents' didn't appear to me to look like the hardened terrorists that everyone says they are. These were mostly teenage boys and young men who looked like they were from the local community."[75] Private First Class Vincent Emanuele of Indiana described shooting an insurgent in the head at close range. Two weeks after the shooting, Emanuele's convoy encountered the body where he had left it, and a fellow marine took a picture of the mutilated head to use as a screen saver for his laptop. Though largely ignored by the media,

Winter Soldier did yield an invitation from the Congressional Progressive Caucus to testify in Washington, DC, and IVAW's membership increased by 25 percent in the two months after the hearings.[76]

In August 2008, IVAW performed Operation First Casualty on the streets of Denver, Colorado, cite of the Democratic National Convention. The group also delivered to Barack Obama's campaign headquarters its demands for the immediate withdrawal of US troops, reparations payments to the Iraqi people, and full health care for all veterans.[77]

But despite the nationwide mantra of "support the troops," antiwar veterans were publicly shunned. At a 2005 protest at Fort Bragg in North Carolina, IVAW members were called "traitors," while a passerby in Chicago called Operation First Casualty "pathetic." In October 2007, Young Republicans in Seattle called protests featuring IVAW members "sedition" and "a disgrace" while holding signs reading, "Give War a Chance," "Stop Global Whining," and "Stop Smoking Marijuana." The next month, spectators at a Veteran's Day parade in Denver turned their backs on an IVAW contingent. In 2006, Army Lieutenant Ehren Watada (not affiliated with IVAW) refused to deploy to Iraq, stating, "My moral and legal obligation is to the Constitution and not those who would issue unlawful orders. . . . It is my job to serve and protect those soldiers, the American people, and innocent Iraqis with no voice. . . . It is my conclusion as an officer of the Armed Forces that the war in Iraq is not only morally wrong but a horrible breach of American law."[78] Rebecca Davis, co-founder of the prowar group Military Families Voice of Victory, called Watada "a coward and a traitor," a sentiment echoed in editorials and blogs nationwide. Like Cindy Sheehan and other bereaved military (and 9/11) families, soldiers and veterans were regarded as heroes only when they toed the official line.[79]

CODE PINK

A third group from the period, Code Pink: Women for Peace, started in November 2002, just before the invasion of Iraq, when its members launched a four-month-long, twenty-four-hour-per-day peace vigil in front of the White House. The vigil culminated with fifty protests around the US on March 8, 2003, National Women's Day. Among the twenty-five women arrested at the Washington, DC, protest were Alice Walker, author of *The Color Purple*, and Amy Goodman, host of *Democracy Now!* Like GSFP and IVAW, Code Pink was organized around a common identity as well as a political goal. The group's name was a jab at the Bush administration's color-coded terror alert system, an embrace of the femininity of the color pink, and a parental call to arms ("Code Pink" also being the hospital term for an infant-abduction emergency). Bright pink clothing, hats, and accessories soon became the group's calling card, and it grew to include nearly two hundred autonomous chapters nationwide.[80]

Code Pink engaged in a wide variety of antiwar activities. The group participated in congressional lobby days, prepared reports on the conditions of Iraqi women, organized eight separate protests of one hundred thousand or more people, helped bring a delegation of Iraqi women to the US, coordinated humanitarian visits to Iraq and Afghanistan, and donated over $500,000 in medical supplies and humanitarian aid to refugees of Fallujah, Iraq. During December 2004 and 2005, Code Pink also campaigned against GI Joes and other military-inspired toys as Christmas gifts, echoing IVAW with the slogan, "War is not a game." Code Pink's expertise, however, was in disruptive actions, such as banner drops and attempted citizen's arrests of government officials.[81]

With calls to end the war, Code Pink interrupted several speaking engagements and official addresses by Bush administration officials, including Condoleezza Rice, Donald Rumsfeld, John Bolton, Dick Cheney, and Karl Rove. At the 2004 Republican National Convention, undercover Code Pink activists disrupted speeches by President Bush and California Governor Arnold Schwarzenegger. A few months later, Code Pink struck again during Bush's second inauguration ceremony. The group also interrupted testimony by General David Petraeus, Senate hearings on Guantanamo Bay, and a Federal Communications Commission (FCC) meeting at which the agency further deregulated American media ownership.[82]

Code Pink's protests, in the tradition of ACT UP and Earth First!, were predictably unpopular with people in power. However, the backlash against the group was not limited to the usual prowar voices such as Fox News, against whom Code Pink organized pickets. Self-professed liberals, including *Daily Kos*'s Markos Moulitsas, also criticized Code Pink activists because they targeted all of the war's supporters—not just Republicans. Code Pink issued "pink slips" to Democratic Senators Hillary Clinton and Dianne Feinstein for their support of the US invasion, while giving "badges of honor" to those who voted against it. Group members also disrupted speeches by Clinton, House Speaker Nancy Pelosi, and others, and they camped out in front of Pelosi's San Francisco home.[83]

In fall 2007, Code Pink became entangled in a struggle between the federal government and the city of Berkeley, California. For years, Berkeley High School had maintained a policy against allowing military recruiters on campus, but Bush's 2001 No Child Left Behind Act removed local control by attaching federal education funding to recruiter access. Under threat of a lawsuit from the Pentagon, the school district finally complied in 2007. The same year, Berkeley passed a resolution in support of prosecuting Defense Secretary Donald Rumsfeld for war crimes. In October, Code Pink and Grandmothers Against the War, among others, began picketing a Marine Corps recruitment center, which had recently relocated to downtown Berkeley. Counterdemonstrators, led by a conservative local radio personality, soon joined them.[84]

As tensions between the two sides escalated, the Berkeley City Council intervened, passing a series of resolutions in January 2008. The council assigned parking spots directly in front of the recruitment center to Code Pink, requested that the city attorney investigate legal means to oust the recruitment center, and classified the recruiters as "uninvited and unwelcome intruders." In response, incensed state and federal lawmakers, notably Senator Jim DeMint of South Carolina, proposed a series of laws to cut funding for Berkeley's schools, transportation, and children's lunch programs. Many of the bills' supporters were southern conservatives, who apparently found no irony in advocating for federal intervention. The Berkeley city council responded with a new resolution, clarifying that its opposition was to the war, not to the troops. Mayor Tom Bates, himself a US Army veteran, apologized for any offense to soldiers and affirmed that the recruiters had the legal right to stay in downtown Berkeley, though, he added, "we wish they would leave."[85]

* * *

Even more so than Earth First!'s campaign to stop the Mount Graham telescope project or the Coalition of Immokalee Workers' campaign to change Taco Bell's labor policies, assessing the successes and failures of entire movements is incredibly difficult, especially in the case of peace movements. Many factors shape and scale foreign-policy decisions, and even successful campaigns to end wars often take many years.

The Iraq War peace movement ultimately achieved its objective of troop withdrawal, as the last US soldiers were removed from Iraq at the end of 2011 (at least officially). The movement also had a clear impact on national politics, if not in concrete policy changes. The occupation of Iraq was not as significant of an issue in the 2008 presidential elections as the sinking US economy, but Senator Hillary Clinton's campaign for the Democratic nomination suffered for her early support for the war, and Republican nominee John McCain's endorsement of a hundred-year US military presence in Iraq was not widely embraced.[86]

However, many aspects of the "War on Terror," both domestically and abroad, continued and expanded under the Obama administration. In addition to growing the US troop presence in Afghanistan and interventions in countries such as Libya and Syria, Obama also renewed key portions of the PATRIOT Act, authorized the National Defense Authorization Act (NDAA), and expanded the use of Predator drones. Moreover, the conclusion of the eight-year occupation of Iraq can only be celebrated halfheartedly, given the enormous loss of life, the continued presence of contractors, and the uncertain future that the country faces with the rise of ISIS/ISIL.[87]

Building on the organizing networks established by the global justice movement in the decade prior, organizations such as UFPJ, ANSWER, GSFP, IVAW, and Code Pink used mass protest to pursue two major, overlapping goals: to build public support for peace and to apply political pressure on the war makers. At the first task, the peace movement was quite successful. For while prowar voices remained well amplified, public opinion on the war shifted substantially between early 2003 and the fall 2008 elections. According to opinion polls by the Pew Research Center, CNN, Gallup, CBS, and the *New York Times*, public support for US military action in Iraq was just over 70 percent at the time of the invasion. From there, it steadily dwindled, dipping below 50 percent by the end of 2004 and below 40 percent by the end of 2006. Between 2006 and 2008, public support for the ongoing occupation hovered between 30 and 40 percent.[88]

This accomplishment is especially impressive given that, in addition to overt support for the war from the likes of Clear Channel and Fox News, the Bush administration also enjoyed considerable influence with other corporate media. CBS's Katie Couric, for example, reported feeling "pressure from government officials and corporate executives to cast the war in a positive light," while the *Washington Post* ran 140 front-page stories that highlighted administration officials' often baseless claims about Iraq in the six months before the invasion. The Bush administration wielded an enormous budget for influencing public opinion and directly paid journalists to promote its policies. During Bush's first term, the administration spent $250 million on public relations contracts, nearly doubling the $128 million spent during Clinton's second term. Among the Bush administration's most well-known propaganda scandals were misleading reports about Private Jessica Lynch's capture and rescue in March 2003 and the death of Corporal Pat Tillman, a former NFL football player, in 2004. Though Tillman was actually killed by "friendly fire," his death was trumpeted as an act of heroism. He was awarded the Silver Star, and his funeral was broadcast nationally.[89]

Internationally, Bush's "Coalition of the Willing"—much of which was limited to token participation—steadily shrunk as the occupation went on. In 2004, the Dominican Republic, Honduras, Hungary, Iceland, New Zealand, Nicaragua, the Philippines, Spain, and Thailand withdrew their troops from Iraq. In 2005, the Netherlands and Portugal also withdrew, followed by Italy, Japan, and Norway in 2006. In 2007, Denmark and Slovakia pulled out. In 2008, Albania, Armenia, Azerbaijan, Bosnia/Herzegovina, Bulgaria, the Czech Republic, Georgia, Kazakhstan, South Korea, Latvia, Lithuania, Macedonia, Moldova, Mongolia, Poland, Singapore, Tonga, and the Ukraine removed their troops. In 2009, Australia, El Salvador, Estonia, and Romania withdrew. And in

2011, the last troops from the UK and US left, as well. Many factors contributed to the participation and defection of coalition members, including US foreign aid and political developments in Iraq, but political pressure from peace movements around the world also played a role.[90]

In terms of military recruitment in the US, declining support for the war repeatedly caused recruiters to miss their quotas. In April 2005, for example, the US Army missed its goal by 42 percent. The increasing aggressiveness of recruitment campaigns during the period also reflects the difficulty of these efforts. In 2003, there were 279 substantiated cases of misconduct by US Army recruiters, and there were another 320 in 2004. In 2005, the Army spent $100 million to revitalize its image and sponsor outreach at music concerts and sporting events. Between 2003 and 2006, the US military also provided more than one hundred thousand "moral waivers" to previously ineligible recruits—including nine hundred waivers for felony convictions in 2006 alone. However, the direct influence of peace activists' counterrecruitment efforts is unclear, as the dwindling job opportunities and rapidly increasing college tuition costs of the Post-Liberal economy favored recruiters.[91]

But while the American public turned against the occupation, the offerings from the two major political parties were minimal. Paralleling public support for the war, the 2002 midterm elections veered Republican, while the 2006 midterm elections gave Democrats the majority of both congressional houses. The 2004 presidential election did not feature an antiwar candidate, though one of the most prominent attacks of the campaign (especially curious given the backgrounds of Bush and Cheney) was an assault on the military record of Democratic presidential nominee John Kerry, who had received three Purple Hearts, the Silver Star, and the Bronze Star during the Vietnam War—and was later active in Vietnam Veterans Against the War. Even in 2008, Democratic nominee Barack Obama's commitments to ending Bush's wars were gradual and long term. If his election was a victory for the peace movement, it was a soft one.[92]

Arguably, the peace movement was most successful at challenging the Bush administration's positions on torture and large-scale military action. The Obama administration immediately reversed the US's policy on the former and clearly favored using special forces, drones, and proxies in lieu of the latter. The movement was decidedly less successful at undermining the neoliberal assumptions at the core of Bush administration policies. Public shaming forced Blackwater to change its name and pushed CACI International to withdraw from the interrogation business; but on a larger scale, US corporate interests were not pressed to abandon their war efforts, nor was their influence in the government curbed.

In many ways, the war industry parallels the decentralized vulnerabilities of the global corporations discussed in chapter 3. However, unlike Taco Bell, companies such as Lockheed Martin and Halliburton have proven virtually immune to public pressure. For while they are intimately involved in the decisions of the US government—through both political contributions (legal and otherwise) and a revolving door of public/private executives—the US government is also their primary customer. They cannot be boycotted by the public, unless the peace movement can rival their influence with government officials—an unlikely prospect, given bipartisan support for the war industry. Ultimately, the unstable US occupation of Iraq was a deadly disaster for the Iraqi people and a failure in neoliberal nation-building, but it quite clearly achieved its more immediate neoliberal goal of publicly financing corporate profits. It also developed new models of privatized security that were adapted to disaster-response efforts in New Orleans after Hurricane Katrina and are now accepted components of US foreign policy. The Bush administration's policies, including its wars, also created trillions of dollars in debt that have since been cited as justification for further privatization and cuts to public services—and may be for generations to come—while also leaving a legacy of destabilization in the Middle East that has already been used to rationalize additional military interventions.

For these reasons, as well as the war's massive human costs—perhaps a million deaths from the US's "War on Terror" as a whole—it is difficult to celebrate US withdrawal from Iraq as more than a bittersweet victory, either for the people of Iraq or for peace activists around the world. Like environmental destruction, war is easiest to measure in its losses. However, exerting any level of democratic influence over the foreign policy of the most powerful empire in human history is a massive and complicated task, and it is one largely without historical precedent. Forcing a partial US withdrawal from Iraq, even after eight years, is thus both a tiny accomplishment, when compared to the war machine as a whole, and a substantial victory, given just how unconcerned with the public that machine generally is.

As movement author Rebecca Solnit notes, the millions of people who marched in streets all over the world were, tragically, unable to stop the US invasion of Iraq. "Instead came the nightmare of burned and maimed children, bombed civilians, soldiers incinerated by depleted-uranium rounds, history itself wiped out when the United States permitted the looting of Baghdad's National Museum and the burning of its National Library, [and] US soldiers picked off a few at a time during the months of occupation and insurrection."[93] Nonetheless, she argues, "The war we got was not the war that would have transpired with universal public acquiescence."[94]

Indeed, the global peace movement prevented the neoconservatives of the Bush administration from rolling out their entire wish list, which included the failed TIPS program and the expansion of their wars into additional countries—Syria, Iran, and North Korea, among them. To some degree, the movement also renewed the "Vietnam syndrome," the American public's general reluctance to support large-scale misadventures abroad. While far short of achieving peace, the antiwar movement of the early 2000s, like its 1960s counterpart, saved countless lives by pressuring US elites to scale back their imperial endeavors, even if only temporarily.

5

EVICTION AND OCCUPATION

AUSTERITY AND THE GLOBAL RECESSION

The point is, today everyone can see that the system is deeply unjust and careening out of control. Unfettered greed has trashed the global economy. And it is trashing the natural world as well. We are overfishing our oceans, polluting our water with fracking and deepwater drilling, turning to the dirtiest forms of energy on the planet, like the Alberta tar sands. And the atmosphere cannot absorb the amount of carbon we are putting into it, creating dangerous warming. The new normal is serial disasters: economic and ecological. These are the facts on the ground.
—Naomi Klein

I'm so scared of this anti–Wall Street effort. I'm frightened to death. . . . They're having an impact on what the American people think of capitalism.
—Frank Luntz, Republican strategist

BY THE END OF GEORGE W. BUSH'S PRESIDENCY, THE US economy had experienced three decades of systematic neoliberal policies that cut taxes, eliminated protective regulations, and syphoned public wealth through privatization. During the 1980s, the Reagan administration undermined the legislative reforms of the Sixties era and shifted the benefits of state resources to the wealthy by defunding regulation enforcement and appointing saboteurs to oversee government agencies. The following decade, the Clinton administration expanded the neoliberal project domestically, deregulating the media industry and investment banks, cutting poverty-assistance programs, and expanding the carceral state.

Clinton also built on the efforts of his predecessors by restructuring the global economy, granting corporations new freedoms across borders while restricting the movement of people. In the first decade of the twenty-first century, the Bush administration deregulated the energy industry, furthered the privatization of public education, and launched a largely privatized war, transferring trillions of dollars in public funds to the defense industry and opening new markets by force.

The collective impacts of these policies—compounded by each administration's additions—were stunning. Decades of liberal policies from the 1930s through 1960s had created one version of American society, however imperfect. As historians Jefferson Cowie and Nick Salvatore note, "The year 1972 [was] the most egalitarian year in US history. . . . Unemployment was at historic lows, and earnings were at their all-time high for male wage earners, having climbed an astonishing forty percent since 1960."[1] The abandonment of New Deal liberalism for the so-called free market in the 1970s, however, created a different America. According to economist Joseph Stiglitz, in the decades since, "those with low wages (in the bottom 90 percent) have seen a growth of only around 15 percent in their wages, while those in the top 1 percent have seen an increase of almost 150 percent and the top 0.1 percent of more than 300 percent."[2] The Post-Liberal economy offered decades of income stagnation or decline for most American workers, but it delivered tremendous benefits to those who were already taking home the most.

These trends continued with the administration of Barack Obama. While burdened with managing the worst economic crisis since the Great Depression and the most expensive war in US history—both of which were neoliberal creations—Obama's signature initiatives also took for granted the wisdom of using public policy to create corporate profits. They notably included an education program that promoted privatized charter schools and health insurance reform that, while expanding Medicaid, required millions of Americans to become customers of the insurance industry. The change that President Obama represented, at least in terms of his policies, was a correction to the two major catastrophes that he inherited from his predecessor—not an abandonment of the bipartisan approach that caused them.

In 2007, Milton Friedman's experiment in unrestrained greed had hit a wall. Wall Street banks, ratings agencies, and insurance companies—deregulated or simply unregulated—had made risky loans on inflated housing prices, offered insurance plans without the funds to cover them, applied safe ratings to unstable transactions, and deliberately sold bad investments to their clients—while betting against them. Many of these gambles were not in stocks or bonds but rather in derivatives markets, in which traders placed bets on the successes and failures of commodities that they did not own (e.g., the future price of oil or someone else's ability to pay their mortgage), often with money that they did not have. When the bets failed, the financial crisis caused tens of trillions of dollars in economic damage worldwide: crashes in retirement funds and home values, losses in gross domestic product and stock prices, layoffs and unemployment, homelessness, poverty, and taxpayer bailouts.

In 2008 alone, 2.6 million Americans lost their jobs, the majority in the last few months of Bush's presidency. Over the next year, that number grew to almost 9 million, while American households lost nearly $19 trillion in wealth. From 2007 to 2012, US banks also foreclosed on 3.6 million American homes. Despite decades of "color-blind" policies intended to ignore racial inequality, the impacts of the recession were also undeniably racialized. In 2009, the median household wealth of white families in the US was $113,149 but just $6,325 for Hispanic families and $5,667 for Black families. The recession cost white families 16 percent of their household wealth, while Hispanic families saw a 66 percent drop and Black families lost 53 percent.[3]

But though the investment banks' own predatory practices were the major cause of the economic crisis, they were rescued by bailouts from the US Treasury Department and the Federal Reserve System ("the Fed"). In Bush's final months, Congress approved the Troubled Asset Relief Program (TARP), a $700 billion program to relieve banks of their bad investments. Much more quietly, the Fed committed as much as $7.7 trillion to the banks, not only covering their losses but also allowing them to give bonuses to top executives and lobby against new regulatory oversight. The banks, which had been allowed to consolidate for decades, had become "too big to fail." Any refusal to cover their losses, they warned, would risk even more catastrophic economic collapse.[4]

The bank bailouts represented privatization in its purest form— the direct transfer of public funds. By many assessments, the bailouts and the trillions of dollars in additional recovery spending stabilized the US economy, saving millions of American jobs, slowing housing evictions, and halting losses to retirement funds. Those benefits did not reach Americans equally, however. By one calculation, the top 1 percent of Americans saw 94.8 percent of the income growth during Obama's first term, while the bottom 90 percent of Americans experienced an average income drop of 15.7 percent. By 2010, the wealthiest 20 percent of Americans held about 85 percent of the nation's wealth, while 15.1 percent of the population lived in poverty. The wealthiest nation in the world also hosted a homeless population of 3.5 million people, while maintaining 18.5 million empty homes.[5]

For the nonelite, the shock to the economy, through foreclosures, layoffs, and government budget crises at various levels, created a new culture of fear, adding tangible anxiety over economic instability to existing, inflated concerns about global terrorism. But rather than confront the neoliberal causes of the economic collapse, policy makers capitalized on Americans' insecurities and the panic of the moment, implementing what Naomi Klein calls the "shock doctrine."[6] They doubled down, demanding further privatization of public resources, additional deregulation, and more cuts to public services ("austerity" cuts)—the very causes of the crisis—claiming that they were necessary for the nation's recovery. Investment banks were effectively reimbursed for their recklessness, and American elites were able to shift much of the blame for the disasters they caused onto their old enemies, namely, labor unions, immigrants, people of color, and the poor—especially after a major sweep of state legislatures in the 2010 elections.[7]

In Wisconsin, Governor Scott Walker and his allies responded to the recession with massive cuts to public education and the elimination of public workers' labor-union rights. In Arizona, politicians and for-profit prison corporations used fear of undocumented immigrants—as both "illegal" criminals and as competitors for dwindling job opportunities—to create an underclass of migrant workers, to mandate racial profiling by police, and to outlaw Mexican American studies courses in Arizona high schools. In North Carolina, public fear allowed policy makers to follow Florida's lead in reinterpreting self-defense laws and expanding public gun use. In Illinois, officials privatized Chicago parking meters, closed or privatized schools and mental hospitals, and demanded concessions from public school teachers. In Texas, economic fears were used to justify deregulating oil and gas extraction. In Pennsylvania, outspoken politicians used unsubstantiated fears of election fraud to pass "voter ID laws," deterring already marginalized Americans from voting.

In just a few years, these laws swept through dozens of states, and they originated with same powerful people: the Koch brothers, the American Legislative Exchange Council (ALEC), and the Heritage Foundation, among others. In addition to American elites' use of the recession to their advantage, they also scored a major victory with the US Supreme Court's 2010 *Citizens United v. Federal Election Commission* decision. By a 5–4 majority, the court's Reagan, Bush I, and Bush II appointees ruled that limiting the political contributions of corporations infringed on their First Amendment rights. Just as neoliberal principles had been applied to government agencies, trade, Wall Street, education, and warfare in previous decades, *Citizens United* deregulated the electoral process itself. And like "free" trade, the "freedom" of speech that it offered was to those who have the most money, effectively allowing them to bribe politicians openly. Two years after the decision, US Senator Bernie Sanders noted its impact by publishing a list of just twenty-six American billionaires whose disclosed political campaign contributions for 2012 topped $61 million—in the first six months of the year alone. The Koch brothers' political networks, meanwhile, announced plans to spend $300 million on the midterms in 2014 and just under $1 billion to shape the 2016 elections.[8]

This expansion of elite power did not go uncontested, however. In 2011, mass protests in Egypt, Spain, Greece, and England—as well as in Wisconsin, Ohio, and elsewhere in the US—shifted public narratives around global and domestic economic policy. Though shaped by local factors, these struggles were largely rooted in austerity measures and related issues of economic inequality in the wake of the recession. In August, environmental activists surrounded the White House to protest the building of the Keystone XL oil pipeline, which, if completed, would connect Texas refineries to Alberta, Canada's tar sands. Former NASA climate scientist James Hansen described harvesting the sludgy oil from the region as "game over for the climate."[9] During two weeks of protests, police made more than one thousand arrests, and President Obama eventually agreed to delay the pipeline decision until further environmental studies were conducted.[10]

In September, another extended protest began when activists set up an encampment in New York City's Zuccotti Park, near Wall

Street. While initially focused on student-loan debt and the bank bailouts, the protests quickly became a broader critique of neoliberalism, which Occupy Wall Street (OWS) activists dubbed "mafia capitalism."[11]

OCCUPY WALL STREET

A week into the Wall Street occupation, footage of a New York City police officer calmly pepper-spraying the faces of peaceful protesters circulated widely on television and the Internet. The protesters, crying in pain, had been trapped behind police fences—a law enforcement strategy known as "kettling"—and could not escape the assault. The next week, police arrested seven hundred people on the Brooklyn Bridge following a march into the streets that, to some observers, appeared to have been steered there by the police themselves. In an age of viral social media, these blatant abuses of nonviolent protesters drew scrutiny of police actions and galvanized support for the movement. Within weeks, activists all over the world had declared a day of action.[12]

On October 15, 2011, there were protests and encampments in as many as 950 cities in more than eighty countries. There were marches in cities famous for their civil rights struggles, such as Birmingham, Jackson, and Little Rock. There were demonstrations in Tucson, where Earth First! had challenged the University of Arizona. There were protests in Berkeley and New York City, the homes of 924 Gilman Street and ABC No Rio. There were rallies in Seattle, where protesters shut down the WTO in 1999, and in South Bend and Austin, where students at Notre Dame University and the University of Texas had challenged their schools to "Boot the Bell." In several cities, members of Code Pink and Iraq Veterans Against the War were among those who helped to organize protest events, and Cindy Sheehan was one of nineteen people arrested at a protest in Sacramento.[13]

In Iowa, there were demonstrations in Des Moines, Dubuque, Iowa City, Cedar Falls, and Mason City. In Florida, protesters rallied in St. Petersburg, Tampa, Orlando, Miami, Jacksonville, Daytona Beach, and Tallahassee. In Montana, there were protests in Missoula, Billings, Helena, and Butte. In New Mexico: Albuquerque, Santa Fe, Taos, and Las Cruces. In Illinois: Chicago, Bloomington-Normal, Peoria, Elgin, Aurora, and Rockford. Around the world, there were protests in Tokyo, Hong Kong, London, Rome, Berlin, Manila, Lisbon, Johannesburg, Vienna, Buenos Aires, and Mexico City. In Spain, where an antiausterity movement predated OWS, as many as eighty cities participated in the day's actions.[14]

As the movement spread to cities large and small, efforts to clear encampments became more concerted. On October 25, police in Oakland fired a tear-gas canister directly at Iraq War veteran Scott Olsen's head, fracturing his skull. Police then threw a flash grenade at those who attempted to assist him. As video footage of the day's events circulated online, Oakland, and its long history of police violence, became the focus of nationwide attention. A week later, students, teachers, nurses, and others organized the city's first general strike since 1946. The day culminated in a march that shut down operations at the Port of Oakland.[15]

In November, police violence against Occupy protesters further escalated. Among the many documented cases were the iconic images of pepper-spray attacks on Elizabeth Nichols (age twenty) in Portland, Dorli Rainey (age eighty-four) in Seattle, and a group of vulnerable, seated students at the University of California, Davis. In the aftermath of the UC Davis attack, presidential candidate Newt Gingrich advised protesters to "go get a job right after you take a bath," while Fox News' Megyn Kelly and Bill O'Reilly downplayed the seriousness of police brutality, arguing that pepper spray was "a food product, essentially."[16] In reality, police-grade pepper spray is five times as potent as the strongest naturally grown pepper and has been linked to as many as seventy deaths in the United States.[17]

By December, police had evicted encampments in dozens of cities, and many others were voluntarily dismantled as winter approached. In Houston, police introduced a new tactic, constructing a large red tent around protesters to block photographers from documenting abuse. Elements of OWS continued (some activists shifted their focus to preventing home evictions, for example), but the movement's popularity and media impact faded. OWS's legacy is not entirely clear, particularly regarding concrete policy changes. However, in just a few short months, its class-based "99 percent versus the 1 percent" framework captured the imagination of a broad spectrum of Americans and shifted the national dialogue. Economic issues dominated the political landscape throughout the 2012 elections, and President Barack Obama's reelection campaign painted his opponent, Mitt Romney—who famously stated that his "job was not to worry about" the 47 percent of Americans "who believe that they are entitled to health care, to food, [and] to housing"—as the face of the callous and greedy elite.[18]

Though OWS was short-lived, one early reaction was quite telling. In October 2011, just five weeks after the occupations started, a *New York Times* / CBS News poll found that a majority of Americans were sympathetic to the protesters' cause. In December, Frank Luntz, one of the nation's most highly regarded conservative strategists, addressed a meeting of the Republican Governors Association. Admittedly shaken by the movement's success, Luntz advised his audience to abandon the term "capitalism" in favor of "economic freedom" or "free market," reasoning that the American public increasingly considered capitalism "immoral." He also told Republican leaders to shift their language on such increasingly popular ideas as "raising taxes on the rich" and instead "talk about government taking money from hardworking Americans."

Similarly, he advised replacing the term "government spending" with "waste" and focusing protesters' anger away from Wall Street and toward the White House, so that Republicans could capitalize on popular outrage—and, presumably, use it to justify additional cuts. A few months of anti–Wall Street protests had convinced US elites of their potential, and they quickly began making plans to contain and outmaneuver them.[19]

OWS, however, was just one thread of popular protest against neoliberal policies during the Obama era. Successful teachers' strikes in Chicago and Seattle, as well as antitesting protests by students and parents from New Mexico to New York, challenged the latest steps in the neoliberal assault on public education. In California, Texas, and elsewhere, protesters opposed the *Citizens United* decision by staging mock "funerals for democracy." The diverse, overlapping movements for peace, immigrant rights, social justice, and the environment outlined in previous chapters also confronted neoliberalism at its many points of impact.[20]

THE ENVIRONMENT

Environmental protest in the Obama era primarily focused on issues related to climate change and fossil-fuel extraction: hydraulic fracturing ("fracking"), the Keystone XL and Dakota Access pipelines, offshore drilling, and mountaintop removal. Like Earth First!'s defense of Mount Graham, many environmental campaigns tackled these issues locally, for example, by passing municipal fracking bans in cities in Hawaii, New Mexico, Colorado, New Jersey, Texas, and Pennsylvania, as well as statewide bans in Vermont and New York. But this strategy had limitations. After fracking-related carcinogens were found at a Denton, Texas, playground, residents launched a referendum to ban fracking wells within city limits. It passed, but the fossil-fuel-funded Texas state legislature responded by outlawing all local fracking bans.[21]

Financially, environmental activists were grossly outmatched by corporate interests. According to one estimate, groups pushing for the Keystone XL pipeline—including the US Chamber of Commerce, the Business Roundtable, and ExxonMobil—boasted lobbying budgets totaling almost $200 million, about forty times that of the pipeline's opponents. A 2013 Drexel University study, meanwhile, estimated that the top climate-change-denial organizations in the US, backed by wealthy conservative donors and the fossil-fuel industry, worked from an annual budget of as much as $900 million. From 2003 to 2010, 140 elite backers—including the Koch brothers, the Lynde and Harry Bradley Foundation, and the Devos family—financed $558 million in climate-change denial. The Koch brothers alone funneled some $25 million into organizations opposed to climate-change legislation between 2005 and 2008. In 2015, then the hottest year in recorded history, an investigation revealed that ExxonMobil, a major funder of climate-change denial for several decades, had understood the realities of climate change as early as the 1970s.[22]

Despite the disadvantage in funds of national groups such as 350.org, they challenged the Keystone XL pipeline with protests at the federal level, including sit-ins and pickets outside the White House. Meanwhile, other activists, including Earth First! and the indigenous activist networks Idle No More and Moccasins on the Ground, disrupted pipeline construction from Canada to Texas with road blockades, tree-sits, and other acts of civil disobedience. Arrests were widespread. In North Dakota, indigenous allies, progressive labor unions, and a group of US military veterans were among those to join the Standing Rock Sioux–led campaign against the Dakota Access Pipeline (DAPL). Despite worldwide attention, arrests and police violence were ubiquitous there, as well.

In 2015, with the cost of oil plummeting, the Obama administration announced its rejection of the Keystone XL pipeline's northern leg. In the meantime, however, the administration had fast-tracked the southern leg from Oklahoma to the Gulf of Mexico, while oil companies expanded existing pipelines to increase their capacity. The Obama administration also urged modest fracking regulations, such as requiring companies to reveal which chemicals they were using on federal land. Those regulations were trumped, however, by George W. Bush–era laws that had given fracking companies exemptions to the Clean Water and Safe Drinking Water Acts since 2005. Before leaving office, Obama also temporarily halted DAPL construction, but he did so knowing that his successor, Donald Trump, had promised to complete it.[23]

SOCIAL JUSTICE

In the 1980s and 1990s, punk rockers at 924 Gilman Street and ABC No Rio openly challenged bigoted behavior in their own communities, demanding "No Racism, No Sexism, and No Homophobia"—and ABC No Rio has since added "No Transphobia" to the fliers for its shows. These mantras for equality drew on Sixties-era movements' efforts against white supremacy and patriarchy, and they were far afield of the contemporary political mainstream. The Reagan administration openly mocked the AIDS crisis, while the more sympathetic Clinton administration endorsed the softer discrimination of "Don't Ask, Don't Tell." On many social justice issues, the Obama administration was one of the most progressive in US history, establishing clear differences between Democrats and Republicans on the decades-long wedge issues of women's and LGBT rights—and obscuring the similarities in the two parties' economic platforms.

In 2010, Obama expanded federal hate-crime enforcement to include gender, gender identity, and sexuality. The next year, his administration discontinued "Don't Ask, Don't Tell" and announced that it would not defend the limited definition of mar-

riage in the Defense of Marriage Act (DOMA). Over the course of
Obama's presidency, he also gradually shifted his public position
on marriage equality. In 2015, when the US Supreme Court ruled
same-sex marriage bans unconstitutional in *Obergefell v. Hodges*,
the White House was illuminated in rainbow colors in celebration.
In May 2016, Obama's Departments of Education and Justice also
issued a joint directive that US schools "provide a safe and nondis-
criminatory environment for all students, including transgender
students," and thus allow them to use the bathrooms corresponding with their identity.[24]

But though the Obama era represented a significant shift in
both federal policy and public opinion, legislative attacks on LGBT
rights at the state level were constant, from California's Proposition 8 ban on same-sex marriage in 2008 to Virginia's 2012 law
allowing adoption agencies to discriminate against same-sex parents to Indiana's 2015 Religious Freedom Restoration Act, which
allowed business owners to use their religious beliefs to discriminate against customers. Dozens of other states passed similar laws,
and these coordinated efforts were challenged in the courts, as well
as in the streets. In response to Proposition 8, thousands of protesters marched throughout California and all over the country: in
Boston and Chicago; in Austin, Houston, Dallas, and Arlington,
Texas; in Boulder and Denver, Colorado. There were also protests
in Salt Lake City, Utah, targeting the Church of Jesus Christ of
Latter-Day Saints, whose members canvassed for, and donated
millions of dollars to, the discriminatory California initiative. In
response to Indiana's law, thousands took to the streets of Indianapolis, and the law was widely panned by prominent business
leaders nationwide. Within a week, the legislature amended it to
protect LGBT customers.[25]

In 2016, North Carolina passed the Public Facilities Privacy
and Security Act, banning transgender individuals from using the
bathrooms corresponding with their identities. Just as Texas had

passed legislation to undermine local fracking bans, the North Carolina law trumped the efforts of the Charlotte city government, undercutting its LGBT rights initiatives as well as attempts to raise the minimum wage. In response to the law, the National Basketball Association moved its 2017 All-Star Game from Charlotte, and the NCAA threatened to withhold championship events for four years. Bruce Springsteen and Ringo Starr canceled North Carolina appearances, while other performers, including Cyndi Lauper and the punk band Against Me!, used their concerts as platforms to condemn the law and raise funds for LGBTQ causes.[26]

Assaults on women's rights followed a similar pattern. In 2012, Wisconsin Governor Scott Walker repealed the state's Equal Pay Enforcement Act. A month earlier, his close ally state senator Glenn Grothman proposed legislation to classify single parents as child abusers. The same year, Republican officials around the country, including Congressman Todd Akin of Missouri, Indiana state treasurer Richard Mourdock, Wisconsin state representative Roger Rivard, and presidential candidate Ron Paul, also made a variety of public statements about women's propensity to lie about rape, revealing their ignorance about sexual violence as well as basic reproductive science. Meanwhile, between 2010 and 2014, US state legislatures passed 231 laws restricting abortion rights, establishing mandatory waiting periods and ultrasounds, enforcing medically unnecessary regulations on service providers, and legally requiring doctors to lie to their patients. In 2015, the antiabortion group Center for Medical Progress released heavily edited "undercover" video footage of discussions with representatives of Planned Parenthood. Though the videos were discredited, the filmmakers were charged with a variety of crimes, and investigations by several state governments found no wrongdoing by Planned Parenthood, legislatures in Kansas, Texas, Utah, Louisiana, Ohio, and five other states used them to justify defunding women's health clinics, including those that did not offer abortion services.[27]

Women's rights activists responded to these attacks with lawsuits and other protests. In 2012, hundreds of people picketed the state capitols in Kansas and Oklahoma to protest abortion rights restrictions. The same year, after radio host Rush Limbaugh called law student Sandra Fluke a "slut" and a "prostitute" for offering testimony on the importance of affordable birth control, activists pressured more than one hundred companies, including Subway, Ford, Office Depot, Walgreens, and Wells Fargo, to cancel their advertisements on his Clear Channel Communications radio program. A similar campaign responded to the Susan G. Komen for the Cure foundation's decision to sever its ties with Planned Parenthood, quickly prompting Komen officials to reconsider. In 2013, a live Internet stream of Texas state senator Wendy Davis's eleven-hour filibuster against abortion restrictions drew national attention, and thousands of supporters flooded the state capitol in support. The bill passed, but it was later overturned by the US Supreme Court.[28]

A complex and vicious combination of backlash to the first Black US president, growing awareness of clear shifts in the demographics of US voters, and xenophobic fears about terrorism and the economic recession also created an incredibly hostile racial environment. During the 2010 election cycle, a national campaign by conservatives decried President Obama's supposed approval of a "mosque at Ground Zero" in New York City. Though fictitious (like similarly racist narratives about Obama's birth certificate), the accusations proved useful to Obama's political opponents during the election. The campaign also inspired a wave of hate crimes, including the stabbing of a taxi driver in New York City, arson at a mosque in Tennessee, and attacks on Muslims in rural New York. The same year, officials in Oklahoma baited anti-Muslim bigotry by introducing the "Save Our State" referendum to prevent a takeover by Sharia law, despite less than 1 percent of the state's population practicing Islam—and the existence of the US Constitution.

The measure passed with 70 percent voter support, though it was later ruled unconstitutional.[29]

In addition to Islamophobic political campaigns and new laws targeting immigrant communities (discussed in the next section), racial conflict during the Obama era manifested itself most clearly around issues of police violence. In 2012, Florida neighborhood-watch volunteer George Zimmerman shot to death Trayvon Martin, an unarmed Black teenager. Despite the fact that Zimmerman had initiated contact with the teen and admitted that he was guided by racial stereotypes, he claimed self-defense under Florida's "Stand Your Ground" laws and initially was not charged with any crime. Students at thirty-four Miami-area schools walked out of class in protest. Members of the Miami Heat basketball team posted sympathetic social media messages, and an online petition demanding charges against Zimmerman collected two million signatures. Zimmerman was eventually charged (and acquitted), and his defense fund received donations from all over the country, after being promoted by Fox News.[30]

Two years later, Ferguson, Missouri, police officer Darren Wilson shot to death Michael Brown, also an unarmed Black teenager. Following the November announcement that Wilson would not be indicted, National Guard–occupied Ferguson erupted into protests and riots. Meanwhile, in St. Louis, hundreds of people took to the streets and blocked traffic. In New York City, where police had recently shot to death Akai Gurley and strangled to death Eric Garner (both of whom were Black and unarmed), hundreds more marched and blocked traffic. In Oakland, where transit police shot to death Oscar Grant (also Black and unarmed) in 2009, hundreds of demonstrators blocked portions of I-580, and forty-three people were arrested. The next night, another ninety-two people were arrested, as protests became riots. In Los Angeles, nearly two hundred people were arrested during three straight days of protest. There were also protests in Chicago, Denver, Seattle, San Diego, Philadelphia, Austin, Washington, DC, and dozens of other cities. In the following weeks, as a grand jury announced that Garner's killers also would not be indicted, protest chants of "Hands Up, Don't Shoot" (in reference to Michael Brown) and "I Can't Breathe" (which Eric Garner gasped as he was strangled) swept the country. Students and teachers at high schools, colleges, and law schools all over the US walked out or staged "die-ins." High school, college, and NBA basketball players appeared before games in shirts emblazoned with "I Can't Breathe." NFL football players entered the field with their hands in the air.[31]

The Movement for Black Lives (#BlackLivesMatter) responded to dozens of other prominent killings by police, as well, drawing public attention to racial disparities in policing methods and to police forces' lack of public accountability. President Obama offered cautious support, both praising the work of police and supporting federal investigations that ultimately revealed widespread, blatant racism in the police forces of Ferguson and Chicago. At the same time, #BlackLivesMatter received angry backlash in the form of FBI surveillance, as well as "Police Lives Matter" and "All Lives Matter" counterprotests, widespread vandalism of Black churches, and a variety of related hate crimes. In 2016, the Louisiana legislature expanded its list of hate-crime-protected groups to include police officers.[32]

IMMIGRATION AND GLOBALIZATION

The immigrant rights movement of the Obama era faced similar racial hostilities and was forced to navigate a complex combination of state- and federal-level politics. While opposing the steady barrage of the US government's record-breaking mass deportation programs—which expelled more than one and a half million people during Obama's first term and more than two and a half million overall—protesters also scrambled to respond to aggressive, xenophobic state-level legislation that targeted immigrant communities. The resulting environment for millions of American immigrants—undocumented and otherwise—was nicknamed "Juan Crow," a wordplay on the Jim Crow system that terrorized African Americans after the US Civil War and maintained a severely marginalized workforce of second-class citizens.

In 2010, the Arizona legislature passed Senate Bill (SB) 1070, requiring Arizona officials to prosecute immigration laws to their fullest extent and mandating that law enforcement seek documentation from all suspected immigrants. The following year, Alabama passed a similar law, House Bill (HB) 56, which additionally required public schools to determine the immigration status of K–12 students and voided undocumented immigrants' ability to enter legally binding contracts. State governments in Georgia, Indiana, South Carolina, and Utah passed similar legislation, and "copycat" bills were considered in California, Texas, Oklahoma, Nebraska, Mississippi, Kentucky, Florida, Michigan, and elsewhere. The model legislation, like others that swept the country, was promoted by ALEC, whose members included the Corrections Corporation of America, a private prison company that stood to profit from the resulting increased detention of undocumented immigrants. Thirty of the thirty-six legislators who sponsored the Arizona bill received financial contributions from private prison companies or their lobbyists.[33]

Activists targeted these anti-immigrant laws, and Arizona's in particular, with a variety of legal challenges and other protests. On May 1, 2010, May Day marches in as many as seventy US cities—with reported crowds of fifty thousand in Los Angeles, twenty-five thousand in Dallas, and ten thousand each in Milwaukee and Chicago—focused attention on SB 1070. Additional opposition to the law included economic boycotts of Arizona by prominent musicians and city governments around the country, as well as a picket of Chicago's Wrigley Field during a baseball game between the Cubs and the visiting Arizona Diamondbacks. Georgia's copy-cat law, HB 87, required all workers in the state to verify their legal status (and threatened up to fifteen years in prison for using false documentation). In response, migrant farmworkers, including members of the Coalition of Immokalee Workers, avoided the state altogether, creating a labor shortage and an estimated $300 million in lost crops.[34]

Protesters also challenged the Obama administration's deportation policies. In 2013, activists in Phoenix chained themselves to the fence of a federal immigration detention center and blocked traffic to prevent a bus from leaving. The next month, seven people were arrested for chaining themselves to the fence of the White House. In 2015, protesters marched from Democratic National Committee headquarters to the White House, chanting, "Obama! Obama! Do not deport my mama!" The next year, protesters marched on the US Immigration and Customs Enforcement (ICE) office in Los Angeles, and eight were arrested for blocking traffic.[35]

Publicly, the Obama administration presented its immigration policies as nuanced, focusing deportation efforts on serious criminals and providing deferments for undocumented youth (the "DREAMers").[36] Like the administration's fracking guidelines, these policies, too, were challenged and overturned in court, with devastating effects. From 2010 to 2012, more than 20 percent of those who were deported—over two hundred thousand people—were parents of US citizens. At the same time, increased border security led those who attempted to enter the country to take increasingly dangerous routes through the deserts of Arizona and Texas. In 2012, the bodies of 171 people were recovered in Pima County, Arizona, alone. The same year, another 129 were found in Brooks County, Texas. While restricting the rights of human beings across borders, the Obama administration, like its predecessors, expanded corporations' freedoms to move freely around the world. Building on Clinton-era "free"-trade initiatives such as NAFTA and the WTO, Obama signed agreements with South Korea, Panama, and Colombia, bringing the number of countries with direct US deals to twenty. With bipartisan support, the Obama administration also negotiated the Trans-Pacific Partnership (TPP), a trade agreement intended to link the US to Chile, Peru, Singapore, Vietnam, Australia, New Zealand, Malaysia, and Brunei—and eventually expand to include China, Japan, and Mexico. However, the TPP failed after becoming a focal point of the 2016 presidential election.[37]

THE "WAR ON TERROR"

During Senator Barack Obama's first presidential campaign in 2008, he used his opposition to the invasion of Iraq and the subsequent "troop surge" to differentiate himself both from his opponents and from President George W. Bush. Upon Obama's election, his administration oversaw a substantial reduction in the US presence in both Iraq and Afghanistan, though the latter followed a surge that tripled US troop levels. US interventions in both countries continued to rely on private contractors. As of January 2016, the Department of Defense employed more than thirty thousand contractors in Afghanistan and more than two thousand in Iraq.[38]

In contrast with the George W. Bush administration's large-scale occupations, the Obama administration's approach to the "War on Terror" was broad but largely covert, relying on assassinations and kidnappings by US Special Operations squads and their proxies (in as many seventy-five countries), as well as the use of attack drones. Tallies of the number of people killed in US drone strikes vary, but 2012 estimates were around three thousand people killed and one thousand injured, perhaps 20–30 percent of them civilians. A nine-month study by the law schools of Stanford and New York University determined that only about

2 percent of those killed were "high-level" targets. Another investigation found that US drones killed 176 children in Pakistan between 2004 and 2012.[39]

With Obama's assurances that the occupation of Iraq would end, and the US's foreign interventions largely out of the view of the American public, the massive peace movement of the previous decade all but disappeared. Sporadic protests continued, however, including a series of demonstrations during the 2012 NATO meeting in Chicago. One of the week's featured events involved veterans of the Iraq and Afghanistan wars symbolically returning their service medals and publicly apologizing to the people of those countries. The next year, in conjunction with a hunger strike by detainees at the prison in Guantanamo Bay, Cuba, several US veterans and other activists engaged in hunger strikes and solidarity protests. In May 2013, Code Pink founder Medea Benjamin interrupted a speech by President Obama to protest both his drone policies and the ongoing, indefinite detention at Guantanamo Bay.[40]

The most revelatory protests against the "War on Terror" came from individuals—government insiders, computer hackers, and other whistleblowers. In early 2010, US Army Private Chelsea Manning leaked thousands of classified documents to the public through the activist-journalist network WikiLeaks. The documents ranged from diplomatic cables to official estimates of the civilian death toll from the US invasion of Iraq. The leaks also included video footage of a controversial 2007 helicopter attack in Baghdad, in which two unarmed journalists were killed. Among the other revelations in the documents were attempts by the US government to spy at the United Nations, to pressure foreign governments to abandon climate-change agreements, and to force the European Union to accept genetically modified foods. The leaks also revealed US awareness of widespread torture in Iraqi prisons, as well as previously unacknowledged civilian casualties and "friendly fire" incidents. Manning described the leaks as an attempt to "spark a domestic debate on the role of the military and our foreign policy in general . . . [and] related to Iraq and Afghanistan." Though acting on behalf of the American public, rather than a foreign enemy, she was charged with espionage and sentenced to a thirty-five-year prison term. In President Obama's last days in office, he commuted her sentence.[41]

Two years after Manning's leaks, activist Jeremy Hammond was arrested for hacking and leaking the internal e-mails of the for-profit spy company Strategic Forecasting (Stratfor) through WikiLeaks. The e-mails included details about the Department of Homeland Security spying on OWS activists, as well as companies such as Coca-Cola and Dow Chemical hiring Stratfor to spy on protesters. Hammond faced the threat of life imprisonment, before pleading guilty in exchange for a ten-year sentence.[42]

In 2013, following revelations that the Obama administration had spied on journalists, the *Washington Post* and the *Guardian* began releasing classified documents related to warrantless wiretapping by the National Security Agency (NSA). The source, Edward Snowden, was a former contractor for the NSA and CIA and an employee of the private security contractor Booz Allen Hamilton. The leaks included information about the Bush-era "President's Surveillance Program," which allowed the NSA to collect user information from Internet service providers and telephone companies. They also outlined a more recent program called "PRISM," which involved the NSA and FBI "tapping directly into the central servers of nine leading US Internet companies, [and] extracting audio and video chats, photographs, e-mails, documents, and connection logs."[43] Through the PRISM program, surveillance agencies developed intimate alliances with companies such as Google/Gmail, Facebook, Hotmail, Yahoo!, Apple, Skype, and YouTube. In response to public concern, the NSA issued a fact sheet outlining the supposed checks and balances on its programs, but it quickly withdrew the document when the claims were challenged by two US senators. The US Justice Department charged Snowden with several counts of espionage, and at the time of this writing, he remains in exile in Russia.[44]

Building on the neoliberal policies of the previous three decades, the Obama era included a clear expansion of corporate power through state-corporate cooperation in surveillance, "free"-trade agreements, "bailouts" for predatory banks, and the deregulation of political contributions. The Obama era was also marked by a Republican-orchestrated standstill at the federal level, while hyperaggressive austerity, deregulation, privatization, and disenfranchisement swept state-level governments—on a tide of race-baiting and fear-mongering that often focused at Obama himself. On social issues, Obama's humane public positions (and, to a limited extent, policies) were a departure from his predecessor, but they also exposed the reality that neoliberal economic policies exacerbate existing social inequalities, with disproportionately negative impacts on minority groups.

TO SEEK THE UNATTAINABLE

Neoliberalism expands economic inequality by transferring public resources into a few private hands while placing private costs on public shoulders. To accomplish these tasks, neoliberal tax cuts, austerity cuts, deregulation, and privatization have been applied to nearly every aspect of American society over the past several decades, with tremendous benefits for some people and horrific consequences for many others. Some of these impacts have been immediate and clear, but others are perhaps less obvious.

For example, in 2010, British Petroleum's *Deepwater Horizon* oil rig exploded, killing eleven workers and spewing roughly two hundred million gallons of oil into the Gulf of Mexico. The effects for wildlife—sea turtles, whales, dolphins, birds, and others—were devastating. The explosion was not just a tragic accident, however, as it followed specific, deliberate acts of federal deregulation. The Bush administration lifted a ban on offshore drilling in 2008, and the Obama administration issued the BP/Halliburton project an exemption from environmental law the next year. During the period covered in this book, the US also became the most imprisoned society on the planet, growing from a prison population of roughly three hundred thousand people in 1980 to more than two million by 2000. One of the many factors driving this explosion was the privatization of prisons, which added a tremendous profit incentive for increased incarceration. For several decades, for-profit prison companies (and those using cheap prison labor) have, unsurprisingly, supported politicians of both parties who promised harsh, "tough on crime" prison sentences and reduced labor regulations for prison workers.[45]

At first glance, the BP oil spill and mass incarceration may not seem like connected issues, but they are both very much products of neoliberal policies that value profit no matter the social or environmental costs and that are justified by public insecurities—fears of economic precariousness and racialized criminality, in this case. The connections do not end there. For example, thousands of the firefighters who battle annual forest fires in California—where droughts are made worse by climate change—are prisoners, who are paid two dollars per hour for their labor. Environmental activists and advocates for prison reform may have more in common than they think.[46]

Both sets of activists should also find common cause with global justice and immigrant rights activists, as the prison industry increasingly looks to target the undocumented, while "free"-trade policies wreak environmental havoc on countries all over the world. Similarly, the militarization of US police forces over the past several decades—including those who attacked Occupy Wall Street and the Water Protectors at Standing Rock—is also a product of this peculiar economic and political moment. It, too, offers a bridge issue for activists across many movements.[47]

During the Post-Liberal Era, US protest movements (those in this book and many others) have responded to a range of neoliberal policy shifts. Activists have won some significant victories, for example, moving public opinion on the occupation of Iraq and pushing the Obama administration to embrace LGBT rights. Their sustained impact on national politics, however, has been otherwise quite limited. Most importantly, they have been unable to counter the neoliberal "free-market" ideology that both major parties use to regulate the economy in favor of the people at the top. In the 1990s, neither party offered a fair-trade alternative to NAFTA. A decade later, neither party offered clear opposition to the growing surveillance state of the "War on Terror." And while these examples say much about the deficiencies of the "establishment" and the two-party political system, they also clearly reflect the failure of protest movements to rival corporate political influence in electoral politics. That the movements of the Post-Liberal Era face impossible odds is an explanation, but it cannot be an excuse. Protest movements in previous periods of US history also confronted hostile political parties and incredibly well-funded opponents. These dynamics are inherent to struggles against the powerful.

The protesters of the Post-Liberal Era have not received the historical accolades of their predecessors, in part because they cannot yet claim the wide-reaching, concrete accomplishments of earlier movements: national independence, the end of slavery, the New Deal, or civil rights legislation. And they may not ever. They have been primarily defensive efforts, focused on stopping, minimizing, or temporarily slowing the attacks against them. As a result, their victories have been barely visible—the absence of change or a less severe negative change than could have been. But they have been no less a part of the political process, and they certainly have not lacked size. While it is difficult to measure the exact number of people involved in any given movement, the global justice movement of the 1990s, the peace movement of the early 2000s, and the brief Occupy Wall Street movement a decade later were easily comparable to, if not larger than, the more famous movements of the 1960s period. Their protests were widespread, frequent, and large.

These movements are, of course, even more substantial when considered together, as expressions of the same broad movement against neoliberalism. While discussing this book project over the past several years, numerous friends and colleagues (many of them historians or activists themselves) expressed confusion at my inclusion of farmworkers, environmentalists, punks, and Iraq War veterans in the same story. I suspect many of the people in those groups would share that skepticism. My hope, though, is that the book sheds some light on the overlap in their grievances and in their efforts—or at least shows that they have often shared the same opponents, guided by the same ideological assumptions. I think such a realization makes for a more cogent and useful history. For me personally, it also offers a more hopeful present and future.

The brutal realities of poverty and growing wealth disparity, modern-day slavery and sweatshop labor, catastrophic climate change, perpetual warfare, and violent racism, sexism, homophobia, and transphobia are, frankly, overwhelming. Those who not only acknowledge but dare to confront these injustices face impossible odds, but they are in good company. The movements against slavery, child labor, and Jim Crow racism also demanded the impossible. So, too, did the movements that won voting and reproductive rights for women, organized unions in hostile factories and fields, attempted to end wars in foreign lands, and tried to save old-growth forests from destruction. This is the nature of the fight.

The people who continue to struggle for a more humane world, despite their chances and the risk of violence, may seem naïve, but they continue fighting because they know what they will get otherwise—a continuation of the unacceptable. They fight. They defy. They disrupt. They demand the impossible, and they seek the unattainable. And they do so, like those before them, to avoid the unimaginable.

EPILOGUE

ON FRIDAY, JANUARY 27, 2017, PRESIDENT DONALD TRUMP issued Executive Order 13769, barring refugees from entering the US for 120 days, blocking refugees from war-torn Syria indefinitely, and halting all US entry by citizens from seven predominantly Muslim countries for 90 days. The next morning, as the "Muslim ban" was implemented, travelers were detained all over the country. Protesters soon swarmed New York City's John F. Kennedy International Airport, then Boston's Logan International, Washington, DC's Dulles International, O'Hare International in Chicago, Dallas–Fort Worth International, Los Angeles International, and Seattle-Tacoma International, as well as the Newark, Portland, Detroit, and San Diego airports over the course of the weekend. Among the protesters were scores of lawyers volunteering to help people impacted by Trump's order. In some cases, elected officials also offered their support. In New York, taxi drivers temporarily suspended their airport pickups to express solidarity with the protests. Within days, judges responding to legal challenges from the states of Washington and Minnesota ruled the travel ban unconstitutional.[1]

Building on a résumé that included bragging about sexually assaulting women and making uninvited entrances into women's dressing rooms, as well as spearheading the racist "birther" conspiracy theory against President Obama, Donald Trump ran one of the most openly authoritarian, racist, and misogynistic US presidential campaigns in modern history. He threatened journalists and political opponents, and he centered his candidacy on the demonization of Mexican immigrants and Syrian refugees. Upon taking office, Trump renewed his promise to build a multibillion-dollar wall on the US-Mexico border, signed a wave of executive orders that included the travel ban, and revoked Obama administration protections of the rights of transgender schoolchildren.[2]

Trump's presidential bid received endorsements from a number of prominent white supremacists and white nationalists, including former Ku Klux Klan Imperial Wizard David Duke, Breitbart News head Steve Bannon, and US Senator Jeff Sessions. Bannon and Sessions were close advisers to the campaign and became members of the administration. After Trump's election, empowered American racists committed a rash of hate crimes. The Southern Poverty Law Center counted more than twelve hundred in a four-month period, including pro-KKK and Nazi vandalism and the open bullying of Latino/a and Muslim students at grade schools, high schools, and universities across the country. Among the more than three hundred anti-Semitic incidents documented by ProPublica during the period were the desecration of Jewish cemeteries in Missouri, New York, and Pennsylvania and several waves of bomb threats that forced the evacuation of dozens of Jewish community centers in California, Nevada, Arizona, Delaware, Indiana, Alabama, Rhode Island, and elsewhere—twenty-four states in all. Mosques in Texas, Washington, and Florida were destroyed by arsonists; others received death threats. In Kansas, a white male shot two Indian immigrants, reportedly believing them to be Iranian, as well as a bystander who intervened. During a two-month period, LGBTQ drop-in centers and advocacy offices in California, Oklahoma, Wisconsin, Florida, and New Jersey also either had windows or doors smashed or were vandalized with hateful graffiti.[3]

Echoing murderous purges from the French Revolution to Stalinist Russia, Trump declared critical media "the enemy of the

American people."[4] Parroting the slogan of 1930s-era US Nazi sympathizers, Trump announced that his policies would prioritize "America First."[5] Trump also borrowed heavily from more recent figures, including Ronald Reagan, who originally used the "Make America Great Again" campaign slogan to wipe the civil rights movement, women's liberation, and the Vietnam peace movement from the public conscience.

Also like Reagan, Trump appointed saboteurs to lead federal agencies. To head the EPA, Trump selected Scott Pruitt, an oil- and gas-industry-funded climate-change denier with a history of suing the EPA. As education secretary, Trump appointed Betsy Devos of the megadonor Devos family, a proponent of defunding public schools through vouchers and charter schools—and the sister of Blackwater founder Erik Prince. Trump's initial proposal for head of the Labor Department was Andrew Puzder, an opponent of raising the minimum wage and CEO of the parent company of Hardee's and Carl's Jr. restaurants. To direct the Office of Civil Rights, Trump appointed the Heritage Foundation's Roger Severino, a vocal critic of transgender rights and same-sex marriage. As secretary of the Treasury, Trump appointed Steve Mnuchin, a former Goldman Sachs partner who became known as the "Foreclosure King" for his role at OneWest bank during the recession. Trump appointed Rick Perry to head the Department of Energy, which Perry had publicly expressed interest in eliminating. Many of Trump's advisers also had direct ties to organizations funded by the Koch brothers. As Steve Bannon remarked at the 2017 Conservative Political Action Conference, "If you look at these cabinet appointees, they were selected for a reason and that is . . . deconstruction."[6]

Like George W. Bush, Trump established direct ties to the fossil-fuel industry, appointing Secretary of State Rex Tillerson, the former CEO of ExxonMobil, whose key investment interests include North Dakota, the Alberta tar sands, and Russia. Like both Reagan and Bush, Trump also proposed transferring public funds to the war industry through a massive increase in defense spending and accompanying cuts to domestic programs. While Reagan used fear of the Soviet Union and Bush pointed to Al-Qaeda and the "Axis of Evil," Trump drummed up fear of ISIS/ISIL, Iran, North Korea, refugees, undocumented immigrants, and other "bad hombres."[7]

The Trump administration recycled Reagan- and Bush-era strategies and reused dated political slogans, but many of Trump's actual policy proposals were just aggressive expansions of those of the Obama era. Trump's immigration orders, though cruel and accompanied by xenophobic bravado, were not otherwise major departures from Obama's mass deportations. Trump criticized Democratic nominee Hillary Clinton for her close ties to Goldman Sachs, but, like Obama, he filled his administration with Goldman alums, Bannon and Mnuchin among them. Through Betsy DeVos, the Trump administration will presumably use vouchers to funnel public money to for-profit charters and hedge-fund managers, but the Obama administration had already promoted charter schools through its "Race to the Top" program. Trump signed presidential memoranda in support of the Keystone XL and Dakota Access Pipelines to spite Obama and environmentalists. The impacts will be devastating for the environment—and for people—but the gesture itself was largely symbolic. Though Obama, unlike Trump, acknowledged the realities of global climate change, his administration also approved many oil and gas pipelines and oversaw a huge expansion in "fracking." Even Trump's threats against government employees and critical media were escalations of Obama's hostile treatment of journalists and their whistleblower sources, not new directions.

The Trump administration's open embrace of white supremacists may very well represent a step toward authoritarianism and protofascism, but its policies are otherwise clearly neoliberal. Trump has proposed massive tax cuts that primarily benefit the wealthy. He issued an executive order to encourage deregulation for its own sake, signed a memorandum against Obama administration restrictions on predatory stockbrokers, and proposed drastic cuts to the EPA and other federal agencies. The Trump administration also promised a renewed expansion of private prison programs, massive defense spending, and the building of the border wall (by private contractors). Republicans in Congress, meanwhile, combined these neoliberal goals in their first attempt at repealing the Affordable Care Act, which, according to a congressional analysis, would have produced $144 billion in tax breaks for American millionaires. Trump also bragged about the net worth of his inexperienced billionaire and multimillionaire cabinet members, leaving little doubt about whose interests they would serve or who would suffer most from their policies.[8]

The Trump administration's fearmongering and scapegoating of immigrants, refugees, and the media, among others, are perfectly in line with several decades of Republican Party strategy, from "welfare queens" to the "Axis of Evil." Trump's attacks are noteworthy, however, for their overt hostility, the popularity of which seems to be a simultaneous response to the first Black US president, an outgrowth of cable news and social media culture, and a result of polarizing 2010 redistricting efforts. Importantly, "Trumpism" is also the culmination of a generation-long process in which administrations of both parties picked the meat from the bones of the Liberal Era welfare state and robbed the bulk of the US population to line the pockets of the very wealthy. Democrats have offered hope, and Republicans have offered rage; but, quite simply, there is less left to pillage than there was during the Reagan years. There are fewer and fewer pension funds to raid, and on a long enough timeline, tax cuts and austerity eventually undermine the profit-padding goals of privatization. Perhaps that is why the open embrace of corporate rule and the depraved political sales pitches used to justify it have become so brazen and unrestrained. If President Trump's transparent greed and seething mean-spiritedness are something new in recent US political history, it may just be because he is the latest step in the steady march to a new Gilded Age.

But Trump's many personal and political attacks on women, immigrants, refugees, the pope, #BlackLivesMatter, Muslims, public education, the LGBTQ community, journalists, the environment, government workers, scientists, science, the disabled, American Indians, a prominent POW, a civil rights icon, movie stars, Gold Star families, protesters, musicians, the elderly, Democrats, and even other Republicans have also provoked a movement of movements—and, perhaps, of unlikely alliances.

Trump's inauguration ceremony was greeted with disruptive demonstrations in Washington, DC, and in several other US cities. The next day, more than four million people marched for women's rights in over six hundred US cities and towns (and one hundred other cities around the world), from Ketchikan, Alaska, to Tenant's Harbor, Maine, to Esperanza, Puerto Rico.[9]

A week later, protesters occupied the country's major airports. A week after that, Yemeni Americans in New York City closed hundreds of bodegas and rallied to protest Trump's travel ban. Two weeks later, businesses in Milwaukee, Philadelphia, San Francisco, New York, Chicago, Los Angeles, Boston, Atlanta, Detroit, Austin, and elsewhere closed their doors, as thousands of workers went on strike for "A Day without Immigrants."[10]

Responding to attacks on Jewish cemeteries and synagogues, several American Muslims, including US military veterans, offered to stand guard. After the Victoria, Texas, Islamic Center was burned down, a local Jewish congregation offered the use of its synagogue. Students at high schools and universities all over the country walked out of class to protest Trump's travel-ban and border-wall proposals. Despite the Trump administration's edicts, protests against the Dakota Access Pipeline continued, including votes by the city governments of Seattle and San Francisco to divest $3 billion and $1.2 billion, respectively, from pipeline backers. Churches offered protection to the undocumented. Mayors and university officials around the country, in the face of threats to cut their funding, declared their cities and campuses sanctuaries from Trump's deportation forces. Employees from the State Department circulated a petition against the travel ban, while the social media accounts of other federal agencies defied White House directives by posting information about climate change. Meanwhile, all over the country, protests by angry constituents compelled Republican lawmakers to cancel town hall meetings that they had hoped would be victory laps for the election.[11]

On the eve of Trump's inauguration, Frances Fox Piven predicted that resisting his agenda would require movements to "throw sand in the gears of everything" and that protesters would "have to aim not at winning, but at halting or foiling initiatives that threaten harm . . . by redistributing wealth to the very top, . . . by eliminating existing political rights, . . . or by jeopardizing established protections and benefits."[12] This effort is under way, and the people in power are aware of its potential.

To delegitimize dissent, Trump accused protesters of being paid actors, disparaged and threatened critical journalists and judges, and claimed, without evidence, that the popular vote tally—which he lost by nearly three million—was skewed by voter fraud. Meanwhile, in the months immediately following the election, legislators in Arizona, Arkansas, Colorado, Florida, Indiana, Iowa, Michigan, Minnesota, Mississippi, Missouri, North Carolina, North Dakota, Oklahoma, Oregon, South Dakota, Tennessee, Virginia, and Washington introduced new laws to discourage public protest. Their various proposals included harsher penalties for blocking traffic and trespassing related to oil pipelines, reduced punishments for drivers who run over protesters, and the expansion of police power to arrest protesters—preemptively—for demonstrations that might become destructive. The powerful excel at dominating public narratives and reshaping the law to their advantage. The work of protest movements must be to counter these efforts, to use their strength in numbers, and to present an alternate vision for the future.[13]

ACKNOWLEDGMENTS

ONE OF THE MAJOR ASSUMPTIONS OF NEOLIBERALISM IS that everything and everyone can be, and should be, monetized. To me, this thinking is both silly on its surface and monstrous in its implications. I find the idea of applying price tags to, say, ocean sunsets, old-growth forests, knowledge, love, health care, or safe drinking water—and then keeping them from people without means—obscene. With that in mind, it is my pleasure here to act on an altogether different set of assumptions, by offering my gratitude to a great many people, not for their monetary worth but for the wealth of generosity, patience, and wisdom that they shared with me throughout the long process of writing this book. The mistakes are all my own, but without assistance and encouragement from family members, friends, colleagues, scholars, and others (some of whom are not mentioned here), I would never have completed it.

First and foremost, I am deeply grateful to my wonderful partner, Beth Robinson. No one has had to hear more about this project or read more drafts of it. No one in my adult life has challenged me more to rethink my worldview, either, with the possible exception of our daughter, Genora. Beth, you are a terrific teacher, historian, and friend.

Much of my interest in the book's subject matter, and my thinking about it, was influenced by the late Tom Hayden. References throughout the book pay homage to Tom and his friends, the young activists of a previous generation, who were inspired by the civil rights movement and in turn inspired many others—including me. Tom was generous to me with his time and insightful with his comments. He was also a tremendous example of lifelong dedication to improving the lives of others. He did so pragmatically and strategically, often in the face of criticism from both his opponents and his allies. My first exposure to his writing was just after the US invasion of Iraq. It included a quote from several decades earlier, when he was younger than I am now. "Fascism will come to America by compromise," he wrote. "Not through the strength of reaction, but through the weakness of the good people." Borrowing heavily from a similar statement by Martin Luther King Jr., Tom's prophetic warning was a call to action. Its relevance continues to haunt and embolden me.

For much of the past decade, Joe Austin has been a close adviser, teacher, mentor, and ally. Throughout this period, higher education—especially in Wisconsin—has been mauled by the greedy claws of austerity, privatization, and precarious, exploitative employment. Joe has been wise and supportive in these challenging times, sharing both his skepticism and cautious optimism about the academy as a force for good. I am deeply grateful for his friendship and counsel. The activist-scholar tradition that he, Rachel Ida Buff, and Robert S. Smith exemplify has shaped me tremendously, both personally and as a teacher. America's colleges and universities are not, in fact, what Scott Walker and his ilk say they are, but their accusations do give us all something to aspire to.

Without the commitments and sacrifices of Earth First!, 924 Gilman Street, ABC No Rio, the Coalition of Immokalee Workers, the Student-Farmworker Alliance, Code Pink, Iraq Veterans Against the War, Gold Star Families for Peace, Occupy Wall Street, #BlackLivesMatter, and others, I would not have had a book to write. I am thankful both as an author and as someone who lives in the world that they have attempted to shape. They did not ask me to tell their stories, and I hope that I have done them some justice. I am especially grateful to Kamala Parks, Branwyn Bigglestone, Chris Boarts, Esneider, Bill Fletcher Jr., and Jean Eisenhower for taking the time to share their memories with me.

The research for this book relied heavily on the efforts of librarians and other workers at the University of Wisconsin–Milwaukee, the Southern California Library for Social Studies and Research, the Wisconsin State Historical Society, the University of Illinois, the University of Washington, and New York University. I also benefited greatly from a generous research fellowship from the University of Wisconsin–Milwaukee Graduate School, as well as the hospitality of the many friends and family members who hosted me as I traveled the country researching, writing, and editing. My thanks to Kyle Waters, Ginny Mies, Kelly and Clementine Weiss, Cassie Morgan, Drew McDowell, Mark Rudd, Tim Mead, Maureen Fitzgerald, Chris Reject, Brian Averill, Jared and Lindsey Madigan, Jason Whisler, Lori and Katie Mann, Katie and Patrick Bell, David Michels and family, Lindsey Dayton, Jimmy Singleton, John and Melissa Terry, Mike Malin, Jay Burseth, Joanna Demas, Dominic and Nikki Henning, and the Robinson and Barrett families—especially my wonderful, supportive parents.

A number of people also offered their thoughts on various drafts of these chapters. Among those not already mentioned are Michael Gordon, David Hoeveler, Aims McGuinness, Joe Rodriguez, Carolyn Eichner, Nicolas Lampert, Kevin Suemnicht, Kyle Schulz, Trevor Smith, Joe Walzer, Tom Alter, David Gray, Heather Ann Thompson, Jefferson Cowie, Randal Jelks and Avery Dame at *American Studies*, Joseph Tohill and Louis Hyman, Daniel Nasset at University of Illinois Press, David Shulman at Pluto Press, Katie Keeran at Rutgers University Press, Brandon Proia at UNC Press, and several anonymous readers.

Thanks as well to Steve Garrison, my high school history teacher, for changing my life by introducing me to the work of Howard Zinn, and to Joe Biel at Microcosm Publishing, for opening my eyes to other projects when this one seemed to have run its course.

I am also deeply grateful to my many wonderful students, teachers, and colleagues at the University of Wisconsin–Milwaukee and Del Mar College—especially the troublemakers. Teaching and learning are both hard work. They are also both important services to the public, and they are too rarely acknowledged as such.

This book took a long road to where you found it. That it is in front of you, and not just in front of me, is largely thanks to Clara Platter, Amy Klopfenstein, Andrew Katz, and everyone else at NYU Press, and I am incredibly grateful. My thanks as well to Nat Damm, whose artwork graces the book's cover (and who is one of the most amazing drummers I have ever heard), and to Aaron Cynic, on whose photo the cover art is based.

Lastly, I thank you, the reader. I hope that you find this history as useful for navigating our world as I have. We have work to do.

NOTES

PROLOGUE

Epigraphs: Giroux, "Terror of Neoliberalism," 2; Tony Schultz, "Farmer Labor Solidarity Tractorcade, Madison 3/12/11 Remarks," *Family Farm Defenders*, Summer 2011, 6.

1. Scott Bauer, "Thousands Protest Anti-Union Bill in Wisconsin," Associated Press, February 16, 2011; Kurt Raether, "Rufus King Students Self-Organize," *UWM Post*, February 21, 2011; Abby Sewell, "Protesters Out in Force Nationwide to Oppose Wisconsin's Anti-union Bill," *Los Angeles Times*, February 26, 2011, www.latimes. com; Lyndsey Layton, "Ralliers Welcome Back Wisconsin Democrats," *Washington Post*, March 13, 2011, www.washingtonpost.com.

2. Mary Bottari, "ALEC Bills in Wisconsin," Center for Media and Democracy, www. prwatch.org; Samantha Abernethy, "Gov. Scott Walker Repeals Wisconsin Equal Pay Law," *Chicagoist*, April 8, 2012, www.chicagoist.com; Thomas Content, "Budget-Repair Bill Would Enable No-Bid Sales of Power Plants," *Milwaukee Journal Sentinel*, February 25, 2011; "Walker Gins Up 'Crisis' to Reward Cronies," *Madison (WI) Capital Times*, February 16, 2011.

3. Sabrina Tavernise and A. G. Sulzberger, "Thousands March on State Capitols as Union Fight Spreads," *New York Times*, February 22, 2011, www.nytimes.com; Mark Niquette, "Public Worker Protests Spread from Wisconsin to Ohio," *Washington Post*, February 18, 2001, www.washingtonpost.com; Daniel Bice, Bill Glauber, and Ben Poston, "From Local Roots, Bradley Foundation Builds Conservative Empire," *Milwaukee Journal Sentinel*, November 19, 2011, www. jsonline.com. For more on the Koch brothers and the Bradley Foundation, see Mayer, *Dark Money*, 307–312.

4. Connolly, "Evangelical-Capitalist Resonance Machine," 869–886.

5. Schwartz, "Democracy against the Free Market," 1097–1123. According to David Graeber, Occupy Wall Street activists adopted the term "mafia capitalism" in order to capture the system's use of extortion, gambling, and loan-sharking. Graeber, *Democracy Project*, 107. The Russian economist Aleksandr Buzgalin uses the term "Jurassic Park capitalism" specifically to describe the ruthlessness of the modern Russian economy. Buzgalin, *Russia*.

6. Wacquant, "Three Steps," 72 (emphasis in original); see also Vogel, *Freer Markets, More Rules*; Harvey, *Brief History of Neoliberalism*.

7. Connie Heckman, "The War in the Trenches," in Hart, *Third Generation*, 144; Jane Mayer, "Covert Operations: The Billionaire Brothers Who Are Waging a War against Obama," *New Yorker*, August 30, 2010, www.newyorker.com.

8. Piketty and Saez, "Income Inequality in the United States," 1–39; David Cay Johnston, introduction to Johnston, *Divided*, xi; Joseph E. Stiglitz, "Inequality Is Holding Back the Recovery," in Johnston, *Divided*, 46; Stiglitz's figure comparing a typical income in 1968 and 2011 is for a male worker.

INTRODUCTION

Epigraph: Students for a Democratic Society, *Port Huron Statement*.

1. Thomas Dressler, "How Many Law Enforcement Agencies Does It Take to Subdue a Peaceful Protest?," American Civil Liberties Union, November 22, 2016, www.aclu.org; Oliver Milman, "Dakota Access Pipeline Company and Donald Trump Have Close Financial Ties," *Guardian* (Manchester), October 26, 2016, www.theguardian.com; Josh Fox, "The Arrest of Journalists and Filmmakers Covering the Dakota Pipeline Is a Threat to Democracy—and the Planet," *Nation*, October 14, 2016, www.thenation.com; "Native Nations Rally in Support of Standing Rock Sioux," *Indian Country Today*, August 16, 2016, www.indiancountrymedianetwork.com.

2. Wolff, *Capitalism's Crisis Deepens*, 232.

3. Ibid., 96.

4. Piven and Cloward, *Poor People's Movements*, 1.

5. Chowla, "Comparing Corporate and Sovereign Power," 1–5. My thanks to Bethany Moreton for bringing Chowla's piece to my attention during her talk at the 2013 meeting of the Organization of American Historians.

6. Piven and Cloward, *Poor People's Movements*, 23–32. On the American Revolution, see Raphael, *People's History of the American Revolution*, 11–46; Cornell, *Other Founders*, 109–120, 200–213, 230–237.

7. "A Declaration of the Causes Which Impel the State of Texas to Secede from the Federal Union," in Winkler, *Journal of the Secession Convention of Texas, 1861*. On abolitionists, see Piven, *Challenging Authority*, 70; J. Stewart, *Holy Warriors*, 60–72, 95–177; Karl Gridley, "'Willing to Die for the Cause of Freedom in Kansas': Free State Emigration, John Brown, and the Rise of Militant Abolitionism in Kansas," in McCarthy and Stauffer, *Prophets of Protest*, 147–164; Hannah Geffert with Jean Libby, "Regional Black Involvement in John Brown's Raid on Harpers Ferry," in McCarthy and Stauffer, *Prophets of Protest*, 165–179.

8. Among many other sources on resistance, see Dunbar-Ortiz, *Indigenous Peoples' History*; Hunter, *To 'Joy My Freedom*; Kelley, "We Are Not What We Seem," 75–112; Gilmore, *Defying Dixie*. On the early 1970s as the pinnacle for the American working classes, see Cowie and Salvatore, "Long Exception," 20.

9. For more on the complexities of this turning point, see Cowie, *Great Exception*.

10. Michael Rosenow estimates that workplace fatalities at the turn of the century, when the US population was only about seventy-six million people, "ranged

between 25,000 to 80,000 per year, while between 300,000 and 1.6 million workers sustained serious injuries." Rosenow, *Death and Dying in the Working Class*, 8. On strike repression, see Brecher, *Strike!*, 13–37, 69–114; Green, *Devil Is Here in These Hills*; Murolo and Chitty, *From the Folks Who Brought You the Weekend*, 150; Shoemaker, *White Court*, 176.

11. Palmer, "Outside the Law," 416–440; Mettler, *Dividing Citizens*; Lipsitz, *Possessive Investment in Whiteness*, 5–7; Onkst, "First a Negro," 517–543; Canaday, "Building a Straight State," 935–957.

12. Among many other sources, see W. Jones, *March on Washington*; Sullivan, *Lift Every Voice*; Morris, *Origins of the Civil Rights Movement*, 40–62; Polletta, *Freedom Is an Endless Meeting*, 39, 47–48; Ransby, *Ella Baker and the Black Freedom Movement*; Carson, *In Struggle*, 19–30; Hogan, *Many Minds, One Heart*; Payne, *I've Got the Light of Freedom*; Arsenault, *Freedom Riders*; Sugrue, *Sweet Land of Liberty*. The movement's media savviness was especially important. Over the course of the 1950s, the percentage of American households with a television rose from around 10 percent to nearly 90 percent. Putnam, *Bowling Alone*, 221.

13. Breines, *Community and Organization in the New Left*; Hall, *Rethinking the American Anti-war Movement*; Lynd and Ferber, *Resistance*; Swerdlow, *Women Strike for Peace*; Polletta, *Freedom Is an Endless Meeting*, 149–174; Evans, *Personal Politics*; Rosen, *World Split Open*; Echols, *Daring to Be Bad*; Nelson, *Women of Color and the Reproductive Rights Movement*; Smith and Warrior, *Like a Hurricane*; Hoffman, *Soon to Be a Major Motion Picture*; Muñoz, *Youth, Identity, and Power*; D'Emilio, *Sexual Politics, Sexual Communities*; Ganz, *Why David Sometimes Wins*.

14. The surveillance and violence directed at Sixties-era movements was ubiquitous. See McGuire, *At the Dark End of the Street*; Hayden, *Whole World Was Watching*; Haas, *Assassination of Fred Hampton*; Churchill and Wall, *Agents of Repression*; Cunningham, *There's Something Happening Here*; Newton, *War against the Panthers*; Olmsted, *Challenging the Secret Government*; Orleck, *Rethinking American Women's Activism*; McMillen, *Citizens' Council*.

15. See Sale, *Green Revolution*.

16. Western and Rosenfeld, "Unions, Norms, and the Rise in US Wage Inequality," 513–537; Glasmeier, *Atlas of Poverty in America*; Thompson, "Why Mass Incarceration Matters," 703–734; Alexander, *New Jim Crow*; Shannon Hall, "Exxon Knew about Climate Change Almost 40 Years Ago," *Scientific American*, October 26, 2015; Damian Carrington and Jelmer Mommers, "'Shell Knew': Oil Giant's 1991 Film Warned of Climate Change Danger," *Guardian* (Manchester), February 28, 2017, www.theguardian.com; Douglas Fischer, "'Dark Money' Funds Climate Change Denial Effort," *Scientific American*, December 23, 2013; National Aeronautics and Space Administration, "2016 Climate Trends Continue to Break Records," July 19, 2016, www.nasa.gov; Alvaredo et al., "Top 1% in International and Historical Perspective," 3–20.

17. On how and why movements succeed and fail, my thinking is primarily influenced by the work of Frances Fox Piven, Richard Cloward, and Tom Hayden, though I also incorporate some of James C. Scott's ideas about the "weapons of the weak," especially their application in the work of Tera Hunter, Tricia Rose, Joe Austin, and others. Scott, *Weapons of the Weak*; Rose, *Black Noise*; Hunter, *'To Joy My Freedom*; Evans and Boyte, *Free Spaces*; Austin, *Taking the Train*; Piven and Cloward, *Poor People's Movements*; Tom Hayden, "Ending the War in Afghanistan (Part 4)," Peace and Justice Resource Center, March 10, 2011, www.tomhayden.com; Hayden, *Long Sixties*. Influential scholarship on the Post-Liberal Era includes the work of David Harvey, Naomi Klein, and Kim Phillips-Fein, but I draw on many others, across several disciplines, throughout the book, including Loïc Wacquant, Henry Giroux, Robert Reich, David Graeber, and Michelle Alexander. Phillips-Fein, *Invisible Hands*; Harvey, *Brief History of Neoliberalism*; Klein, *Shock Doctrine*.
18. Students for a Democratic Society, *Port Huron Statement*.

CHAPTER 1. THE FORESTS FOR THE TREES
Epigraphs: Faludi, *Backlash*, 237; Grover Norquist, "A Conservative New Deal," in Hart, *Third Generation*, 157.

1. James E. Hinish Jr., "Regulatory Reform: An Overview," in Heatherly, *Mandate for Leadership*, 701.
2. Norquist, "Conservative New Deal," 160.
3. Harvey, *Brief History of Neoliberalism*, 43–44; Sale, *Green Revolution*, 49; Saloma, *Ominous Politics*, 23.
4. Gonzales and Delgado, *Politics of Fear*, 22, 29. For more on the Business Roundtable and the Chamber of Commerce in the 1970s, see Phillips-Fein, *Invisible Hands*, 192–211. In 2004 alone, the Chamber of Commerce spent $24.5 million lobbying the federal government on behalf of American businesses. "Washington in Brief: Chamber Spent Record $53 Million in Lobbying," *Washington Post*, February 15, 2005, www.washingtonpost.com.
5. Saloma, *Ominous Politics*, 14.
6. Ibid., 8, 14, 15. The 1,093-page *Mandate for Leadership* provides a step-by-step guide for applying neoliberal principles to dozens of federal agencies, ranging from the Departments of Education, Energy, Labor, and Justice to regulatory agencies such as the Federal Communications Commission and the Environmental Protection Agency. Heatherly, *Mandate for Leadership*.
7. For example, see Edward Morgan's discussion of "political correctness," postfeminism, and racial meritocracy in *What Really Happened to the 1960s*, 294–305.
8. Hacker and Pierson, *Winner-Take-All Politics*, 118.
9. Ibid., 128–132; Saloma, *Ominous Politics*, 15–16.
10. Nash, Taggart, and Grisham, *Mississippi Politics*, 117–120; Rick Perlstein, "Exclusive: Lee Atwater's Infamous 1981 Interview on the Southern Strategy,"

Nation, November 13, 2012, www.thenation.com. Thank you to my good friend John Terry for bringing the Atwater interview to my attention.

11. Marable, *Race, Reform, and Rebellion*, 179, 195, 196. For more on Reagan's Supreme Court appointments, see Scott A. Merriman, "The 'Real' Right Turn: The Reagan Supreme Court," in Moffitt and Campbell, *1980s*, 65–87; and Robert P. Weiss, "Privatizing the Leviathan State: A 'Reaganomic' Legacy," in Moffitt and Campbell, *1980s*, 90–92.

12. Faludi, *Backlash*, xix, 257, 259–262.

13. Marable, *Race, Reform, and Rebellion*, 178; Whittaker, *Child Labor in America*, 16–20.

14. On homelessness, see Jencks, *Homeless*, 13, 37; Marable, *Race, Reform, and Rebellion*, 179; Alexander, *New Jim Crow*, 49.

15. Gonzales and Delgado, *Politics of Fear*, 128.

16. Faludi, *Backlash*, 237.

17. Frank, *Wrecking Crew*, 128–129, 155–157.

18. Dunlap, "Polls, Pollution, and Politics Revisited," 10, 34–35; Alexander, *New Jim Crow*; Thompson, "Why Mass Incarceration Matters," 703–734; Kousser, *Colorblind Injustice*; Piven, Minnite, and Groarke, *Keeping Down the Black Vote*, 164–203.

19. Pring and Canan, *SLAPPs*, 83–104.

20. Sale, *Green Revolution*, 23, 33.

21. Ibid., 35–38.

22. Ibid., 50–51; Frank, *Wrecking Crew*, 159; Hays, *Beauty, Health, and Permanence*, 493–498.

23. Lash, Gillman, and Sheridan, *Season of Spoils*, 236–237, 243–244, 258, 321–322; Robert W. Crandall and Paul R. Portney, "Environmental Policy," in Portney, *Natural Resources and the Environment*, 47–82. Incidentally, both Watt and Gorsuch were forced to resign their posts following scandals at their agencies. Even while accepting their resignations, Reagan continued to praise their work.

24. Epstein, *Political Protest and Cultural Revolution*; Smith, *Resisting Reagan*; Scarce, *Eco-Warriors*, 47–56, 97–113; Butler and McHenry, *Food Not Bombs*. See also Vellela, *New Voices*; Martin, *Other Eighties*.

25. Scarce, *Eco-Warriors*, 71, 82–83.

26. Blackstock, *COINTELPRO*; Olmsted, *Challenging the Secret Government*, 88–177; Ivan Greenberg, "Reagan Revives FBI Spying," in Moffitt and Campbell, *1980s*, 43–63; Scarce, *Eco-Warriors*, 276–280.

27. Zakin, *Coyotes and Town Dogs*, 335.

28. "5 Environmentalists Go on Trial: US Accuses Them of Conspiring to Sabotage Nuclear Plants," *Dallas Morning News*, June 11, 1991; Bari, *Timber Wars*, 286–328; Scarce, *Eco-Warriors*, 83–86; *Forest for the Trees*.

29. "The Ever-Expanding Earth First! Contact List," *Earth First! Journal*, June 21, 1982; "The Earth First! Directory," *Earth First! Journal*, December 21, 1988; Jean

Eisenhower, e-mail interview by author, October 17, 2012. All references in the notes to the *Earth First! Journal* from 1981 through 1990 are from microfilms at the Wisconsin Historical Society in Madison, 4146P, P90–3694, P90–3695 2n.

30. Mike Roselle, "Burger King Protest Set," *Earth First! Journal*, March 20, 1984; Jay Moore, "Tropical Rainforests and the 'Hamburger Connection,'" *Earth First! Journal*, September 23, 1986; Karen Pickett, "Stop Rainforest Destruction! May Is Whopper Stopper Month," *Earth First! Journal*, May 1, 1987; Karen Pickett, "Whopper Stopper Month Strikes Again—and Continues . . . ," *Earth First! Journal*, June 21, 1987; Karen Pickett, "Hamburger Connection Broken: Major Victory," *Earth First! Journal*, August 1, 1987.

31. Peter Warshall and William DeBuys provide excellent overviews of the Mount Graham conflict: Warshall, "Biopolitics of the Mt. Graham Red Squirrel," 977–988; DeBuys, *Great Aridness*, 268–297. For an in-depth look at the Mount Graham campaign with especially well-articulated focuses on Apache struggles, environmental history, and the role of the Vatican, see Helfrich, "Mountain of Politics," 38–117, 176–285, 287–357.

32. Ed Abby and Pablo Desierto, "Earth First! Proposes 6 Million Acres National Forest Wilderness in Arizona," *Earth First! Journal*, May 1, 1984, 8; John Davis, "Arizona Earth First! Defends on a Broad Front," *Earth First! Journal*, September 22, 1985, 1; John Davis, "Critters Oppose Scopes on Mt. Graham," *Earth First! Journal*, November 1, 1985, 1. See also M. Mitchell Waldrop, "The Long, Sad Saga of Mt. Graham," in Istock and Hoffmann, *Storm over a Mountain Island*, 9–18.

33. Raven (a whole flock) Madd, "Mount Graham," *Earth First! Journal*, September 22, 1988, 7.

34. John Lancaster, "Endangered Squirrel Has Astronomers, Biologists at Odds," *Washington Post*, March 8, 1990, A1.

35. Madd, "Mount Graham"; Jean Eisenhower, "The Continuing Battle for Mt. Graham: Profiles of Courage and Complicity," *Earth First! Journal*, February 2, 1993, 11–12; Steve Lipsher, "Arizona's Star Wars," *Denver Post*, May 18, 1997, 12; Norma Coile, "Squaring Off over Squirrels: Ecosystem Caught in Scientific Feud," *USA Today*, March 13, 1990, 3A; John Lichfield, "Astronomers Brought Down by the Red Squirrel," *Independent* (London), March 26, 1990. In 1993, in an attempt to discredit environmental protesters, conservative radio and TV host Rush Limbaugh instead revealed his own ignorance of the area when he mused that the Mount Graham red "squirrels are idiots. You can simply move them to a different desert and they'll never know the difference." Rush Limbaugh, on the *Rush Limbaugh* television show, July 8, 1993.

36. Madd, "Mount Graham"; "Mt. Graham & Laws Lose in Congress: Women's Action Group Won't Take Mo Shit," *Earth First! Journal*, November 1, 1988, 1; Elizabeth Pennisi, "Astronomers vs. Conservationists: Astronomers Ask Congress for Mountain Top," United Press International, August 27, 1988; Colman McCarthy, "Politics, the Pope, and Red Squirrels," *Washington Post*, March 30,

1990, A25; Charles J. Babbitt, "Plans to Build Telescopes Worry Environmentalists," *Washington Times*, January 1, 1990, D2.

37. Dale Turner, "EF! Carries Mt. Graham to Washington," *Earth First! Journal*, March 20, 1990, 1; B. Bear and M. Graham, "Telescopes Dealt a Double Blow," *Earth First! Journal*, May 1, 1991, 7; McCarthy, "Politics, the Pope, and Red Squirrels"; "Smithsonian Board Chooses Hawaii over Arizona as Site of New Telescope," Associated Press, May 6, 1991. All references in the notes to the *Earth First! Journal* from 1991 to 1996 are from microfilms at the University of Illinois, Urbana-Champaign, FILM071.3A182.

38. "Mount Graham Comes Alive," *Earth First! Journal*, March 20, 1990, 1; Lancaster, "Endangered Squirrel Has Astronomers, Biologists at Odds."

39. Dale Turner, "Mt. Graham Sleaze Flows through Halls of Congress," *Earth First! Journal*, August 1, 1990, 8.

40. Ibid.

41. Arthur H. Rotstein, "Lawmakers Call for Review of Observatory's Impact on Endangered Squirrel," Associated Press, June 29, 1990; John Lancaster, "Lujan: Endangered Species Act 'Too Tough,' Needs Change," *Washington Post*, May 12, 1990, A1; Donald A. Falk, "What Kind of Stewards of the Planet Are We?," *New York Times*, June 5, 1990, A28.

42. Jim Leonard, "Trees Cut on Mt. Graham! Ecowarriors Act like a Mountain," *Earth First! Journal*, November 1, 1990, 12; Harriett Hindman, "Work Begins on Controversial Arizona Observatory," United Press International, October 2, 1990.

43. Leonard, "Trees Cut on Mt. Graham"; Dwight Metzger, "Mount Graham Update," *Earth First! Journal*, December 21, 1990, 10; Erik Ryberg, "Lessons from Mt. Graham," *Earth First! Journal*, February 2, 1991, 8–9.

44. C.B., "Quit? I'd Rather Die! Ohio EF! Takes on Mt. Graham," *Earth First! Journal*, March 20, 1991, 1; Copperbelly, Ohio EF!, "Of Squirrels, Squabbles, and Scalawags," *Earth First! Journal*, November 1, 1991, 11.

45. George V. Coyne, "Vatican Observatory Statement on MGIO and American Indian Peoples," Vatican Observatory, March 1992, www.vaticanobservatory.va.

46. "Mount Graham Insert," *Earth First! Journal*, May 1, 1993; Jean Eisenhower, e-mail interview by author, October 17, 2012.

47. Colman McCarthy, "Mountain of Contention," *Washington Post*, May 2, 1992, A27.

48. "Mount Graham Insert," *Earth First! Journal*, May 1, 1993.

49. Jean Eisenhower, "Tucson Businessmen Attack Apache—Again: Another History of Mt. Graham," *Earth First! Journal*, November 2, 1992, 8; Jason Torrance, "Earth First! in UK Joins the Fight for Mount Graham," *Earth First! Journal*, November 2, 1992, 8. Curiously, at least some of the Vatican's interest in the project stemmed from more than just scientific pursuits. Father Coyne, in fact, acknowledged more than a passing interest in the possibility of baptizing extraterrestrials. Steve Yozwiak, "Will Vatican Telescope Help Bring Aliens Closer to God?," *Orange County (CA) Register*, December 25, 1992, A46.

50. According to the Earth First! version of the story, the twenty-five arrestees issued a plea of "no compromise." "Mount Graham Updates," *Earth First! Journal*, June 21, 1993, 34; Karen Pickett, "On Top of Mt. Graham," *Earth First! Journal*, August 1, 1993, 1, 8; Freida Bea of AZEF!, "University of Arizona Hosts Earth First! Occupation," *Earth First! Journal*, August 1, 1993, 9.

51. *Earth First! Journal*, June 21, 1993, 34.

52. Paul Roland, "Activists Crash Scope Dedication," *Earth First! Journal*, November 1, 1993, 1, 7; Cardinal Knowledge, "The Pope Sins on Mt. Graham," *Earth First! Journal*, September 22, 1993, 24; "Protesters Delay Observatory Dedication," Associated Press, September 20, 1993.

53. "U of A Clock Tower Occupation!," *Earth First! Journal*, March 20, 1994, 7.

54. University of Arizona Faculty Senate Minutes, January 10, 1994, University of Arizona Campus Repository, http://hdl.handle.net; "U of A Clock Tower Occupation!"; Wallace Immen, "U of T Opts Out of Telescope Project: Finances, Apache Protests Change Focus on Arizona Scheme," *Globe and Mail* (Toronto), January 19, 1994.

55. Jay, "MSU Backs Out," *Earth First! Journal*, May 1, 1994, 26; "Mt. Graham Day of Action!," *Earth First! Journal*, May 1, 1994, 1, 26; The Pitt Panthers, "Mt. Graham Victory," *Earth First! Journal*, May 1, 1994, 26; Slugthang, "Six Foot Squirrel Visits Portland," *Earth First! Journal*, May 1, 1994, 26; Ralph K. M. Haurwitz, "Catholic Support of Arizona Observatory Criticized," *Austin American-Statesman*, April 6, 1994; Don Hopey, "Apache Sets Sights on Pitt: O'Connor Hears Opposition to Telescope Project Role," *Pittsburgh Post-Gazette*, March 2, 1993, B5; Don Hopey, "6 Pitt Students Cited for Office Sit-In," *Pittsburgh Post-Gazette*, December 9, 1993, C6.

56. Al Knight, "Environmental Lawsuits Can Make Things Worse," *Denver Post*, September 4, 1994, E-01.

57. Tigger and Whaley, "Mt. Graham: Permanent Scope Injunction!," *Earth First! Journal*, August 1, 1994, 4; "Victory! Ninth Circuit Court Rules in Favor for Mt. Graham," *Earth First! Journal*, September 22, 1994, 12; "Conservationists Win Mount Graham Lawsuit in Arizona, Make Progress on Endangered Species in California," *Business Wire*, July 28, 1994. For an in-depth look at the campaign at the University of Minnesota, see Helfrich, "Mountain of Politics," 359–421.

58. Lipsher, "Arizona's Star Wars"; Joan Moody, "Defenders of Wildlife Praises President Clinton for Saying 'No' to Ecological Blackmail," US Newswire, December 18, 1995; "Embattled Mountaintop Telescope Can Be Built, Court Rules," Associated Press, June 18,1996.

59. "Future of Mount Graham Telescope Rosier with Addition of Partners," Associated Press, February 22, 1997; Irene Hsaio, "Notre Dame Joins U. Arizona to Build Largest Telescope Ever Made," *Arizona Daily Wildcat* (University of Arizona), University Wire, August 25, 1999; "Apaches Ask U. Va. Not to Invest in Arizona Telescope Project," Associated Press, January 28, 2002; Deborah Locke, "Religion vs. Science: Some Apaches Believe a Telescope Being Built on an

Arizona Mountain Will Destroy a Sacred Place," *St. Paul (MN) Pioneer Press*, January 31, 2002, A13; Bill Baskervill, "Virginia Indians Protest Arizona Telescope Project," Associated Press, June 26, 2002; Sara Hebel, "On a Mountaintop, a Fight between Science and Religion," *Chronicle of Higher Education*, June 28, 2002, 21; Natasha Altamirano, "U. Virginia Agrees to Join Mt. Graham Telescope Project," *Cavalier Daily* (University of Virginia), University Wire, October 10, 2002; Brand Unangst, "U. Minnesota Approves Telescope Deal amid Angry Protests," *Minnesota Daily* (University of Minnesota), University Wire, October 14, 2002; Arthur Rotstein, "Long-Embattled Mount Graham Telescope Being Dedicated in Arizona," Associated Press, October 15, 2004.

60. Kauffman, *Direct Action*; Benjamin Shepard, "Introductory Notes on the Trail from ACT UP to the WTO," in Shepard and Hayduk, *From ACT UP to the WTO*, 11–16; Starhawk, "How We Really Shut Down the WTO," in Shepard and Hayduk, *From ACT UP to the WTO*, 52–56; and Stephen Duncombe, "Stepping off the Sidewalk: Reclaim the Streets/NYC," in Shepard and Hayduk, *From ACT UP to the WTO*, 215–228; Carlsson, Elliott, and Camarena, *Shift Happens!* See also Best and Nocella, *Terrorists or Freedom Fighters?*; Best and Nocella, *Igniting a Revolution*.

61. Norquist, "Conservative New Deal," 158, 162–163.

CHAPTER 2. REBEL SPACES
Epigraphs: Mike K., in Edge, *924 Gilman*, 106; Chris Larson, *Slug & Lettuce* 37 (December 1994).

1. Kelley, *Yo Mama's Disfunktional!*, 46, 50–51.
2. Austin, *Taking the Train*, 16, 17, 80, 88, 130, 267, 269.
3. Rose, *Black Noise*, 35.
4. See Rose, *Black Noise*, 7, 50, 73, 90, 183; Marable, *Race, Reform, and Rebellion*, 172–173; Alexander, *New Jim Crow*, 98; George Lipsitz, "The Hip Hop Hearings: Censorship, Social Memory, and Intergenerational Tensions among African Americans," in Austin and Willard, *Generations of Youth*, 400–403.
5. Moore, "Friends Don't Let Friends Listen to Corporate Rock," 446; Duncombe, *Notes from Underground*, 118–121; Andersen, *All the Power*.
6. Rothschild and Whitt, *Cooperative Workplace*, 17.
7. Breines, *Community and Organization in the New Left*, 53. See also Evans and Boyte, *Free Spaces*, 42–43, 61, 102–103, 187; John Clarke, Stuart Hall, Tony Jefferson, and Brian Roberts, "Subcultures, Cultures, and Class: A Theoretical Overview," in Hall and Jefferson, *Resistance through Rituals*, 43–47; Bey, *T.A.Z.*
8. Out of the many punk projects in the US, I chose to examine 924 Gilman Street and ABC No Rio both because of their prominence and because the collectives themselves have taken an interest in documenting their histories. In 2004, former Gilman volunteer Brian Edge published a compilation of Gilman's internal documents, press clippings about the venue, and seventy-eight essays by former Gilman workers. The ABC No Rio collective, meanwhile, has used its webpage to

store several news articles and internal documents from various periods in its history. Edge, *924 Gilman*; ABC No Rio, "ABC No Rio History," www.abcnorio.org; Boulware and Tudor, *Gimme Something Better*, 280–402; S. Stewart, *In Every Town*, 105–117, 149–165.

9. Though the exact source of this quote is unclear, several people trace it to Schlafly's *Eagle Forum* column; Frank Rich, "The GOP's Bitter Pill," *New York Times*, February 12, 1997, www.nytimes.com.

10. A. Jones, *Losing the News*, 37.

11. Saloma, *Ominous Politics*, 53; Farber, *Rise and Fall of Modern American Conservatism*, 119–157.

12. Faludi, *Backlash*, 244.

13. Ibid., 232.

14. Gonzales and Delgado, *Politics of Fear*, 8; Faludi, *Backlash*, 232–233; Saloma, *Ominous Politics*, 52. The Reverend Pat Robertson, host of the *700 Club* and founder of the Christian Coalition, best summed up this position in a 1992 fund-raising letter: "The feminist agenda is not about equal rights for women. It is about a socialist, anti-family political movement that encourages women to leave their husbands, kill their children, practice witchcraft, destroy capitalism and become lesbians." "Equal Rights Initiative in Iowa Attacked," *Washington Post*, August 23, 1992.

15. *American Hardcore*; Tim Gosling, "'Not for Sale': The Underground Network of Anarcho-Punk," in Bennett and Peterson, *Music Scenes*, 170–174; Leblanc, *Pretty in Punk*, 48–54; Jake Filth, in Edge, *924 Gilman*, 43. Many of the roots of the punk politics that influenced 924 Gilman and ABC No Rio can be traced to the English feminist, vegetarian, antiwar, anarchist band/commune/activist troupe Crass. See McKay, *Senseless Acts of Beauty*, 75, 80–82, 86; Cross, "Hippies Now Wear Black," 25, 32, 34, 37–38.

16. Kamala Parks, interview by author, September 9, 2012.

17. Mike K., in Edge, *924 Gilman*, 106; Devon M., in Edge, *924 Gilman*, 47; Brian Edge, in Edge, *924 Gilman*, 67; Law, *Enter the Nineties*, 23.

18. Martin Sprouse, in Edge, *924 Gilman*, 14.

19. Kamala P. [Parks], in Edge, *924 Gilman*, 40.

20. Jonathan Denlinger, in Edge, *924 Gilman*, 83, 86; Tim Y. [Yohannon], in Edge, *924 Gilman*, 11; Ben S., in Edge, *924 Gilman*, 156; Parks, interview by author, September 9, 2012.

21. Anthony S, letter to the editors, *Maximum RocknRoll* 90 (November 1990).

22. Law, *Enter the Nineties*, 7, 29; Jim Testa, "Interview with Mike Bullshit," *Jersey Beat* 39 (1989); Chris Boarts Larson, e-mail interview by author, September 9, 2007; Esneider, e-mail interview by author, August 20, 2007.

23. Michael D., in Edge, *924 Gilman*, 133.

24. Lauren L., in Edge, *924 Gilman*, 252–253.

25. Photographs by Susan S., in Edge, *924 Gilman*, 285.

26. Athena K., in Edge, *924 Gilman*, 120; Rachel Siebert, in Edge, *924 Gilman*, 281–282, 284–285; Jane G., in Edge, *924 Gilman*, 19; Celia S., in Edge, *924 Gilman*, 217; Adrienne D., in Edge, *924 Gilman*, 27; Lauren L., in Edge, *924 Gilman*, 253. For more on the Riot Grrrl movement, see *Don't Need You*; Moore, "Friends Don't Let Friends Listen to Corporate Rock," 465–466; Andersen and Jenkins, *Dance of Days*.

27. Jim Testa, "The Hardcore Matinees Today: Still DIY after All These Years," *Jersey Beat* 77 (2005).

28. Mike Goodbar, in Edge, *924 Gilman*, 181.

29. Clayton M., in Edge, *924 Gilman*, 234; Kerith Pickett, in Edge, *924 Gilman*, 49; Mike Goodbar, in Edge, *924 Gilman*, 181; Tim Yohannon, in Edge, *924 Gilman*, 9; Brian Edge, in Edge, *924 Gilman*, 66; Branwyn Bigglestone, e-mail interview by author, December 4, 2012.

30. Kerith Pickett, in Edge, *924 Gilman*, 49; Tim Yohannon, in Edge, *924 Gilman*, 7; Jonathan D., in Edge, *924 Gilman*, 88–89.

31. Law, *Enter the Nineties*, 9; Testa, "Interview with Mike Bullshit"; Jim Testa, "ABC No Rio: The Rise and Fall (& Rise Again) of NYC's Only All-Ages Non-Racist, Non-Sexist, Non-Homophobic Punk Scene," *Jersey Beat* 56 (Spring 1996); Chris Boarts, *Slug & Lettuce* 32 (November 1993); David Powell, letter to the editor, *Jersey Beat* 58 (Fall 1996); Vikki, "Tell Me about the First Time You Came to ABC No Rio" (self-published, 2006).

32. Tim Y. [Yohannon], in Edge, *924 Gilman*, 8; John H., in Edge, *924 Gilman*, 168; Edge, in Edge, *924 Gilman*, 159.

33. Michael Diehl, in Edge, *924 Gilman*, 133; Edge, in Edge, *924 Gilman*, 158–164.

34. John H., in Edge, *924 Gilman*, 170–171.

35. Ibid., 171.

36. Ibid.; Charles L., in Edge, *924 Gilman*, 228; "Letter from Alex K. to Berkeley Zoning Board," in Edge, *924 Gilman*, 337; Arnold, *Kiss This*, 122–129.

37. John H., in Edge, *924 Gilman*, 172.

38. Ibid.; A. Clay Thompson, "Seen but Not Heard," *San Francisco Bay Guardian*, 6 January 1999, in Edge, *924 Gilman*, 320–321.

39. John H., in Edge, *924 Gilman*, 172–3; Chris S., in Edge, *924 Gilman*, 279; Chris H., in Edge, *924 Gilman*, 216.

40. Alan Moore and Marc Miller, "The ABCs of ABC No Rio and Its Times," in Moore and Miller, *No Rio Dinero*; Committee for the Real Estate Show, "MANI-FESTO or Statement of Intent," in Moore and Miller, *No Rio Dinero*, 56; ABC No Rio, "Statement by the Organizers of the Real Estate Show," January 1980, www.abcnorio.org; Chris Oliver, "Heave-Ho Ends Sit-In on Eastside," *New York Post*, January 3, 1980; Josh Barbanel, "Artists Ejected in Occupation of a Storefront," *New York Times*, January 9, 1980; Sarah Ferguson, "The Struggle for Space: 10 Years of Turf Battling on the Lower East Side," in Patterson, *Resistance*, 141–165; "Third Officer Charged in Tompkins Melee," *New York Times*, November 5, 1988;

Lisa W. Foderaro, "9 Held in Protest near Tompkins Square Park," *New York Times*, April 2, 1989; Jesus Rangel, "Protest in Tompkins Square Park Draws 300 Officers and 16 Arrests," *New York Times*, May 3, 1989; John Kifner, "New York Closes Park to Homeless," *New York Times*, June 4, 1991, A1; Thomas Morgan, "New York City Bulldozes Squatters' Shantytowns," *New York Times*, October 16, 1991, A1.

41. Law, *Enter the Nineties*, 2–3, 13; Chris Boarts Larson, e-mail interview by author, September 14, 2007; New York City Council, "In the Matter of the Regularly Scheduled Meeting of the Permits, Dispositions, and Concessions Committee," November 14, 1995, available at www.abcnorio.org; Steven Wishnia, "ABC Community Center Fights for Survival," *Shadow*, December 1995.

42. Vivian S. Toy, "Differing Viewpoints on the Squatters Next Door," *New York Times*, May 31, 1995, B2; Shawn G. Kennedy, "Riot Police Remove 31 Squatters from Two East Village Buildings," *New York Times*, May 31, 1995; David Stout, "The Tenement Battle Is Over, but Not the Fight," *New York Times*, July 6, 1995.

43. Wishnia, "ABC Community Center Fights for Survival."

44. Claude Solnick, "ABC No Rio Fights Eviction by a Nonprofit," *Manhattan Mirror*, October 10, 1996.

45. New York City Council, "In the Matter of the Regularly Scheduled Meeting"; Sarah Ferguson, "ABC No RIP," *Village Voice*, October 8, 1996; Wishnia, "ABC Community Center Fights for Survival."

46. Solnick, "ABC No Rio Fights Eviction by a Nonprofit"; Steve Ellman, "Blame It on Rio," *Time Out New York*, October 10, 1996; Robin Goldsmith, letter to the editor, *Time Out New York*, October 26, 1997; New York City Council, "In the Matter of the Regularly Scheduled Meeting."

47. Steven Wishnia, "Arts Center Fights Eviction," *Tenant*, February 1997; Andrew Jacobs, "What a Difference Two Decades Makes," *New York Times*, January 12, 1997; Michael Haberman, "5 Arrested in ABC No Rio Protest," *Villager*, January 22, 1997; Andrew Jacobs, "Arts Group Wins Eviction Battle," *New York Times*, February 23, 1997.

48. Jacobs, "Arts Group Wins Eviction Battle"; Robert Kolker, "Spare Some Change?," *Time Out New York*, March 20, 1997; Colin Moynihan, "For $1, a Collective Mixing Art and Radical Politics Turns Itself into Its Own Landlord," *New York Times*, July 4, 2006; ABC No Rio, "ABC No Rio News: ABC No Rio to Receive Funding for Building Project," June 26, 2009, www.abcnorio.org; James Trimarco, "ABC No Rio," *Brooklyn Rail*, February 2008, www.brooklynrail.org.

49. Liza Kirwin, "Oral History Interview with Steven Englander," September 7–October 10, 2007, Archives of American Art, Smithsonian Institute, www.aaa.si.edu.

50. Chris Boarts Larson, e-mail interview by author, September 14, 2007.

51. Marable, *Race, Reform, and Rebellion*, 171.

52. Most of these institutions have a web presence. See also Stewart Varner, "Youth Claiming Space: The Case of Pittsburgh's Mr. Roboto Project," in Hodkinson and

Deicke, *Youth Cultures*, 161–174; Profane Existence, *Making Punk a Threat Again*; S. Stewart, *In Every Town*.

53. Solidarity Books Collective, "Patriot Acts in Indianapolis," *Bloomington Alternative*, August 17, 2003; Tom Spalding, "Protest Group Angry over Police Search of Indianapolis Bookstore," *Indianapolis Star*, August 15, 2003; John the Baker, "Burnt Ramen Closing," Burnt Ramen, accessed July 14, 2010, www.burntramen.com; 69.

CHAPTER 3. LINKS IN THE CHAIN

Epigraphs: Clinton made the statement just before he signed NAFTA into law in 1993; William J. Clinton, *Public Papers of the Presidents of the United States, William J. Clinton, 1993, Bk. 2, August 1 to December 31, 1993*, National Archives and Records Administration, Office of the Federal Register (Washington, DC: Government Printing Office, 1994), 2142. Benitez's statement, ten years later, was at the Robert F. Kennedy Human Rights Awards Ceremony, November 20, 2003, available at http://blogs.nysut.org.

1. Working closely with Republicans in Congress, Clinton also furthered the privatization of government services, including through the Federal Activities Inventory Reform (FAIR) Act of 1998, which required that federal agencies regularly produce lists of their services that could be handed to the private sector. Clinton-era deregulation notably included the Telecommunications Act, which essentially removed barriers to US media monopolies and resulted in huge conglomerates such as Clear Channel Communications, as well as the 1999 Financial Services Modernization Act, which "modernized" financial services by repealing key components of the 1933 Glass-Steagall Act. For more on the significance of media mergers, see Bagdikian, *New Media Monopoly*; Baker, *Media Concentration and Democracy*, 76–87. On the roles of Bush and Clinton, see MacArthur, *Selling of "Free Trade,"* 58–166; Howard J. Wiarda, "The US Domestic Politics of the US-Mexico Free Trade Agreement," in Baer and Weintraub, *NAFTA Debate*, 121, 130–131; Von Bertrab, *Negotiating NAFTA*, 30. For more on Citizens for a Sound Economy, see Mayer, *Dark Money*, 161–164.

2. Cornelius, "Death at the Border," 661, 669–670; Stuart Anderson, "How Many More Deaths? The Moral Case for a Temporary Work Program," policy brief, National Foundation for American Policy, March 2013; Estabrook, *Tomatoland*, xv, 75–100.

3. Saskia Sassen, "Global Cities and Survival Circuits," in Ehrenreich and Hochschild, *Global Woman*, 267.

4. Johann Hari, "It's Not Just Dominique Strauss-Kahn: The IMF Itself Should Be on Trial," *Independent* (London), June 3, 2011.

5. Jorn Madslien, "Debt Relief Hopes Bring Out the Critics," BBC News, June 29, 2005; Stiglitz, *Globalization and Its Discontents*, 53–88.

6. Public Citizen, "The Ten Year Track Record of the North American Free Trade Agreement: US Workers' Jobs, Wages, and Economic Security," February 2004, www.citizen.org; Giroux, "Terror of Neoliberalism," 3.

7. Public Citizen, "Ten Year Track Record: US Workers' Jobs, Wages, and Economic Security"; Public Citizen, "The Ten Year Track Record of the North American Free Trade Agreement: US, Mexican and Canadian Farmers and Agriculture," February 2004, www.citizen.org.

8. Hing, *Ethical Borders*, 9–28; Corp Watch, "Maquiladora Industry Fact Sheet," October 20, 1999, Acc. #5177–3, Box 1, Folder 77, WTO Seattle Collection, University of Washington, Seattle; Evelyn Nieves, "To Work and Die in Juarez," *Mother Jones*, May–June 2002; Molly E. Moore, "Nightmare in a City of Dreams," *Washington Post*, July 2000, www.washingtonpost.com; Livingston, "Murder in Juárez," 59–76; Public Citizen, "The Ten Year Track Record of the North American Free Trade Agreement: The Mexican Economy, Agriculture, and the Environment," February 2004, www.citizen.org.

9. Cornelius, "Death at the Border," 661, 669–670; Tim Vanderpool, "Price of Admission: Along the Border, Sexual Assault Has Become Routine," *Tucson Weekly*, June 5, 2008.

10. Public Citizen, "The Ten Year Track Record of the North American Free Trade Agreement: Undermining Sovereignty and Democracy," February 2004, www.citizen.org.

11. International Forum on Globalization, "The World Trade Organization vs. the Environment, Public Health, and Human Rights," 2003, www.ifg.org; Wallach and Sforza, *Whose Trade Organization?*

12. Hawken, *Blessed Unrest*, 117–122, 127–131; Juliette Beck and Kevin Danaher, "Top Ten Reasons to Oppose the World Trade Organization," in Danaher and Burbach, *Globalize This!*, 98–102; Valentine M. Moghadam, "Bringing the Third World In: A Comparative Analysis of Gender and Restructuring," in Moghadam, *Democratic Reform*, 337; *Life and Debt*; Sassen, "Global Cities and Survival Circuits."

13. The theorization of the power structure of global capitalism is hotly contested, notably including the work of Michael Hardt and Antonio Negri, who present a borderless, "*decentered* and *deterritorializing* apparatus of rule that progressively incorporates the entire global realm within its open, expanding frontiers." Hardt and Negri, *Empire*, xii (emphasis in original). Other scholars, including Ellen Meiksins Wood, dismiss the narrative of the declining power of states. According to Wood, "the world today is more than ever a world of nation-states. . . . The very essence of globalization is a global economy administered by a global system of multiple states and local sovereignties, structured in a complex relation of domination and subordination." Wood, *Empire of Capital*, 6, 141. Samir Amin, meanwhile, sees a new "collective imperialism" in the form of a "triad of the United States, Europe, and Japan." Amin, *World We Wish to See*, 30. For workers, the concrete realities are less open to debate; see, for example, the film *Global Assembly Line*.

14. Tom Hayden, "In Chiapas," in Hayden, *Zapatista Reader*, 76–79; Luis Hernández Navarro, "Mexico's Secret War," in Hayden, *Zapatista Reader*, 63–65; Keck and Sikkink, *Activists beyond Borders*, 8, 12–14; Gabriel García Marquéz and Cambio, "Marcos Speaks," in Hayden, *Zapatista Reader*, 182; Elizabeth "Betita" Martínez and Anoldo García, "What Is Zapatismo? A Brief Definition for Activists," in D. Solnit, *Globalize Liberation*, 213–216; and Manuel Callahan, "Zapatismo Beyond Chiapas," in D. Solnit, *Globalize Liberation*, 217–228.

15. Alex Khasnabish calls this influence between movements "resonance." Khasnabish, *Zapatismo beyond Borders*, 22–24, 123–128.

16. Starhawk, *Webs of Power*, 16–20; Ana Nogueira, "The Birth and Promise of the Indymedia Revolution," in Shepard and Hayduk, *From ACT UP to the WTO*, 290–297. For more on DAN, see Graeber, *Direct Action*. The WTO protest archives at the University of Washington also include examples of lighthearted protest, including a children's coloring contest. WTO Seattle Collection, University of Washington, Seattle.

17. Sweatshop Watch, "Student Organizing against Sweatshops," October 20, 1999, Acc. #5177-3, Box 1, Folder 74, WTO Seattle Collection, University of Washington, Seattle.

18. Featherstone, *Students against Sweatshops*, 28–31; Klein, *No Logo*, 59–61, 63–85, 345–358.

19. Oxfam America, *Like Machines in the Field*; Estabrook, *Tomatoland*; Coalition of Immokalee Workers, "Consciousness + Commitment = Change," in D. Solnit, *Globalize Liberation*, 347–360.

20. Fine, *Worker Centers*, 9–22, 104–105, 171–179, 239–243; Evans and Boyte, *Free Spaces*, 42–43, 61, 102–103, 187; Elly Leary, "Immokalee Workers Take Down Taco Bell," *Monthly Review*, October 2005; Kari Lydersen, "Farm Workers Walk for Freedom," *AlterNet*, November 17, 2003; Rob Augman, "The Coalition of Immokalee Workers and the IWW," Industrial Workers of the World, May 12, 2001, www.iww.org; David Solnit, "Taco Bell Boycott Victory—A Model of Strategic Organizing: An Interview with the Coalition of Immokalee Workers," *Left Turn*, August 1, 2005; Rob Gurwitt, "Power to the Pickers," *Mother Jones*, July 1, 2004; Coalition of Immokalee Workers, "About CIW," accessed November 5, 2009, www.ciw-online.org.

21. Johnston and Laxer, "Solidarity in the Age of Globalization," 64–67.

22. Edid, *Farm Labor Organizing*, 37–38, 58–59.

23. Leary, "Immokalee Workers Take Down Taco Bell"; D. Solnit, "Taco Bell Boycott Victory"; Katrina vanden Heuvel, "Sweet Victory: Yo Quiero Justice!," *Nation*, March 11, 2005.

24. Student/Farmworker Alliance, "March 12, 2005 Press Release: Taco Bell Concedes to Boycott Pressure, Commits to End Sweatshop Conditions in the Fields of Florida," March 12, 2005, www.sfalliance.org. For an enlightening examination of corporate structure, see Bartow Elmore's study of Coca-Cola, an incredibly destructive company that was ahead of its time in many ways. Elmore, *Citizen Coke*.

25. Lauren Sage Reinlie, "Students Join Farmworkers to Boot the Bell at UT," *UT Watch*, November 2003.

26. Courtney Morris, "Students Join 3-Day Protest of Taco Bell," *Daily Texan* (University of Texas at Austin), December 1, 2001; Elizabeth Esfahani, "Students Protest Practices of Fast Food Chain," *Daily Texan*, November 1, 2002; "Viewpoint: Yo No Quiero Taco Bell," *Daily Texan*, October 7, 2003; Reinlie, "Students Join Farmworkers to Boot the Bell at UT."

27. Sarah Michel, "Student Group Encourages Taco Bell Boycott," *Daily Texan*, October 29, 2004.

28. Ibid.; "Viewpoint: Stop—What's in Your Taco?," *Daily Texan*, November 10, 2004; Rev. Lou Snead and Rev. Tom Heger, "Churches Join Bell Boycott," *Daily Texan*, January 19, 2005.

29. Dirk Dozier, "Taco Bell's Response to Boycott," *Daily Texan*, February 1, 2005; Melissa Mixon, "Union Board to Consider Taco Bell's Fate," *Daily Texan*, January 31, 2005; Lauren Sage Reinlie, "Taco Bell Boycott Continues . . . but Is Student Demand Subsiding?," *UT Watch*, February 2005.

30. Mixon, "Union Board to Consider Taco Bell's Fate"; Patrick George, "Forum Addresses Taco Bell," *Daily Texan*, February 8, 2005; Reinlie, "Taco Bell Boycott Continue"; Adrienne Lee, "Taco Bell Faces Final Union Vote," *Daily Texan*, February 25, 2005; "Viewpoint: Rotten Tomatoes," *Daily Texan*, February 24, 2005; Laura Heinauer, "Taco Bell Isn't Facing Expulsion from UT," *Austin American-Statesman*, February 25, 2005; Melissa Mixon, "Unanimous Board Vote Keeps Taco Bell in Union," *Daily Texan*, February 28, 2005; "Put Bell on the Ballot," *Daily Texan*, March 2, 2005; Adrienne Lee, "Taco Bell Boycott Finally Over," *Daily Texan*, March 9, 2005.

31. Giagnoni, *Fields of Resistance*, 103–107.

32. The Notre Dame Student/Farmworker Alliance, "Take Charge of Your Taco," *Notre Dame Observer*, April 4, 2001; Kamaria Porter, "Boycotts Benefit Farmworkers," *Notre Dame Observer*, September 29, 2003; Maria Smith, "Partners in the Fight for Justice," *Notre Dame Observer*, March 30, 2004.

33. Smith, "Partners in the Fight for Justice."

34. Claire Heininger, "Protests Prompt Taco Bell Response," *Notre Dame Observer*, April 5, 2004; Observer Viewpoint, "Voicing Dissent," *Notre Dame Observer*, April 6, 2004; Claire Heininger, "PSA Descends on Office of the President," *Notre Dame Observer*, April 15, 2004; Kamaria Porter, "Staying on the Path," *Notre Dame Observer*, April 20, 2004.

35. Porter, "Staying on the Path."

36. Claire Heininger, "Notre Dame Issues Statement on Taco Bell," *Notre Dame Observer*, April 28, 2004.

37. Claire Heininger, "Taco Bell to Respond to ND Letter," *Notre Dame Observer*, April 19, 2004; Porter, "Staying on the Path"; Heininger, "Notre Dame Issues Statement on Taco Bell."

38. Claire Heininger, "ND Cancels Contract with Taco Bell," *Notre Dame Observer*, August 26, 2004.

39. William J. Clinton, *Public Papers of the Presidents of the United States, William J. Clinton, 1993, Bk. 2, August 1 to December 31, 1993,* National Archives and Records Administration, Office of the Federal Register (Washington, DC: Government Printing Office, 1994), 2142.

CHAPTER 4. INVASION AND OCCUPATION

Epigraphs: Matt Kelley, "Rumsfeld Says US Ready for Iraqi Terrorist Attacks: Defense Secretary Says If Military Force Used, Conflict Will Be Brief," *Alameda (CA) Times-Star*, November 15, 2002; Leon Harris, "CNN Live Event/Special: Bush Speaks in Milwaukee," CNN, October 3, 2003, www.cnn.com.

1. Donnelly, Kagan, and Schmitt, *Rebuilding America's Defenses*, 51.

2. Project for the New American Century, "Letter to President Clinton on Iraq," January 26, 1998, www.newamericancentury.org.

3. Contrary to US general Tommy Franks's remark in 2002 that "we don't do body counts," the US military's classified records, released by WikiLeaks in 2010, acknowledge 66,081 civilian deaths directly caused by military action in Iraq from 2004 to 2009. Other estimates vary widely, based on methodology, time frame, whether they seek to calculate deaths directly or indirectly caused by the war, and whether they seek numbers for civilians or all Iraqis. Associated Press, Iraq Body Count, and World Health Organization estimates range from approximately 104,000 to 151,000. A study published in the *Lancet* puts the figure at 654,965 through June 2006, while a poll by the Opinion Research Business estimated violent deaths at anywhere from 946,000 to 1,120,000. John M. Broder, "US Won't Be Tallying Iraqi Army Death Toll," *New York Times*, April 3, 2003, www.nytimes. com; Joshua Holland, "Iraq Death Toll Rivals Rwanda Genocide, Cambodia Killing Fields," *AlterNet*, September 17, 2007, www.alternet.org; Sarah Boseley, "151,000 Civilians Killed since Iraq Invasion," *Guardian* (Manchester), January 9, 2008, www.theguardian.com; David Leigh, "Iraq War Logs Reveal 15,000 Previously Unlisted Civilian Deaths," *Guardian* (Manchester), October 22, 2010; Iraq Body Count, www.iraqbodycount.org; David Brown and Joshua Partlow, "New Estimate of Violent Deaths among Iraqis Is Lower," *Washington Post*, January 10, 2008, www.washingtonpost.com. See also Bennis, *Ending the War in Iraq*, 11–15; Nicholas D. Kristof, "A Veteran's Death, the Nation's Shame," *New York Times*, April 14, 2012, www.nytimes.com; Tanielian and Jaycox, *Invisible Wounds of War*, xxi.

4. Ernesto Londoño, "Study: Iraq, Afghan War Costs to Top $4 trillion," *Washington Post*, March 28, 2013, www.washingtonpost.com.

5. Wilson and Beach, *Economic Impact of President Bush's Tax Relief Plan*.

6. Piven, *Challenging Authority*, 8; Piven, *War at Home*, 41, 71; Wall Street Journal Staff, "Bush on Jobs: The Worst Track Record on Record," *Real Time Economics* (blog), *Wall Street Journal*, January 9, 2009, www.wsj.com; US Department of Treasury, "Historical Debt Outstanding—Annual 2000–2010," accessed June 27, 2012, www.treasurydirect.gov.

7. David E. Sanger, "President Asserts Shrunken Surplus May Curb Congress," *New York Times*, August 25, 2001, www.nytimes.com.

8. See, for example, Bruce Bartlett, "Tax Cuts and 'Starving the Beast': The Most Pernicious Fiscal Doctrine in History," *Forbes*, May 7, 2010, www.forbes.com.

9. Dan Morgan, "House Approves Energy Measure," *Washington Post*, November 19, 2003, www.washingtonpost.com.

10. Meier and Wood, *Many Children Left Behind*; Ravitch, *Life and Death of the Great American School System*; Public Citizen, "The Best Energy Bill Corporations Could Buy: Public Citizen's Analysis of the Domenici-Barton Energy Policy Act," 2005, www.citizen.org; Kennedy, *Crimes against Nature*, 96–99, 144; Kate Sheppard, "Fracking Halliburton," *Mother Jones*, November 10, 2010. See also *Gasland*.

11. Marcy Gordon, "Bush Team May Have Feared Enron Aid," Associated Press, January 14, 2002; Schwartz, "Democracy against the Free Market," 1098, 1100–1101.

12. Schwartz, "Democracy against the Free Market," 1098, 1100–1101; "Largest US Bankruptcies," *Toronto Star*, June 2, 2009. See also *Enron: The Smartest Guys in the Room*.

13. Kennedy, *Crimes against Nature*, 40.

14. Additional Bush appointees with ties to the energy industry included assistant secretary of land and minerals management Rebecca W. Watson, assistant secretary of water and science Bennett Raley, and Jeffrey D. Jarrett, director of the Office of Surface Mining Reclamation and Enforcement. President Bush himself had been the head of an oil-exploration company, while Vice President Cheney was the former CEO of Halliburton and eventual secretary of state Condoleezza Rice was the former head of Chevron's Committee on Public Policy. Kennedy, *Crimes against Nature*, 32–39, 129–142; Susan Schmidt and James V. Grimaldi, "Ex-Official at Interior Hid His Ties to Abramoff," *Washington Post*, March 24, 2007, www.washingtonpost.com; Matt Apuzzo, "Former Interior Official Gets Prison," *Washington Post*, June 26, 2007, www.washingtonpost.com; Goodman, *Exception to the Rulers*; Klein, *Shock Doctrine*, 370–385.

15. Charles Babington and Dafna Linzer, "Bolton Assures Senators of Commitment to UN," *Washington Post*, April 12, 2005, www.washingtonpost.com.

16. "Full Text: George Bush's Speech to the American Enterprise Institute," *Guardian* (Manchester), February 27, 2003; Finlay, *George W. Bush and the War on Women*, 24–27.

17. West, "Institutionalization of Regulatory Review," 32–34.

18. Howell and Keefe, *History of Federal Abstinence-Only Funding*; Laura Sessions Step, "Study Casts Doubt on Abstinence-Only Programs," *Washington Post*, April 14, 2007.

19. Richard Benedetto, "Faith-Based Programs Flourishing, Bush Says," *USA Today*, March 9, 2006, www.usatoday.com; Mike Allen and Alan Cooperman, "Bush

Backs Amendment Banning Gay Marriage," *Washington Post*, February 25, 2004, www.washingtonpost.com.

20. Bob Woodward, "CIA Told to Do 'Whatever Necessary' to Kill Bin Laden: Agency and Military Collaborating at 'Unprecedented' Level; Cheney Says War against Terror 'May Never End,'" *Washington Post*, October 21, 2001, www.washington-post.com.

21. John Diamond, "US Assertions Go Beyond Its Intelligence," *USA Today*, September 17, 2002, www.usatoday.com; Holsti, *American Public Opinion on the Iraq War*, 31, 43, 44.

22. Gordon, *Invisible War*.

23. Johnson, *Nemesis*, 5–6, 139; Blum, *Killing Hope*, 242–244, 320–338.

24. "Eyes on Iraq; In Cheney's Words: The Administration Case for Removing Saddam Hussein," *New York Times*, August 27, 2002, www.nytimes.com.

25. "Threats and Responses; Bush's Speech on Iraq: 'Saddam Hussein and His Sons Must Leave,'" *New York Times*, March 18, 2003, www.nytimes.com.

26. C. J. Chivers, "The Secret Casualties of Iraq's Abandoned Chemical Weapons," *New York Times*, October 14, 2014, www.nytimes.com.

27. Ron Hutcheson, "Cheney: 'Clear' Proof of Threat; He Said Evidence of Increased Iraq Weapons Activity Obtained within the Last 14 Months Convinced Him of the Need to Act," *Philadelphia Inquirer*, September 9, 2002.

28. Joyce Howard Price, "US Reprisal on Iraq to Be 'Annihilation'; Saddam Warned Not to Strike," *Washington Times*, September 9, 2002, www.washingtonpost.com.

29. Holsti, *American Public Opinion on the Iraq War*, 45; Matt Kelley, "Rumsfeld Says US Ready for Iraqi Terrorist Attacks: Defense Secretary Says If Military Force Used, Conflict Will Be Brief," *Alameda (CA) Times-Star*, November 15, 2002; "Rumsfeld Briefs Press," CNN, January 19, 2003, www.cnn.com.

30. Office of the Assistant Secretary of Defense, "DoD Announces Top Contractors for Fiscal Year 2003," www.defense.gov; Tim Weiner, "Lockheed and the Future of Warfare," *New York Times*, November 28, 2004; Tim Weiner, "Boeing Hires a Legal Team to Handle Scandal Cases," *New York Times*, February 4, 2005; Renae Merle, "Northrop Agrees to Settle Charges of Inflating Prices: Government Contractor to Pay $62 Million," *Washington Post*, March 2, 2005; see also Hartung, *Prophets of War*.

31. Jason Linkins, "Meet the Senators Who Voted against the Franken Amendment," *Huffington Post*, March 18, 2010, www.huffingtonpost.com.

32. Chatterjee, *Iraq, Inc.*, 23, 39; Jim Miklaszewski, "Pentagon Audit Reveals Halliburton Overcharges," NBC News, March 15, 2005, www.nbcnews.com; James Risen, "Soldier's Electrocution in Iraq Was Negligent Homicide, Army Concludes," *New York Times*, January 23, 2009, www.nytimes.com; Chris McGreal, "Rape Case to Force US Defence Firms into the Open," *Guardian* (Manchester), October 16, 2009, www.theguardian.com; Linkins, "Meet the Senators Who Voted against the Franken Amendment."

33. Nicholas Kralev, "Security Firm Banned by Iraq after Deaths: Tough Call for Embassy," *Washington Times*, September 18, 2007; Sudarsan Raghavan and Steve Fainaru, "US Repeatedly Rebuffed Iraq on Blackwater Complaints," *Washington Post*, September 23, 2007, www.washingtonpost.com; Karen DeYoung, "Other Killings by Blackwater Staff Detailed: State Dept. Papers Tell of Coverup," *Washington Post*, October 2, 2007, www.washingtonpost.com; James Glanz and Andrew W. Lehren, "Use of Contractors Added to War's Chaos in Iraq," *New York Times*, October 23, 2010, www.nytimes.com; Michael Hirsh, "The Age of Irresponsibility: How Bush Has Created a Moral Vacuum in Iraq in Which Americans Can Kill for Free," *Newsweek*, September 20, 2007; Scahill, *Blackwater*, 9–13; Nathan Hodge, "Company Once Known as Blackwater Ditches Xe for Yet Another Name," *Wall Street Journal*, December 12, 2011, www.wsj.com.

34. Seymour Hersh, "Torture at Abu Ghraib," *New Yorker*, May 10, 2004, www. newyorker.com; Kate Zernike, "Detainees Describe Abuses by Guard in Iraq Prison," *New York Times*, January 12, 2005, www.nytimes.com; Duncan Gardham and Paul Cruickshank, "Abu Ghraib Abuse Photos 'Show Rape,'" *Telegraph* (London), May 27, 2009; Renae Merle, "Titan Admits Bribery in Africa: Contractor Will Pay $28.5 Million to Settle Criminal, SEC Cases," *Washington Post*, March 2, 2005, www.washingtonpost.com; Griff Witte, "L-3 to Pay $2 Billion Cash for Titan," *Washington Post*, June 4, 2005; Ellen McCarthy, "CACI Plans to Drop Interrogation Work: Firm Was Entangled in Abu Ghraib," *Washington Post*, September 15, 2005, www.washingtonpost.com; Reuters, "Torture Case against Iraq Contractors Is Dismissed," *New York Times*, September 12, 2009. See also *Ghosts of Abu Ghraib*; *Iraq for Sale*.

35. T. Christian Miller, "Contractors Outnumber Troops in Iraq," *Los Angeles Times*, July 4, 2007, www.latimes.com.

36. Patrick E. Tyler, "After the War: Rebuilding; US Says Bank Credits will Finance Sale of Goods to Iraq," *New York Times*, May 27, 2003, www.nytimes.com.

37. Naomi Klein, "Bring Halliburton Home," *Nation*, November 24, 2003, www. thenation.com.

38. Rod Nordland, "Puppets or Players?," *Newsweek*, June 7, 2004.

39. Bremer, "Coalition Provisional Authority Order Number 12."

40. Juhasz, *Bush Agenda*, 200–226; Klein, "Bring Halliburton Home"; Fiona Fleck, "Iraq Is Granted Observer Status at the WTO," *New York Times*, February 12, 2004, www.nytimes.com.

41. "A Nation Challenged: President Bush's Address on Terrorism before a Joint Meeting of Congress," *New York Times*, September 21, 2001, www.nytimes.com.

42. Jeffrey Tobin, "Crackdown: Should We Be Worried about the New Antiterrorism Legislation?," *New Yorker*, November 5, 2001, www.newyorker.com.

43. Cole and Dempsey, *Terrorism and the Constitution*; Cole, *Enemy Aliens*, 25–26; Jarice Hanson, "Selling the Bush Doctrine: Persuasion, Propaganda, Public Relations, and the Patriot Act," in Conron and Hanson, *Constructing America's War Culture*, 51–55.

44. John Schwartz, "US to Drop Color-Coded Terror Alerts," *New York Times*, November 24, 2010, www.nytimes.com; Brian Bennett, "Homeland Security Scrapping Color-Coded Alert System," *Los Angeles Times*, April 21, 2011, www.latimes.com.

45. "What Is Operation TIPS?," *Washington Post*, July 14, 2002, www.washingtonpost.com.

46. Amy Goodman, "Peace Group Infiltrated by Government Agent," *Democracy Now!*, October 9, 2003, www.democracynow.org; Richard Gonzales, "Oakland Police Spy on Anti-war Group," National Public Radio, August 8, 2006, www.npr.org; Nick Madigan, "Spying Uncovered: Documents Show State Police Monitored Peace and Anti–Death Penalty Groups," *Baltimore Sun*, July 18, 2008, www.baltimoresun.com; Matthew Rothschild, "FBI Infiltrates Iowa City Protest Group," *Progressive*, May 26, 2009, www.progressive.org; Gene Johnson, "Wash. Peace Group Sues over Infiltration," *Seattle Times*, January 13, 2010, www.seattletimes.com; Amy Goodman, "Government Spy Infiltrated Antiwar Groups before FBI Raids," *Democracy Now!*, January 13, 2011; "What Is Operation TIPS?"; Ellen Sorokin, "Planned Volunteer-Informant Corps Elicits '1984' Fears: Accessing Private Homes Is Objective of 'Operation TIPS,'" *Washington Times*, July 16, 2002; Nat Hentoff, "The Death of Operation TIPS," *Village Voice*, December 17, 2002, www.villagevoice.com.

47. Thomas Fitzgerald, "Ridge to Lead Newly Created Office of Homeland Security," *Philadelphia Inquirer*, September 21, 2001; US Department of Homeland Security, "2004 Budget in Brief"; Dana Priest and William M. Arkin, "Monitoring America," *Washington Post*, December 20, 2010; Radley Balko, "A Decade after 9/11, Police Departments Are Increasingly Militarized," *Huffington Post*, September 12, 2011, www.huffingtonpost.com; Arthur Rizer and Joseph Hartman, "How the War on Terror Has Militarized Police," *Atlantic*, November 7, 2011; Rania Khalek, "Why Do the Police Have Tanks? The Strange and Dangerous Militarization of the US Police Force," *AlterNet*, July 5, 2011, www.alternet.org.

48. Lisa Davis, "Not Your Mother's Peace Movement; Major Anti-war Groups Change Strategy, Hoping to Win Over Mainstream Voters the Bush Administration Can't Ignore," *SF Weekly*, November 6, 2002, www.sfweekly.com; Amy Westfeldt, "Anti-war Protesters Announce Feb. 15 Rally for 'Millions,'" Associated Press, January 29, 2003; Stephanie Ho, "Anti-war Protests," *Voice of America News*, December 10, 2002; Allen G. Breed, "Diverse Groups Protest Possible Iraq War," Associated Press, December 11, 2002; Evelyn Nieves, "Antiwar Sentiment Galvanizes Thousands: Groups See Numbers Rise as They Reach Out to Supporters via Internet, E-Mail," *Washington Post*, January 19, 2003, www.washingtonpost.com; Manny Fernandez and Justin Blum, "Thousands Oppose a Rush to War: Chill Doesn't Cool Fury over US Stand on Iraq," *Washington Post*, January 19, 2003, www.washingtonpost.com.

49. "Millions Protest around the World against War on Iraq," *Channel NewsAsia*, February 15, 2003; "Around Globe, Millions Protest War," *St. Petersburg Times*,

February 16, 2003; "Thousands Rally against Iraq War in Thailand," Agence France-Presse (English), February 1, 2003; Giles Hewitt, "Huge Anti-war Protest near UN Headquarters in New York," Agence France-Presse (English), February 16, 2003; "Cities around World Cry for Peace: Demonstrations Mostly Peaceful; Millions Turn Out," *Chattanooga Times Free Press*, February 16, 2003; Julia Duin, "Protests for Peace: Anti-war Movement Built on Broader Base," *Washington Times*, February 16, 2003; David Paul Kuhn, "New Yorkers to Take Lead in Nationwide Antiwar Rallies," *Daily Yomiuri* (Tokyo), February 15, 2003.

50. "80 Arrested in San Francisco Anti-war Protest," Agence France-Presse (English), March 15, 2003; Manny Fernandez, "Demonstrators Use More Active Tactics," *Washington Post*, March 18, 2003.

51. Sean D. Hamill and David Heinzmann, "Chicago Anti-war Demonstration Shuts Down City," *Chicago Tribune*, March 21, 2003, www.chicagotribune.com; Chronicle Staff, "Protest Creates Gridlock on SF Streets," *San Francisco Chronicle*, March 20, 2003; Tara Burghart, "Protesters Arrested, Officers Injured in Antiwar March," Associated Press, March 23, 2003; Fawn Vrazo, "Anti-war Protests Smaller, Angrier: Demonstrators Target McDonald's in France; US, British Embassies Draw Violent Crowds," *Akron Beacon Journal*, March 23, 2003.

52. George Packer, "Smart-Mobbing the War," *New York Times*, March 9, 2003, www.nytimes.com; Josh Richman, "Antiwar Movement Unites Varied Groups of Activists," *Alameda (CA) Times-Star*, March 22, 2003; "More than 100 Anti-War Protests in 35 States Will Mark International Human Rights Day Dec. 10," US Newswire, December 9, 2002; Nieves, "Antiwar Sentiment Galvanizes Thousands"; Patrick Anidjar, "Coalition of the Unwilling Rallies in US against War," Agence France-Presse (English), February 13, 2003; "United for What?," *New York Sun*, February 13, 2003; Bill Fletcher Jr., interview by author, November 4, 2012.

53. Davis, "Not Your Mother's Peace Movement"; Nieves, "Antiwar Sentiment Galvanizes Thousands"; Evelyn Nieves, "Peace Movement Reawakened," *Hackensack (NJ) Record*, December 8, 2002; "More than 100 Anti-war Protests"; Mary Brown Malouf, "Utahns on the March: SLC Demonstration Brings Out Thousands against Iraq Attack; Peace March Attracts 3,000 in S.L. City," *Salt Lake Tribune*, January 19, 2003; Kristen Klein, "Notre Dame Students Plan Iraq-War Protest in New York City," *Notre Dame Observer*, February 14, 2003.

54. Ron Hutcheson, Diego Ibarguen, and Martin Merzer, "Bush: War Protests Won't Affect Policy," *Philadelphia Inquirer*, February 19, 2003.

55. Kate Donnolly, Barbie Dutter, Marcus Warren, David Blair, Bruce Johnston, and Philip Smucker, "Wave of Protest Ripples around the World," *Daily Telegraph* (London), February 17, 2003.

56. Julia Hartley-Brewer and Tim Shipman, "Opponents of Conflict with Iraq 'Will Have Blood on Their Hands': Blair's Attack on Peace Marchers," *Sunday Express* (London), February 16, 2003; Sandra Laville and Barbie Dutter, "Protest Has Rattled Number 10, Say March Organisers," *Telegraph* (London), February 17, 2003.

57. Bill Lambrecht, "Standing Firm: Presidents Often Discount Protests, but Historians Say They Have Affected Policy," *St. Louis Post-Dispatch*, February 23, 2003.

58. Duncan Campbell, "One Year On: Relatives Protest at War Plans," *Guardian* (Manchester), September 12, 2002; Fernandez and Blum, "Thousands Oppose a Rush to War."

59. Tara Burghart, "Thousands Protest War in March down Broadway," Associated Press, March 22, 2003.

60. Pat Buchanan, "Buchanan & Press for April 24, 2003," *Buchanan & Press*, MSNBC, April 24, 2003.

61. Coulter, *Godless*, 103.

62. Darren Epps, "Fifty Protest Dixie Chicks Performance in Knoxville," *Chattanooga Times Free Press*, May 9, 2003; "Chicks Protesters Were Too Few for Such Attention," *St. Petersburg Times*, May 8, 2003; Jennifer Barrs, "Tampa Fans Welcome Dixie Chicks Warmly," *Tampa Tribune*, May 6, 2003; Charles Passy, "Controversy? What Controversy? Dixie Chicks Wow 'Em in Sunrise," *Palm Beach Post*, May 5, 2003.

63. Alisa Solomon, "The Big Chill: Is This the New McCarthyism?," *Nation*, June 2, 2003, www.thenation.com.

64. "Down to the Wire with Iraq," *New York Daily News*, February 15, 2003.

65. Frank Testa, "Basis of War Protest," *Lancaster (PA) New Era*, March 13, 2003.

66. Byron York, "Reds, Still: The Story No One Wants to Hear about the Antiwar Movement," *National Review*, February 2003; Anidjar, "Coalition of the Unwilling Rallies in US against War."

67. Bob Edwards, "Anti-war Protests Held across the Country Yesterday," *Morning Edition*, National Public Radio, March 21, 2003, www.npr.org; Tara Burghart, "Peace Marchers Rally across United States," AP Online, March 22, 2003; Malouf, "Utahns on the March."

68. Leslie Eaton, "A Nation at War: Rallies; On New York's Streets and across the Nation, Protesters Speak Out," *New York Times*, March 23, 2003, www.nytimes.com; Simon Houpt, "Florida Station Axes Canadian News: Radio Program Aired for Snowbirds among the Early Casualties of War," *Globe and Mail* (Toronto), March 20, 2003.

69. Nearly two thousand people were detained in mass arrests at the 2004 Republican National Convention in New York City. During Bush's reelection campaign, he also made numerous appearances at which audiences were hand-screened and required to pledge oaths of loyalty, while opponents were kept in distant "free-speech zones." Similar policies were implemented at the Democratic National Convention, as well. Lawrence Messina, "Bush, Kerry Camps Pledge No 'Loyalty Oaths' for Future Visits," Associated Press, August 6, 2004; "Tyranny in the Name of Freedom: 'Free Speech Zones' and the Abuse of Executive Power," *Pittsburgh Post-Gazette*, August 13, 2004; "Convention Protesters Describe Stays in Grimy Conditions," *USA Today*, September 2, 2004, www.usatoday.com.

70. Anne E. Kornblut, "Mother's Grief-Fueled Vigil Becomes Nexus for Antiwar Protesters," *New York Times*, August 13, 2005, www.nytimes.com; Ryan Parry, "As Long as the President Who Sent My Son to Die in His Senseless War Is Here, Then This Is Where I Belong: Mum's Vigil at Bush Ranch," *Mirror* (London), August 30, 2005; Mike Allen, "They Are Stardust, and in Texas: At the Crawford Protest Camp, Growing Echoes of Woodstock," *Washington Post*, August 22, 2005, www.washingtonpost.com; Kenneth R. Bazinet, "Rev. Al Will Join Peace Mom," *New York Daily News*, August 26, 2005; Tim Harper, "Americans Rallying behind 'Peace Mom,'" *Toronto Star*, August 18, 2005. See also Smith et al., *Vigil*; David Barsamian, "Cindy Sheehan Interview," *Progressive*, March 2006, www.progressive.org.

71. Sean Hannity and Alan Colmes, "Antiwar Mom Sparks Debate with Vigil," *Hannity & Colmes*, Fox News, August 15, 2005; Michael A. Fletcher, "In Texas, a Time to Circle the Minivans: Activists Protest the War, or Protest the Protesters," *Washington Post*, August 14, 2005, www.washingtonpost.com; Rupert Cornwell, "America and the War in Iraq: The Grieving Mother Who Took on George Bush; Cindy Sheehan's Soldier Son Casey Was Killed near Baghdad," *Independent* (London), August 16, 2005; Elisabeth Bumiller, "Antiwar Vigil in US Moves Closer to Bush; Truck Mows Down Crosses for War Dead," *International Herald Tribune*, August 18, 2005; Andrew Gumbel, "The War in Iraq: Across the Tracks at Crawford, Texas, A Divided Nation Bares Its Pain and Fury," *Independent* (London), August 29, 2005; Sam Coates, "Near the President's Ranch, Protests Expand in the Heat," *Washington Post*, August 28, 2005; Abby Goodnough, "In War Debate, Parents of Fallen Are United Only in Grief," *New York Times*, August 28, 2005, www.nytimes.com; Tom Baldwin, "I'm Not Budging, Says Soldier's Mother Camped at Bush's Door," *Times* (London), August 12, 2005.

72. Kenneth R. Bazinet, "Prez: 'We Will Stay'; Meets Pro-war Military Families, *New York Daily News*, August 25, 2005; Carlos Guerra, "Camp Casey Gets Read for Its Big Road Trip to Nation's Capital," *San Antonio Express-News*, September 1, 2005; Stephanie Mansfield, "'Mrs. Sheehan Goes to Washington'—A New Road Picture?," *Washington Times*, September 22, 2005.

73. Bill O'Reilly, "'Personal Story': O'Reilly Discusses Iraq," *O'Reilly Factor*, Fox News, September 9, 2004; Tavis Smiley, "Former Marine Mike Hoffman Talks about His Changing Views on the War in Iraq," *Tavis Smiley*, National Public Radio, December 7, 2004. See also *Ground Truth*; *Body of War*.

74. Karen Matthews, "Iraq War Veterans Opposed to War Stage Theater Protests in New York," Associated Press, May 27, 2007; David Montgomery, "In Clash with Marines, Reservists Gain Ally in VFW," *Washington Post*, June 2, 2007, www.washingtonpost.com; Robert McCoppin, "Iraq Veterans Protest War but Change Few Minds," *Chicago Daily Herald*, June 19, 2007; Aisha Sultan, "Anti-war Veterans Protest at Black Expo," *St. Louis Post-Dispatch*, August 19, 2007; Andrew H. Gross, "Iraq War Protests Hit Capitol Hill," *GW Hatchet* (George Washington University), University Wire, September 17, 2007; Mike Ferner, "Can We Talk?

Day One of the IVAW's 'Truth in Recruiting' Campaign," *CounterPunch*, September 19, 2007, www.counterpunch.org.

75. Iraq Veterans against the War and Glantz, *Winter Soldier Iraq and Afghanistan*, 77.

76. Ibid., 8–11, 17, 24, 48–49, 78–79, 98–100; Ronald R. Krebs, "Where Are This War's Winter Soldiers?," *Slate*, March 7, 2008.

77. Aaron Leclair, "Iraq Veterans Protest in Denver," Associated Press, August 27, 2008.

78. Aaron Glantz, "Politics-US: More Subpoenas Come Down in Watada Case," Inter Press Service, January 8, 2007.

79. Jonathan Finer, "Iraq War Opponents Stage Protest near Fort Bragg: N.C. Demonstration Is Largest of 800 Held across the US to Mark 2nd Anniversary of Conflict," *Washington Post*, March 20, 2005, www.washingtonpost.com; McCoppin, "Iraq Veterans Protest War but Change Few Minds"; Tom Paulson, "Thousands in Seattle March against Iraq War," *Seattle Post-Intelligencer*, October 27, 2007; "Anti-war Veterans March in Denver's Parade," Associated Press, November 11, 2007; Sam Skolnik and Carol Smith, "Not Going, and Not Going Quietly: Soldier against Iraq War Won't Seek Objector Status," *Seattle Post-Intelligencer*, June 8, 2006; Dean Paton, "Backstory: Dissent of an Officer," *Christian Science Monitor*, February 2, 2007, www.csmonitor.com.

80. Nancy Trejos, "Antiwar Activists Plan to Stay the Course: Women Settling In for Four-Month Vigil," *Washington Post*, November 18, 2002, www.washingtonpost.com; Sylvia Moreno and Lena H. Sun, "In Effort to Keep the Peace, Protesters Declare 'Code Pink,'" *Washington Post*, March 9, 2003, www.washingtonpost.com; "Threats and Response: The Opposition; With Passion and a Dash of Pink, Women Gather to Protest," *New York Times*, March 9, 2003, www.nytimes.com; Kim Ode, "Code Pink for Peace; Women Uniting in Hope They Can Prevent War under Banner of Care for Children," *Minneapolis Star Tribune*, January 11, 2003; Bob Dart, "Code Pink: A Sisterhood Bound by Protests of Iraq War," Cox News Service, March 28, 2007. See also Benjamin and Evans, *Stop the Next War Now*.

81. Cintra Wilson, "Cracking Code Pink," *Salon*, July 17, 2008, www.salon.com; "Peace Delegation Heads for Middle East," *InsideBayArea.com*, December 28, 2004; Amy Doolittle, "Code Pink Fights Sales of GI Joe: Group Pushes Anti-war Toys," *Washington Times*, December 13, 2005.

82. Marc Santora, "With Spare Passes in Hand, Hecklers Found It Surprisingly Easy to Crash the Party," *New York Times*, September 3, 2004, www.nytimes.com; Zachary Coile, "Opposition: Loud, Peaceful Protest Interrupts Bush Speech; Code Pink Activists Access VIP Section—and Get Expelled," *San Francisco Chronicle*, January 21, 2005; Jitendra Joshi, "Fur Flies as Petraeus and Pink Protesters Enliven Congress," Agence France-Presse (English), September 10, 2007; Andrea Billups and Jim McElhatton, "Rice Sees Red and Pink: War Protester Rushes Official before Hearing on Capitol Hill," *Washington Times*, October 25, 2007; S. A. Miller, "Code Pink to Take Aim at Democrats in 2008," *Washington Times*, December 12,

2007; Michele Norris, "FCC Lifts 'Cross-Ownership' Ban Despite Protests," *All Things Considered*, National Public Radio, December 18, 2007, www.npr.org.

83. Omar Melhem, "Anti-war Activists Picket Fox News," United Press International, April 3, 2003; Bill O'Reilly, "Impact," *O'Reilly Factor*, Fox News, April 2, 2009, www.foxnews.com; Julia Duin, "Hillary Given 'Pink Slip' for Stance on Iraq War: Lacy Lingerie a Sign of Feminists' Disdain," *Washington Times*, March 7, 2003; "Pretty Rowdy in Pink: How Some Ladies from S.F. Will Harass Hillary Clinton into Being the Tipping Point against the Iraq War," *SF Weekly*, December 21, 2005; Sean Hannity and Alan Colmes, "Interview with Rae Abileah," *Hannity & Colmes*, Fox News, January 30, 2007; Jesse McKinley, "Home in San Francisco, Pelosi Gets the Crawford Treatment," *New York Times*, March 13, 2007; Sam Youngman, "Code Pink Dogs Clinton on 2008 Trail," *Hill*, March 28, 2007; Nikki Schwab, "Antiwar Liberals Heckle House Speaker Pelosi," CBS News, June 21, 2007, www.cbsnews.com; Lona O'Connor, "Granny the Activist," *Palm Beach Post*, July 4, 2007; James Wensits, "Protesters Target Sen. Bayh: Democrats Seek a Hearing on Troop Withdrawal Planning," *South Bend Tribune*, July 24, 2007.

84. Carolyn Jones, "Code Pink Finds Marine Recruiters in Berkeley—War Protests Begin," *San Francisco Chronicle*, October 4, 2007; Jesse McKinley, "Berkeley Finds a New Way to Make War Politics Local," *New York Times*, February 1, 2008, www.nytimes.com; "Hundreds of Anti-war and Pro-military Supporters in Confrontation outside Berkeley City Hall," *San Jose Mercury News*, February 12, 2008; Carolyn Jones, Christopher Heredia, and Steven Rubenstein, "War of Words; Anti-war, Pro-military Factions Face Off over Berkeley Council's Letter Calling Marines 'Intruders,'" *San Francisco Chronicle*, February 13, 2008; Doug Oakley, "Lawmakers Aim to Punish Berkeley over Anti-Marines Stance," *San Jose Mercury News*, February 7, 2008; Taylor Fife and Jane Shin, "Marines Vote Leads to Threat on City Funds," *Daily Californian* (University of California, Berkeley), February 4, 2008.

85. Kristin Bender, "Berkeley Council Votes to Clarify Language on Marines," *InsideBayArea.com*, February 14, 2008; Berkeley City Council, Regular Meeting Minutes, January 29, 2008, www.cityofberkeley.info; Berkeley City Council, Meeting Minutes, February 12, 2008, www.cityofberkeley.info.

86. "McCain Defends '100 Years in Iraq' Statement," *Larry King Live*, CNN, February 14, 2008, www.cnn.com.

87. "Obama Signs Extension of Patriot Act," *USA Today*, February 27, 2010; Erik Kain, "President Obama Signed the National Defense Authorization Act—Now What?," *Forbes*, January 2, 2012, www.forbes.com; Ryan Gallagher, "Are Guidelines Issued by Drone Industry an Attempt to Avoid Government Regulation?," *Slate*, July 3, 2012, www.slate.com.

88. Holsti, *American Public Opinion on the Iraq War*, 39, 60.

89. Piven, *Challenging Authority*, 9; Holsti, *American Public Opinion on the Iraq War*, 135, 143; Jim Drinkard, "Report: PR Spending Doubled under Bush," *USA Today*, January 26, 2005, www.usatoday.com; *Tillman Story*.

90. For example, see "Spain Withdraws Iraq Troops in 15 Days," United Press International, April 18, 2004; "Italy to Withdraw Troops from Iraq at the Latest Early 2006," Agence France-Presse (English), May 10, 2005; "Coalition in Iraq Continues to Dwindle," *USA Today*, May 30, 2006.

91. "Army Recruiters Step Up Tactics to Meet Quotas," *NewsHour*, PBS, May 12, 2005; "Military Granting More Criminal Waivers," CBS News, February 11, 2009, www.cbsnews.com; Tamara Keith, "A Weak Economy Is Good for Military Recruiting," *All Things Considered*, National Public Radio, July 29, 2011, www.npr.org.

92. Holsti, *American Public Opinion on the Iraq War*, 145–147; Joe Conason, "Republicans' Dishonorable Charge," *Salon*, August 7, 2004, www.salon.com.

93. R. Solnit, *Hope in the Dark*, 59.

94. Ibid., 17.

CHAPTER 5. EVICTION AND OCCUPATION

Epigraphs: Naomi Klein, "Occupy Wall Street: The Most Important Thing in the World Now," *Nation*, October 6, 2011; Chris Moody, "How Republicans Are Being Taught to Talk about Occupy Wall Street," Yahoo! News, December 1, 2011, www.news.yahoo.com.

1. Cowie and Salvatore, "Long Exception," 20.

2. Stiglitz, *Price of Inequality*, 8.

3. David Coldman, "Worst Year for Jobs since '45," CNN Money, January 9, 2009, www.cnn.com; Dennis Cauchon and Barbara Hansen, "Typical US Family Got Poorer during the Last 10 Years," *USA Today*, September 14, 2011, www.usatoday.com; Kevin Fagan, Justin Berton, and Marisa Lagos, "20 Arrested in the Castro," *San Francisco Chronicle*, October 11, 2012; National Law Center on Homelessness & Poverty, *2007 Annual Report*, 2007, www.nlchp.org; Rakesh Kochhar, Richard Fry, and Paul Taylor, "Wealth Gaps Rise to Record Highs between Whites, Blacks, and Hispanics: Executive Summary," Pew Research Center: Social and Demographic Trends, July 26, 2011, www.pewsocialtrends.org.

4. Bob Ivry, Bradley Heoun, and Phil Kuntz, "Secret Federal Loans Gave Banks $13 Billion Undisclosed to Congress," *Bloomberg Markets*, November 27, 2011, www.bloomberg.com; US Department of the Treasury, "The Financial Crisis Response in Charts," April 2012, www.treasury.gov.

5. David Cay Johnston, introduction to Johnston, *Divided*, xii; Steve Inskeep, "Americans Underestimate US Wealth Inequality," *Morning Edition*, National Public Radio, October 7, 2010, www.npr.org; Jann Swanson, "Rental Vacancies at Lowest Point in a Decade, Homeownership Increases," *Mortgage News Daily*, www.mortgagenewsdaily.com.

6. Klein, *Shock Doctrine*.

7. See Street and DiMaggio, *Crashing the Tea Party*; Daley, *Ratf**ked*.

8. Andy Kroll, "The Republicans' Dark-Money-Moving Machine," *Mother Jones*, January–February 2012; Linette Lopez, "A Quick Rundown of How Much Some of Wall Street's Most Famous Billionaires Have Given to Super PACs This Year,"

Business Insider, July 24, 2012, www.businessinsider.com; Bernie Sanders, "America for Sale: A Report on Billionaires Buying the 2012 Election," July 2012, www.sanders.senate.gov; Matea Gold, "An Expanding Koch Network Aims to Spend $300 Million to Shape Senate Fight and 2016," *Washington Post*, June 18, 2014, www.washingtonpost.com; Matea Gold, "Koch-Backed Network Aims to Spend Nearly $1 Billion in Run-Up to 2016," *Washington Post*, January 26, 2015, www.washingtonpost.com.

9. James Hansen, "Game Over for the Climate," *New York Times*, May 9, 2012, www.nytimes.com.

10. Elena Schor, "Protest Makes Canada-to-US Pipeline Project Newest Front in Climate Clash," *New York Times*, August 19, 2011, www.nytimes.com; John M. Broder and Dan Frosch, "US Delays Decision on Pipeline until After Election," *New York Times*, November 10, 2011, www.nytimes.com.

11. Graeber, *Democracy Project*, 107.

12. Colin Moynihan, "80 Arrested as Financial District Protest Moves North," *City Room* (blog), *New York Times*, September 24, 2011; Sarah Maslin Nir, "Video Appears to Show Wall Street Protesters Being Pepper-Sprayed," *City Room* (blog), *New York Times*, September 25, 2011, www.nytimes.com; Al Baker and Joseph Goldstein, "Officer's Pepper Spraying of Protesters Is Under Investigation," *City Room* (blog), *New York Times*, September 28, 2011, www.nytimes.com; Al Baker, Colin Moynihan, and Sarah Maslin Nir, "Police Arrest More than 700 Protesters on Brooklyn Bridge," *City Room* (blog), *New York Times*, October 1, 2011, www.nytimes.com. The many books and collections already emerging about OWS include Chomsky, *Occupy*; Writers for the 99%, *Occupying Wall Street*; Khatib, Killjoy, and McGuire, *We Are Many*; Blumenkranz et al., *Occupy!*; Gitlin, *Occupy Nation*.

13. Brian Chilson, "Occupy Little Rock Marches This Morning," *Little Rock Arkansas Times*, October 16, 2011; "Wall Street Protesters Rally in Phoenix, Tucson," Associated Press, October 16, 2011; "Thousands of Occupy Seattle Protesters March to Pike Place Market," KCPQ/KMYQ-TV, October 15, 2011; Nick Allen, "Occupy Wall Street: Over 80 Arrests as Protests Intensify," *Telegraph* (London), October 16, 2011; Andria Borba, "Cindy Sheehan Speaks to, Stands with Occupy Sacramento," KTXL-TV, October 16, 2011.

14. Jim Winter, "Protesters Occupy Dubuque," *Dubuque (IA) Telegraph Herald*, October 16, 2011; "Iowa Protesters Report Being Assaulted at Park," Associated Press, October 16, 2011; Curtis Krueger and Shelley Rossetter, "Occupy Fever Spreads in Bay," *St. Petersburg Times*, October 16, 2011; Chris Graham, "Nearly 200 Speak Out in Daytona Beach Rally," *Daytona Beach News-Journal*, October 16, 2011; Russell Contreras, "'Occupy' Movement Growing in NM Towns, Cities," Associated Press, October 16, 2011; Patti Welander, "Anti–Wall St. Group Protests at Parade," *Bloomington (IL) Pantagraph*, October 16, 2011; Elena Ferrarin, "Occupy Wall Street Protests Mirrored in Elgin, Aurora," *Chicago Daily Herald*, October 16, 2011; Justin Glawe, "Occupy Peoria Just Getting Going with First

Rally," *Peoria Journal Star*, October 15, 2011; "'Occupy Wall Street' Protests Spread to London, Berlin, and South America: Protests against Corporate Greed and Cutbacks Have Sprung Up across Europe and South American Inspired by the 'Occupy Wall Street' Movement in New York," *Telegraph* (London), October 16, 2011; "Protests Go Global, with Some Violence," *Spokane Spokesman Review*, October 16, 2011.

15. Kristin J. Bender, "Oakland Police Investigation into Scott Olsen Injury Still Ongoing," *Contra Costa Times*, November 28, 2011; Matt Krupnick, Scott Johnson, Sean Maher, and Thomas Peele, "Occupy Oakland: Officials Shift into Damage Control," *San Jose Mercury News*, October 27, 2011; Kristin J. Bender, Sean Maher, and Cecily Burt, "Dozens of Arrests at Occupy Oakland," *Contra Costa Times*, November 2, 2011; Julia Prodis Sulek, Cecily Burt, and Kristin Bender, "Mostly Peaceful Occupy Oakland March Shuts Down Port and Banks," *Contra Costa Times*, November 2, 2011; Terence Chea and Lisa Leff, "Workers, Students Join Occupy Rally in Oakland," Associated Press, November 2, 2011; Robert Mackey, "57 Seconds of Video from Oakland Shows the Power of Citizen Journalism," *The Lede* (blog), *New York Times*, November 10, 2011, www.nytimes.com.

16. "Gingrich Takes GOP Lead, Takes on 'Occupy,'" *Tell Me More*, National Public Radio, November 21, 2011, www.npr.org; "UC Davis Pepper Spray: Bill O'Reilly and Megyn Kelly Defend Police, Say Pepper Spray Makes Protesters Less Confrontational," *International Business Times News*, November 22, 2011.

17. "Here's That Occupy Portland Pepper Spray Photo That Everybody's Talking About," *Business Insider*, November 19, 2011; Chris Grygiel, "Elderly Woman Hit by Spray at Protest: I'm 'Tough,'" Associated Press, November 16, 2011; Mark Trumbull, "UC Davis Pepper Spray, Smear Tactics," *Christian Science Monitor*, November 19, 2001; "Occupy Wall Street, UC Davis: Campus Police Lt. Pepper Sprays Sitting Protesters," *International Business Times News*, November 19, 2011; Brad Knickerbocker, "UC Davis Pepper Spray Incident Goes Viral," *Christian Science Monitor*, November 20, 2011, www.csmonitor.com; Charles Cooper, "Pepper Spray and Its (Painful) Discontents," CBS News, November 23, 2011, www.cbsnews.com.

18. James Pinkerton, "No Clarity on Why Tent Was Used to Cover Arrests of Occupy Activists," *Houston Chronicle*, December 13, 2011; Lucy Madison, "Fact-Checking Romney's '47 Percent' Comment," CBS News, September 25, 2012, www.cbsnews.com. For more on OWS offshoots, see Jobin-Leeds and AgitArte, *When We Fight, We Win!*, 105–117; and Jaffe, *Necessary Trouble*.

19. Judith Scherr, "US: Occupy Group Plans Take-Over of Bank Foreclosures," Inter Press Service, December 7, 2011; Chris Moody, "How Republicans Are Being Taught to Talk about Occupy Wall Street," Yahoo! News, December 1, 2011, www.news.yahoo.com; Wolff, *Capitalism's Crisis Deepens*, 232.

20. Alter, "It Felt Like Community," 11–25; Uetricht, *Strike for America*; Associated Press, "New Mexico High School Students Walk Out in Protest of New Standardized Tests," *Guardian* (Manchester), March 2, 2015, www.theguardian.com; Brett Abrams,

"Wednesday: Funeral Marches in SF and LA Mark the 5th Anniversary of Citizens United Supreme Court Decision," Courage Campaign, January 21, 2015, www.couragecampaign.org; Jim Klein, "6th Annual Funeral for Democracy," Nueces County Democratic Party, January 18, 2016, www.nuecesdemocrats.org.

21. Barry Yeoman, "The Shale Rebellion," *American Prospect*, December 11, 2013, www.prospect.org; Jesse McKinley, "Fracking Fight Focuses on New York Town's Ban," *New York Times*, October 23, 2013, www.nytimes.com; Heather McClain, "Discussing Municipal Bans on Fracking," WESA Pittsburgh, National Public Radio, September 24, 2013, www.wesa.fm; Emily Mathis, "Fracking Emission Carcinogens Found in Denton Playgrounds," *Dallas Observer*, October 1, 2014; Wade Goodwyn, "New Texas Law Makes Local Fracking Bans Illegal," *Morning Edition*, National Public Radio, May 20, 2015, www.npr.org.

22. Josh Israel, "Supporters of Keystone XL Outspend Opponents 35 to 1," *Think Progress*, February 20, 2013, www.thinkprogress.org; "Not Just the Koch Brothers: New Drexel Study Reveals Funders behind the Climate Change Denial Effort," *Drexel Now* (Drexel University), December 20, 2013, www.drexel.edu; Shannon Hall, "Exxon Knew about Climate Change Almost 40 Years Ago," *Scientific American*, October 26, 2015, www.scientificamerican.com; Justin Gillis, "2015 Was Hottest Year in Historical Record, Scientists Say," *New York Times*, January 20, 2016, www.nytimes.com; Eric Holthaus, "Researchers: Exxon, Koch Family Have Powered the Climate-Denial Machine for Decades," *Slate*, December 1, 2015, www.slate.com; Mayer, *Dark Money*, 204–205.

23. Black et al., *Line in the Tar Sands*; Wen Stephenson, "The Grassroots Battle against Big Oil," *Nation*, October 8, 2013, www.thenation.com; Camila Domonoske, "Federal Judge Strikes Down Obama Administration's Fracking Rules," *The Two-Way*, National Public Radio, June 22, 2016, www.npr.org. See also Klein, *This Changes Everything*.

24. US Department of Justice, "Matthew Shepard and James Byrd, Jr., Hate Crimes Prevention Act of 2009," www.justice.gov; Elisabeth Bumiller, "Obama Ends 'Don't Ask, Don't Tell' Policy," *New York Times*, July 22, 2011, www.nytimes.com; Charlie Savage and Sheryl Gay Stolberg, "In Shift, US Says Marriage Act Blocks Gay Rights," *New York Times*, February 23, 2011, www.nytimes.com; Gautam Raghavan, "Obama Administration Statements on the Supreme Court's DOMA Ruling," WhiteHouse.gov, June 27, 2013; US Department of Justice and US Department of Education, "Dear Colleague Letter on Transgender Students," May 13, 2016, www2.ed.gov.

25. Randal C. Archibold and Abby Goodnough, "California Voters Ban Gay Marriage," *New York Times*, November 5, 2008, www.nytimes.com; Michael K. Lavers, "Virginia Anti-Gay Adoption Law Takes Effect," *Washington Blade*, July 18, 2012, www.washingtonblade.com; Suzannah Gonzales, "Thousands Raise Voices to Protest Proposition 8," *Austin American-Statesman*, November 16, 2008; Thadeus Greenson, "Hundreds in Eureka, Thousands across Nation Protest Proposition 8," *Eureka Times Standard*, November 16, 2008; Ethan Thomas, Aaron

Falk, and Joseph M. Dougherty, "Hundreds of Demonstrators in S.L. Protest Proposition 8," *Salt Lake City Deseret Morning News*, November 16, 2008; "Thousands March in Indiana to Protest Law Seen to Be Targeting Gays," Reuters, March 28, 2015; Tony Cook, Tom LoBianco, and Doug Stanglin, "Indiana Governor Signs Amended 'Religious Freedom' Law," *USA Today*, April 2, 2015, www.usatoday.com.

26. Katie Zezima, "'Not about Bathrooms': Critics Decry North Carolina Law's Lesser-Known Elements," *Washington Post*, Mary 14, 2016, www.washingtonpost.com; Tirdad Derakhshani, "Ringo Starr Joins Springsteen in Canceling NC Concert," *Philadelphia Inquirer*, April 14, 2016.

27. Betsy Bloom, "Officials Criticize Repeal of Pay Law," *La Crosse (WI) Tribune*, April 18, 2012; Rick Unger, "Wisconsin GOP Leader Proposes Legislation to Blame Single Parents for Child Abuse and Neglect," *Forbes*, March 2, 2012, www.forbes.com; Gregory J. Krieg and Chris Good, "Mourdock Rape Comment Puts GOP on Defense," ABC News, October 24, 2012, www.abcnews.com; Piers Morgan, "Interview with Ron Paul," *Piers Morgan Tonight*, CNN, February 3, 2012, www.cnn.com; Patrick Marley, "Rep. Roger Rivard Criticized for 'Some Girls Rape Easy' Remark," *Milwaukee Journal Sentinel*, October 10, 2012, www.jsonline.com; Molly Redden, "The War on Women Is Over—And Women Lost," *Mother Jones*, September–October 2015, www.motherjones.com; Leah Jessen, "A 10th State Defunded Planned Parenthood: Why There's So Much Momentum Now," *Daily Signal* (Heritage Foundation), February 23, 2016, www.dailysignal.com.

28. "Statehouse Rally Draws 200 Women," *Topeka Capital-Journal*, April 29, 2012; Juliana Keeping, "Demonstrators Rally for Women's Rights," *Oklahoma City Daily Oklahoman*, April 29, 2012; Brian Steltzer, "Limbaugh Advertisers Flee Show amid Storm," *New York Times*, March 4, 2012, www.nytimes.com; Huma Khan, "Top Susan G. Komen Official Resigns after Planned Parenthood Flap," ABC News, February 7, 2012, www.abnews.com; Andrew Rosenthal, "Rush Limbaugh Is Really Sorry That He Had to Apologize," *Taking Note* (blog), *New York Times*, March 5, 2012, www.nytimes.com; Lynn Arditi, "Warwick; Dozens Protest outside Hobby Lobby," *Providence Journal*, July 6, 2014.

29. Michael D. Shear, "With Document, Obama Seeks to End 'Birther' Issue," *New York Times*, April 27, 2011, www.nytimes.com; Paul Vitello, "Islamic Center Exposes Mixed Feelings Locally," *New York Times*, August 19, 2010, www.nytimes.com; "Muslim Sues Oklahoma over Anti-Shariah Ballot Measure," Fox News, November 4, 2010, www.foxnews.com. For more on the attacks on Muslims that followed the Republican "Ground Zero Mosque" campaign, see Stephanie Rice, "Mosque Furor, Quran Burning: Anti-Islamic Fervor Mobilizes US Muslims," *Christian Science Monitor*, September 10, 2010, www.csmonitor.com.

30. "Students across S. Fla. Walkout for Justice in Trayvon Martin Case," CBS Miami, March 23, 2012, http://miami.cbslocal.com; Rene Stutzman, "O'Mara: We've Spent $300,000 on George Zimmerman and Are Desperate for More Donations," *Orlando Sentinel*, January 30, 2013.

31. "Trouble Erupts after Jury Decision," *Belfast Telegraph Online*, November 25, 2014; Lauren Gambino and Rory Carroll, "Thousands Hit Streets across Nation to Protest against Missouri Grand Jury Decision," *Guardian* (Manchester), November 25, 2014; Natalie Neysa Alund, "Ferguson Protest: 92 Arrests in Oakland during Second Night of Looting Vandalism," *San Jose Mercury News*, November 26, 2014; Julia Terruso, Vernon Clark, and Maria Panaritis, "Ferguson Protests Continue in Philly: 2 Released from Custody," *Philadelphia Inquirer*, November 26, 2014; Philip Jankowski, "Hundreds Protest outside Austin Police HQ," *Austin American-Statesman*, November 26, 2014; Jason Henry, "Third Day of Ferguson Protests in Los Angeles Comes after Nearly 200 Were Arrested," *Whittier (CA) Daily News*, November 26, 2014; "NFL Ferguson Protest," *Morgantown (WV) Dominion Post*, December 2, 2014; Vernon Clark, "Penn Law Students Stage Quick, Quiet Ferguson Protest," *Philadelphia Inquirer*, December 3, 2014; Jesse Paul and Tom McGhee, "Hundreds Walk Out of Four Denver Schools in Ferguson Protest," *Denver Post*, December 4, 2014; J. David Goodman and Al Baker, "Fury after New York Jury Clears Officer: Chanting 'I Can't Breathe,' Protesters Assail Ruling over Chokehold Death," *New York Times*, December 5, 2014; Gavin Aronsen, "Student Groups Plan Ferguson Protests," *Ames (IA) Tribune*, December 9, 2014.
32. Taylor, *From #BlackLivesMatter to Black Liberation*; Mark Berman and Wesley Lowery, "The 12 Key Highlights from the DOJ's Scathing Ferguson Report," *Washington Post*, March 4, 2015, www.washingtonpost.com; Monica Davey and Mitch Smith, "Chicago Police Department Plagued by Systematic Racism, Task Force Finds," *New York Times*, April 13, 2016; Dana Farrington, "In Louisiana, It's Now a Hate Crime to Target Police Officers," *The Two-Way*, National Public Radio, May 26, 2016, www.npr.org.
33. Laura Sullivan, "Prison Economics Help Drive Ariz. Immigration Law," *Morning Edition*, National Public Radio, October 28, 2010, www.npr.org.
34. Julia Preson, "Fueled by Anger over Arizona Law, Immigration Advocates Rally for Change," *New York Times*, May 2, 2010, A22; Associated Press, "About 40 Protesters Outside Wrigley," ESPN, April 29, 2010, www.espn.com; Mark Sherman, "Supreme Court Issues Ruling on SB 1070," Associated Press, June 25, 2012; American Immigration Council Legal Action Center, "*Friendly House v. Whiting* Amicus Briefs," accessed September 5, 2013, www.legalactioncenter.org; Greg Asbed and Sean Sellers, "The High Cost of Anti-Immigrant Laws," *Nation*, October 12, 2011, www.thenation.com. See also Jobin-Leeds and AgitArte, *When We Fight, We Win!*, 77–99; *Precious Knowledge*; Santa Ana and González de Bustamante, *Arizona Firestorm*.
35. Julia Preston, "Young Immigrants Protest Deportations," *New York Times*, August 23, 2013, www.nytimes.com; "Seven Arrested at White House Protesting Deportations," *New Zealand Herald* (Auckland), September 19, 2013; Joe Heim, "Immigration Activists Protest Deportation Plan with March," *Washington Post*, December 31, 2015, www.washingtonpost.com.

36. Initially named for the proposed Development, Relief, and Education for Alien Minors (DREAM) Act, the label "DREAMers" has since been applied rather loosely to the youth wing of the immigrant rights movement. Julia Preston and John H. Cushman Jr., "Obama to Permit Young Migrants to Remain in the US," *New York Times*, June 15, 2012, www.nytimes.com; Nicholls, *DREAMers*.

37. Corey Dade, "Obama Administration Deported Record 1.5 Million People," National Public Radio, December 24, 2012, www.npr.org; Stephen Dinan, "House Rebukes Obama, Challenges Deportation Policy, *Washington Times*, June 6, 2013; Seth Freed Wessler, "Nearly 205K Deportations of Parents of US Citizens in Just Over Two Years," *Colorlines*, December 17, 2012, www.colorlines.com; Associated Press, "Bodies Pile Up in Texas as Immigrants Adopt New Routes over Border," *New York Times*, September 22, 2013; Associated Press, "Obama Signs 3 Free Trade Deals," CBS News, October 21, 2011, www.cbsnews.com; Doug Palmer, "Some Secrecy Needed in Trade Talks: Ron Kirk," Reuters, May 13, 2012; Darrell Issa, "Issa Releases the Trans Pacific Partnership Intellectual Property Rights Chapter on KeeptheWebOpen.com," Darrell Issa's US House webpage, May 15, 2012, www.issa.house.gov; Zach Carter, "Obama Trade Document Leaked, Revealing New Corporate Powers and Broken Campaign Promises," *Huffington Post*, June 13, 2012, www.huffingtonpost.com; Lori Wallach and Ben Beachy, "Obama's Covert Trade Deal," *New York Times*, June 2, 2013, www.nytimes.com.

38. Barack Obama, "Executive Order 13491—Ensuring Lawful Interrogations," WhiteHouse.gov, January 22, 2009; Mark Hosenball, "Exclusive: Senate Probe Finds Little Evidence of Effective 'Torture,'" Reuters, April 27, 2012; Joshua Partlow and Julia Tate, "US Had Advance Warning of Abuse at Afghan Prisons, Officials Say," *Washington Post*, October 30, 2011, www.washingtonpost.com; Glenn Greenwald, "About that Iraq Withdrawal," *Salon*, October 21, 2011, www.salon.com; Deputy Assistant Secretary of Defense (Program Support), "Contractor Support of US Operations in the USCENTCOM Area of Responsibility," Office of the Under Secretary of Defense for Acquisition, Technology and Linguistics, January 2016, www.acq.osd.mil.

39. Sheryl Gay Stolberg and Helene Cooper, "Obama Adds Troops, but Maps Exit Plan," *New York Times*, December 1, 2009, www.nytimes.com; Thom Shanker, "Obama Sends Armed Drones to Help NATO in Libya War," *New York Times*, April 21, 2011, www.nytimes.com; David S. Cloud and Raja Abdulrahim, "Update: US Training Syrian Rebels; White House 'Stepped Up Assistance,'" *Los Angeles Times*, June 21, 2013, www.latimes.com; Andrew Buncombe and Issam Ahmed, "Protests Grow as Civilian Toll of Obama's Drone War on Terrorism Is Laid Bare," *Independent* (London), March 3, 2012, www.independent.co.uk; CNN Wire Staff, "Drone Strikes Kill, Maim, and Traumatize Too Many Civilians, US Study Says," CNN, September 25, 2012, www.cnn.com; Karen DeYoung and Greg Jaffe, "US 'Secret War' Expands Globally as Special Operations Forces Take Larger Role," *Washington Post*, June 4, 2010, www.washingtonpost.com; Scahill, *Dirty Wars*.

40. "Chicago Braces for Final Day of Anti-NATO Protests as Demonstrators March on Boeing HQ," Associated Press, Mary 21, 2012; Mary Wisniewski, "Veterans Symbolically Discard Service Medals at Anti-NATO Rally," Reuters, May 20, 2012, www.reuters.com; Charlie Savage, "Amid Hunger Strike, Obama Renews Push to Close Cuba Prison," *New York Times*, April 30, 2013, www.nytimes.com; "Medea Benjamin v. President Obama: Code Pink Founder Disrupts Speech, Criticizing Drone, Gitmo Policy," *Democracy Now!*, May 24, 2013, www.democracynow.org. See also Benjamin, *Drone Warfare*.

41. D. B. Grady, "Today Is Bradley Manning's 1,000th Day without a Trial," *Atlantic*, February 23, 2013, www.theatlantic.com; Greg Mitchell, "Many in Media Claim Bradley Manning's Leaks Had Little Value—Here's Why They're So Wrong," *Nation*, June 13, 2013, www.thenation.com; Ed Pilkington, "Bradley Manning's Treatment Was Cruel and Inhuman, UN Torture Chief Rules," *Guardian* (Manchester), March 12, 2012, www.guardian.co.uk; Charlie Savage, "Chelsea Manning to Be Released Early as Obama Commutes Sentence," *New York Times*, January 17, 2017, www.nytimes.com.

42. Scott Shane, "Leak Offers Look at Efforts by US to Spy on Israel," *New York Times*, September 5, 2011, www.nytimes.com; Mark Benjamin, "WikiLeakers and Whistleblowers: Obama's Hard Line," *Time*, March 11, 2011, www.time.com. Nick Pinto, "Jeremy Hammond Pleads Guilty in Stratfor Hack, Could Serve Ten Years in Prison," *Village Voice*, May 28, 2013, www.villagevoice.com; Associated Press, "Stratfor Hacker Faces 10 Years in Jail after Pleading Guilty," *Guardian* (Manchester), May 28, 2013, www.theguardian.com; Paul J. Weber and Raphael Satter, "WikiLeaks Publishes Leaked Stratfor Emails, Casting Light on Workings of Private US Intel Firm," Associated Press, February 28, 2012.

43. Barton Gellman and Laura Poitras, "US, British Intelligence Mining Data from Nine US Internet Companies in Broad Secret Program," *Washington Post*, June 7, 2013, www.washingtonpost.com.

44. Mark Sherman, "Gov't Obtains Wide AP Phone Records in Probe," Associated Press, May 13, 2013, www.ap.org; Ann E. Marimow, "A Rare Peek into a Justice Department Leak Probe," *Washington Post*, May 19, 2013, www.washingtonpost.com; "NSA Slides Explain the PRISM Data-Collection Program," *Washington Post*, June 6, 2013, www.washingtonpost.com; Greg Miller and Ellen Nakashima, "NSA Fact Sheet on Surveillance Program Pulled from Web after Senators' Criticism," *Washington Post*, June 25, 2013, www.washingtonpost.com; Robert O'Harrow Jr. and Ellen Nakashima, "President's Surveillance Program Worked with Private Sector to Collect Data after Sept. 11, 2001," *Washington Post*, June 27, 2013, www.washingtonpost.com; Peter Finn and Sari Horwitz, "US Charges Snowden with Espionage," *Washington Post*, June 21, 2013, www.washingtonpost.com; James Ball, "How Obama Took On Six Major Areas of Concern about NSA Surveillance," *Guardian* (Manchester), January 17, 2014, www.theguardian.com.

45. Dan Eggen and Steven Mufson, "Bush Rescinds Fathers' Offshore Ban," *Washington Post*, July 15, 2008, www.washingtonpost.com; Juliet Eilperin, "US

Exempted BP's Gulf of Mexico Drilling from Environmental Impact Study,"
Washington Post, May 5, 2010, www.washingtonpost.com; US Coast Guard, "On
Scene Coordinator Report: *Deepwater Horizon* Oil Spill, Submitted to the
National Response Team," September 2011, 33, www.uscg.mil; Associated Press,
"Rand Paul: Obama BP Criticism 'Un-American,'" NBC News, May 21, 2010,
www.nbcnews.com; NPR Staff, "White House Lifts Ban on Offshore Drilling,"
National Public Radio, October 12, 2010, www.npr.org; Alexander, *New Jim Crow*,
59; Thompson, "Why Mass Incarceration Matters."

46. Julia Lurie, "30 Percent of California's Forest Firefighters Are Prisoners," *Mother
Jones*, August 14, 2015, www.motherjones.com; Justin Gillis, "California Drought
Is Made Worse by Global Warming, Scientists Say," *New York Times*, August 20,
2015, www.nytimes.com. Naomi Klein has highlighted this connection in public
appearances.

47. While contracts for military equipment initially produce enormous profits for
manufacturers, those weapons are also inevitably aimed at civilians, both in
foreign countries and in the US. To give some sense of the scale of police
militarization, between January 1997 and October 1999, the US government
"handled 3.4 million orders of Pentagon equipment from over eleven thousand
domestic police agencies in all fifty states," including airplanes, Blackhawk
helicopters, M-16 rifles, night-vision goggles, and grenade launchers. Alexander,
New Jim Crow, 73.

EPILOGUE

1. Eli Rosenberg, "Protest Grows 'Out of Nowhere' at Kennedy Airport after Iraqis
Are Detained," *New York Times*, January 28, 2017, www.nytimes.com; James
Doubek, "Thousands Protest at Airports Nationwide against Trump's
Immigration Order," NPR News, January 29, 2017, www.npr.org; "Protests Erupt at
US Airports as Trump Order Targeting Refugees & Muslim Immigrants Takes
Effect," *Democracy Now!*, January 28, 2017, www.democracynow.org.

2. Julia Edwards Ainsley, "Trump Border 'Wall' to Cost $21.6 Billion, Take 3.5 Years
to Build: Internal Report," Reuters, February 9, 2017, www.reuters.com; Jeremy W.
Peters, Jo Becker, and Julie Hirschfeld Davis, "Trump Rescinds Rules on
Bathrooms for Transgender Students," *New York Times*, February 22, 2017.

3. Southern Poverty Law Center, "Hate Watch: Post-election Bias Incidence Up to
1,372," February 10, 2017, www.splcenter.org; A. C. Thompson and Ken
Schwencke, "In an Angry and Fearful Nation, an Outbreak of Anti-Semitism,"
ProPublica, March 8, 2017, www.propublica.org; Holly Yan and Mayra Cuevas,
"Spate of Mosque Fires Stretches across the Country," CNN, March 2, 2017, www.
cnn.com; "Four Atlanta-Area Mosques Receive Death Threats," KTLA 5, March 6,
2017, www.ktla.com; Mark Berman, "FBI Investigating Shooting of Two Indian
Men in Kansas as a Hate Crime," *Washington Post*, February 28, 2017, www.
washingtonpost.com; Mary Emily O'Hara, "Wave of Vandalism, Violence Hits
LGBTQ Centers across Nation," NBC News, March 13, 2017, www.nbcnews.com.

4. Andrew Higgins, "Trump Embraces 'Enemy of the People,' a Phrase with a Fraught History," *New York Times*, February 26, 2017, www.nytimes.com; David Jackson, "Trump Again Calls Media 'Enemy of the People,'" *USA Today*, February 24, 2017, www.usatoday.com.

5. Krishnadev Calamur, "A Short History of 'America First,'" *Atlantic*, January 21, 2017, www.theatlantic.com.

6. Additional Reagan ties included Trump's selection of Neil Gorsuch, son of Reagan appointee Anne Gorsuch, for the US Supreme Court and early campaign endorsements from Phyllis Schlafly and Jerry Falwell Jr. Bannon is quoted in Max Fisher, "Stephen K. Bannon's CPAC Comments, Annotated and Explained," *New York Times*, February 24, 2017, www.nytimes.com. For more on the Devos family's long history of political financing, see Mayer, *Dark Money*, 230–237.

7. Michael D. Shear and Jennifer Steinhauer, "Trump to Seek $54 Billion Increase in Military Spending," *New York Times*, February 27, 2017, www.nytimes.com; Lee Fang, "Koch Brothers' Operatives Fill Top White House Positions, Ethics Forms Reveal," *Intercept*, April 4, 2017, www.theintercept.com.

8. Steve Mufson, "Trump Wants to Scrap Two Regulations for Each New One Adopted," *New York Times*, January 30, 2017, www.nytimes.com; Ben Protess and Julie Hirschfeld Davis, "Trump Moves to Roll Back Obama-Era Financial Regulations," *New York Times*, February 3, 2017, www.nytimes.com; Eric Lipton and Binyamin Appelbaum, "Leashes Come Off Wall Street, Gun Sellers, Polluters, and More," *New York Times*, March 5, 2017, www.nytimes.com; Derek Thompson, "The GOP's Plan Is Basically a $600 Billion Tax Cut for Rich Americans," *Atlantic*, March 7, 2017, www.theatlantic.com; Jesse Drucker, "Wealthy Would Get Billions in Tax Cuts under Obamacare Repeal Plan," *New York Times*, March 10, 2017, www.nytimes.com.

9. Barb Darro, "Turns Out Attendance at Women's March Events Was Bigger than Estimated," *Fortune*, January 23, 2017, www.fortune.com; Kaveh Waddell, "The Exhausting Work of Tallying America's Largest Protest," *Atlantic*, January 23, 2017, www.theatlantic.com.

10. Liam Stack, "Yemenis Close Bodegas and Rally to Protest Trump's Ban," *New York Times*, February 2, 2017, www.nytimes.com; Associated Press, "'Day without Immigrants' Protest Closes Restaurants across the US," *Los Angeles Times*, February 16, 2017, www.latimes.com; Doug Stanglin, "Businesses across US Close, Students Skip School on 'Day without Immigrants,'" *USA Today*, February 16, 2017, www.usatoday.com.

11. Doug Criss, "Jews Hand Muslims Keys to Synagogue after Texas Mosque Burns," CNN, February 2, 2017, www.cnn.com; "Muslim Veterans Vow to Protect Jewish Cemeteries amid Anti-Semitic Threats," Fox News, March 2, 2017, www.foxnews.com; Sydney Brownstone, "Seattle Votes to End $3 Billion Relationship with Wells Fargo Because of the Bank's Dakota Access Pipeline Financing," *Stranger*, February 7, 2017, www.thestranger.com; "San Francisco Moves to Divest $1.2B

from Companies Financing Dakota Access Pipeline," CBS SF Bay Area, March 14, 2017.

12. Frances Fox Piven, "Throw Sand in the Gears of Everything," *Nation*, January 18, 2017.

13. Spencer Woodman, "Republican Lawmakers in Five States Propose Bills to Criminalize Peaceful Protest," *Intercept*, January 19, 2017, www.theintercept.com; Christopher Ingraham, "Republican Lawmakers Introduce Bills to Curb Protesting in at Least 18 States," *Washington Post*, February 24, 2017; Traci Yoder, "New Anti-protesting Legislation: A Deeper Look," National Lawyers Guild, March 2, 2017, www.nlg.org.

BIBLIOGRAPHY

Alexander, Michelle. *The New Jim Crow: Mass Incarceration in the Age of Colorblind-ness*. New York: New Press, 2010.

Alter, Tom. "'It Felt like Community': Social Movement Unionism and the Chicago Teachers Union Strike of 2012." *Labor: Studies in Working-Class History of the Americas* 10, no. 3 (2013).

Alvaredo, Facundo, Anthony B. Atkinson, Thomas Piketty, and Emmanuel Saez. "The Top 1% in International and Historical Perspective." *Journal of Economic Perspectives* 27, no. 3 (2013).

American Hardcore. Directed by Steven Blush and Paul Rachmen. Sony Pictures Home Entertainment, 2007.

Amin, Samir. *The World We Wish to See: Revolutionary Objectives in the Twenty-First Century*. New York: Monthly Review Press, 2008.

Andersen, Mark. *All the Power: Revolution without Illusion*. Chicago: Punk Planet Books, 2004.

Andersen, Mark, and Mark Jenkins. *Dance of Days: Two Decades of Punk in the Nation's Capital*. New York: Akashic Books, 2003.

Arnold, Gina. *Kiss This: Punk in the Present Tense*. New York: St. Martin's Griffin, 1997.

Arsenault, Raymond. *Freedom Riders: 1961 and the Struggle for Racial Justice*. New York: Oxford University Press, 2006.

Austin, Joe. *Taking the Train: How Graffiti Art Became an Urban Crisis in New York City*. New York: Columbia University Press, 2001.

Austin, Joe, and Michael Nevin Willard, eds. *Generations of Youth: Youth Cultures and History in Twentieth-Century America*. New York: NYU Press, 1998.

Baer, M. Delal, and Sidney Weintraub, eds. *The NAFTA Debate: Grappling with Unconventional Trade Issues*. Boulder, CO: Lynne Rienner, 1994.

Bagdikian, Ben. *The New Media Monopoly: A Completely Revised and Updated Edition with Seven New Chapters*. Boston: Beacon, 2004.

Baker, C. Edwin. *Media Concentration and Democracy: Why Ownership Matters*. New York: Cambridge University Press, 2007.

Bari, Judi. *Timber Wars*. Monroe, ME: Common Courage, 1994.

Benjamin, Medea. *Drone Warfare: Killing by Remote Control*. London: Verso, 2013.

Benjamin, Medea, and Jodie Evans, eds. *Stop the Next War Now: Effective Responses to Violence and Terrorism*. San Francisco: Inner Ocean, 2005.

Bennett, Andy, and Richard A. Peterson, eds. *Music Scenes: Local, Translocal, and Virtual*. Nashville, TN: Vanderbilt University Press, 2004.

Bennis, Phyllis. *Ending the War in Iraq: A Primer*. Northampton, MA: Olive Branch, 2009.

Best, Steven, and Anthony J. Nocella II, eds. *Igniting a Revolution: Voices in Defense of the Earth*. Oakland, CA: AK Press, 2006.

——, eds. *Terrorists or Freedom Fighters? Reflections on the Liberation of Animals*. New York: Lantern Books, 2004.

Bey, Hakim. *T.A.Z.: The Temporary Autonomous Zone, Ontological Anarchy, Poetic Terrorism*. Brooklyn, NY: Autonomedia, 1991.

Black, Toban, Stephen D'Arcy, Tony Weis, and Joshua Kahn Russell, eds. *A Line in the Tar Sands: Struggles for Environmental Justice*. Oakland, CA: PM Press, 2014.

Blackstock, Nelson. *COINTELPRO: The FBI's Secret War on Political Freedom*. New York: Vintage Books, 1975.

Blum, William. *Killing Hope: US Military and CIA Interventions since World War II*. Monroe, ME: Common Courage, 1995.

Blumenkranz, Carla, Keith Gessen, Mark Greif, Sarah Leonard, Sarah Resnick, Nikil Saval, Eli Schmitt, and Astra Taylor, eds. *Occupy! Scenes from Occupied America*. New York: Verso, 2011.

Body of War. Directed by Ellen Spiro and Phil Donahue. Film Sales Company, 2007.

Boulware, Jack, and Silke Tudor. *Gimme Something Better: The Profound, Progressive, and Occasionally Pointless History of Bay Area Punk from Dead Kennedys to Green Day*. New York: Penguin Books, 2009.

Brecher, Jeremy. *Strike!* Cambridge, MA: South End, 1997.

Breines, Wini. *Community and Organization in the New Left, 1962–1968*. New Brunswick, NJ: Rutgers University Press, 1989.

Bremer, L. Paul. "Coalition Provisional Authority Order Number 12: 'Trade Liberalization Policy.'" Coalition Provisional Authority, June 7, 2003. www.iraqcoalition.org.

Butler, C. T. Lawrence, and Keith McHenry. *Food Not Bombs: How to Feed the Hungry and Build Community*. Tucson, AZ: See Sharp, 2000.

Buzgalin, Aleksandr Vladimirovich. *Russia: Capitalism's Jurassic Park*. Moscow: Economic Democracy, 1999.

Canaday, Margot. "Building a Straight State: Sexuality and Social Citizenship under the 1944 G.I. Bill." *Journal of American History* 90, no. 3 (2003).

Carlsson, Chris, LisaRuth Elliott, and Adriana Camarena, eds. *Shift Happens! Critical Mass at 20*. Oakland, CA: AK Press, 2012.

Carson, Clayborne. *In Struggle: SNCC and the Black Awakening of the 1960s*. Cambridge, MA: Harvard University Press, 1981.

Chatterjee, Pratrap. *Iraq, Inc.* New York: Seven Stories, 2004.

Chomsky, Noam. *Occupy*. Brooklyn, NY: Zuccotti Park, 2012.

Chowla, Peter. "Comparing Corporate and Sovereign Power." *Journal of the Development Studies Institute (DESTIN) Students Society at the London School of Economics* 1, no. 1 (2004–2005).

Churchill, Ward, and Jim Vander Wall. *Agents of Repression: The FBI's Secret Wars against the Black Panther Party and the American Indian Movement*. Boston: South End, 2002.

Cole, David. *Enemy Aliens: Double Standards and Constitutional Freedoms in the War on Terrorism*. New York: New Press, 2005.

Cole, David, and James X. Dempsey. *Terrorism and the Constitution: Sacrificing Civil Liberties in the Name of National Security*. New York: New Press, 2006.

Connolly, William E. "The Evangelical-Capitalist Resonance Machine." *Political Theory* 33, no. 6 (2005).

Conron, Thomas, and Jarice Hanson, eds. *Constructing America's War Culture: Iraq, Media, and Images at Home*. New York: Lexington Books, 2008.

Cornelius, Wayne A. "Death at the Border: Efficacy and Unintended Consequences of US Immigration Control Policy." *Population and Development Review* 27, no. 4 (2001).

Cornell, Saul. *The Other Founders: Anti-Federalism and the Dissenting Tradition in America, 1788–1828*. Chapel Hill: University of North Carolina Press, 1999.

Coulter, Ann H. *Godless: The Church of Liberalism*. New York: Random House, 2006.

Cowie, Jefferson. *The Great Exception: The New Deal and the Limits of American Politics*. Princeton, NJ: Princeton University Press, 2016.

Cowie, Jefferson, and Nick Salvatore. "The Long Exception: Rethinking the Place of the New Deal in American History." *International Labor and Working-Class History* 2008 (74).

Cross, Richard. "'The Hippies Now Wear Black': Crass and the Anarcho-Punk Movement, 1977–1984." *Socialist History* 26 (2004).

Cunningham, David. *There's Something Happening Here: The New Left, the Klan, and FBI Counterintelligence*. Berkeley: University of California Press, 2004.

Daley, David. *Ratf**ked: The True Story behind the Secret Plan to Steal America's Democracy*. New York: Liveright, 2016.

Danaher, Kevin, and Roger Burbach, eds. *Globalize This!* Monroe, ME: Common Courage, 2000.

DeBuys, William. *A Great Aridness: Climate Change and the Future of the American Southwest*. New York: Oxford University Press, 2011.

D'Emilio, John. *Sexual Politics, Sexual Communities: The Making of a Homosexual Minority in the United States, 1940–1970*. Chicago: University of Chicago Press, 1983.

Donnelly, Thomas, Donald Kagan, and Gary Schmitt. *Rebuilding America's Defenses: Strategy, Forces, and Resources*. Washington, DC: Project for the New American Century, 2000.

Don't Need You. Directed by Kerri Koch. Urban Cowgirl, 2005.

Dunbar-Ortiz, Roxanne. *An Indigenous Peoples' History of the United States*. Boston: Beacon, 2014.

Duncombe, Stephen. *Notes from Underground: Zines and the Politics of Alternative Culture*. New York: Verso, 1997.

Dunlap, Riley E. "Polls, Pollution, and Politics Revisited: Public Opinion on the Environment in the Reagan Era." *Environment* 29, no. 6 (1987).

Echols, Alice. *Daring to Be Bad: Radical Feminism in America, 1967–1975*. Minneapolis: University of Minnesota Press, 1989.

Edge, Brian, ed. *924 Gilman: The Story So Far . . .* San Francisco: Maximum RocknRoll, 2004.

Edid, Maralyn. *Farm Labor Organizing: Trends and Prospects.* Ithaca, NY: ILR Press, 1994.

Ehrenreich, Barbara, and Arlie Russell Hochschild, eds. *Global Woman: Nannies, Maids, and Sex Workers in the New Economy.* New York: Henry Holt, 2002.

Elmore, Bartow J. *Citizen Coke: The Making of Coca-Cola Capitalism.* New York: Norton, 2016.

Enron: The Smartest Guys in the Room. Directed by Alex Gibney. Magnolia Pictures, 2005.

Epstein, Barbara. *Political Protest and Cultural Revolution.* Berkeley: University of California Press, 1993.

Estabrook, Barry. *Tomatoland: How Modern Industrial Agriculture Destroyed Our Most Alluring Fruit.* Riverside, NJ: Andrews McMeel, 2012.

Evans, Sara. *Personal Politics: The Roots of Women's Liberation in the Civil Rights Movement and the New Left.* New York: Vintage, 1980.

Evans, Sara M., and Harry C. Boyte. *Free Spaces: The Sources of Democratic Change in America.* Chicago: University of Chicago Press, 1992.

Faludi, Susan. *Backlash: The Undeclared War against American Women.* New York: Crown, 1991.

Farber, David. *The Rise and Fall of Modern American Conservatism: A Short Story.* Princeton, NJ: Princeton University Press, 2010.

Featherstone, Lisa. *Students against Sweatshops.* London: Verso, 2002.

Fine, Janice. *Worker Centers: Organizing Communities at the Edge of the Dream.* Ithaca, NY: ILR Press, 2006.

Finlay, Barbara. *George W. Bush and the War on Women: Turning Back the Clock on Progress.* London: Zed Books, 2006.

Forest for the Trees, The. Directed by Bernardine Mellis. Redbird Films, 2006.

Frank, Thomas. *The Wrecking Crew: How Conservatives Rule.* New York: Metropolitan Books, 2008.

Ganz, Marshall. *Why David Sometimes Wins: Leadership, Organization, and Strategy in the California Farm Worker Movement.* New York: Oxford University Press, 2009.

Gasland. Directed by Josh Fox. New Video Group, 2010.

Ghosts of Abu Ghraib. Directed by Rory Kennedy. HBO Documentary Films, 2007.

Giagnoni, Silvia. *Fields of Resistance: The Struggle of Florida's Farmworkers for Justice.* Chicago: Haymarket Books, 2011.

Gilmore, Glenda Elizabeth. *Defying Dixie: The Radical Roots of Civil Rights, 1919–1950.* New York: Norton, 2009.

Giroux, Henry A. "The Terror of Neoliberalism: Rethinking the Significance of Cultural Politics." *College Literature* 32, no. 1 (2005).

Gitlin, Todd. *Occupy Nation: The Roots, the Spirit, and the Promise of Occupy Wall Street.* New York: It Books, 2012.

Glasmeier, Amy K. *An Atlas of Poverty in America: One Nation, Pulling Apart, 1960–2003.* New York: Routledge, 2006.

Global Assembly Line, The. Directed by Lorraine W. Gray. New Day Films, 1986.

Gonzales, Manuel G., and Richard Delgado. *The Politics of Fear: How Republicans Use Money, Race, and the Media to Win.* London: Paradigm, 2006.

Goodman, Amy. *The Exception to the Rulers.* New York: Hyperion, 2004.

Gordon, Joy. *Invisible War: The United States and the Iraq Sanctions.* Cambridge, MA: Harvard University Press, 2010.

Graeber, David. *The Democracy Project: A History, a Crisis, a Movement.* New York: Spiegel and Grau, 2013.

———. *Direct Action: An Ethnography.* Oakland, CA: AK Press, 2009.

Green, James. *The Devil Is Here in These Hills: West Virginia's Coal Miners and Their Battle for Freedom.* New York: Atlantic Monthly Press, 2015.

Ground Truth, The. Directed by Patricia Foulkrod. Focus Features, 2006.

Haas, Jeffrey. *The Assassination of Fred Hampton: How the FBI and Chicago Police Murdered a Black Panther.* Chicago: Chicago Review Press, 2011.

Hacker, Jacob S., and Paul Pierson. *Winner-Take-All Politics: How Washington Made the Rich Richer—And Turned Its Back on the Middle Class.* New York: Simon and Schuster, 2010.

Hall, Simon. *Rethinking the American Anti-war Movement.* New York: Routledge, 2012.

Hall, Stuart, and Tony Jefferson, eds. *Resistance through Rituals: Youth Cultures in Post-war Britain.* London: Hutchinson University, 1976.

Hardt, Michael, and Antonio Negri. *Empire.* Cambridge, MA: Harvard University Press, 2000.

Hart, Benjamin, ed. *The Third Generation: Young Conservative Leaders Look to the Future.* Washington, DC: Regnery Books, 1987.

Hartung, William D. *Prophets of War: Lockheed Martin and the Making of the Military-Industrial Complex.* New York: Nation Books, 2010.

Harvey, David. *A Brief History of Neoliberalism.* Oxford: Oxford University Press, 2005.

Hawken, Paul. *Blessed Unrest: How the Largest Movement in the World Came into Being and Why No One Saw It Coming.* New York: Viking, 2007.

Hayden, Tom. *The Long Sixties: From 1960 to Barack Obama.* Boulder, CO: Paradigm, 2009.

———. *The Whole World Was Watching: The Streets of Chicago, 1968.* Davis, CA: Panorama West, 1996.

———, ed. *The Zapatista Reader.* New York: Thunder's Mouth, 2002.

Hays, Samuel P. *Beauty, Health, and Permanence.* Cambridge: Cambridge University Press, 1987.

Heatherly, Charles L., ed. *Mandate for Leadership: Policy Management in a Conservative Administration.* Washington, DC: Heritage Foundation, 1981.

Helfrich, Joel T. "A Mountain of Politics: The Struggle for *dzil nchaa si'an* (Mount Graham), 1871–2002." PhD diss., University of Minnesota, 2010.

Hing, Bill Ong. *Ethical Borders: NAFTA, Globalization, and Mexican Migration.* Philadelphia: Temple University Press, 2010.

Hodkinson, Paul, and Wolfgang Deicke, eds. *Youth Cultures: Scenes, Subcultures, and Tribes.* New York: Routledge, 2007.

Hoffman, Abbie. *Soon to Be a Major Motion Picture*. New York: Perigree Books, 1980.

Hogan, Wesley. *Many Minds, One Heart: SNCC's Dream for a New America*. Chapel Hill: University of North Carolina Press, 2007.

Holsti, Ole R. *American Public Opinion on the Iraq War*. Ann Arbor: University of Michigan Press, 2011.

Howell, Marcela, and Marilyn Keefe. *The History of Federal Abstinence-Only Funding*. Washington, DC: Advocates for Youth, 2007.

Hunter, Tera. *To 'Joy My Freedom: Southern Black Women's Lives and Labors after the Civil War*. Cambridge, MA: Harvard University Press, 1997.

Iraq for Sale: The War Profiteers. Directed by Robert Greenwald. Brave New Films, 2006.

Iraq Veterans Against the War and Aaron Glantz. *Winter Soldier Iraq and Afghanistan: Eyewitness Accounts of the Occupations*. Chicago: Haymarket Books, 2008.

Istock, Conrad A., and Robert S. Hoffmann, eds. *Storm over a Mountain Island*. Tucson: University of Arizona Press, 1995.

Jaffe, Sarah. *Necessary Trouble: Americans in Revolt*. New York: Nation Books, 2016.

Jencks, Christopher. *The Homeless*. Cambridge, MA: Harvard University Press, 1994.

Jobin-Leeds, Greg, and AgitArte. *When We Fight, We Win! Twenty-First-Century Social Movements and the Activists That Are Transforming Our World*. New York: New Press, 2016.

Johnson, Chalmers. *Nemesis: The Last Days of the American Republic*. New York: Holt, 2006.

Johnston, David Cay, ed. *Divided: The Perils of Our Growing Inequality*. New York: New Press, 2015.

Johnston, Josée, and Gordon Laxer. "Solidarity in the Age of Globalization: Lessons from the anti-MAI and Zapatista Struggles." *Theory and Society* 32 (2003).

Jones, Alex S. *Losing the News: The Future of the News That Feeds Democracy*. New York: Oxford University Press, 2009.

Jones, William P. *The March on Washington: Jobs, Freedom, and the Forgotten History of Civil Rights*. New York: Norton, 2013.

Juhasz, Antonia. *The Bush Agenda: Invading the World, One Economy at a Time*. New York: Regan Books, 2006.

Kauffman, L. A. *Direct Action: Protest and the Reinvention of American Radicalism*. New York: Verso, 2017.

Keck, Margaret E., and Kathryn Sikkink. *Activists beyond Borders*. Ithaca, NY: Cornell University Press, 1998.

Kelley, Robin D. G. "'We Are Not What We Seem': Rethinking Black Working-Class Opposition in the Jim Crow South." *Journal of American History* 80, no. 1 (1993).

———. *Yo Mama's Disfunktional! Fighting the Culture Wars in Urban America*. Boston: Beacon, 1998.

Kennedy, Robert F., Jr. *Crimes against Nature*. New York: HarperCollins, 2004.

Khasnabish, Alex. *Zapatismo beyond Borders: New Imaginations of Political Possibility*. Toronto: University of Toronto Press, 2008.

Khatib, Kate, Margaret Killjoy, and Mike McGuire, eds. *We Are Many: Critical Reflections on Movement Strategy from Occupation to Liberation*. Oakland, CA: AK Press, 2012.

Klein, Naomi. *No Logo: Taking Aim at the Brand Bullies*. New York: Picador, 1999.

———. *The Shock Doctrine: The Rise of Disaster Capitalism*. New York: Random House, 2008.

———. *This Changes Everything: Capitalism vs. the Climate*. New York: Simon and Schuster, 2014.

Kousser, J. Morgan. *Colorblind Injustice: Minority Voting Rights and the Undoing of the Second Reconstruction*. Chapel Hill: University of North Carolina Press, 1999.

Lash, Jonathan, Katherine Gillman, and David Sheridan. *A Season of Spoils: The Reagan Administration's Attack on the Environment*. New York: Pantheon Books, 1984.

Law, Vicki. *Enter the Nineties: ABC No Rio Poets, Punks, Politics*. Self-published, 2005.

Leblanc, Lauraine. *Pretty in Punk: Girls' Gender Resistance in a Boys' Subculture*. New Brunswick, NJ: Rutgers University Press, 1999.

Life and Debt. Directed by Stephanie Black. New Yorker Films, 2003.

Lipsitz, George. *The Possessive Investment in Whiteness: How White People Profit from Identity Politics*. Philadelphia: Temple University Press, 1998.

Livingston, Jessica. "Murder in Juárez: Gender, Sexual Violence, and the Global Assembly Line." *Frontiers—A Journal of Women's Studies* 25 (January 2004).

Lynd, Staughton, and Michael Ferber. *The Resistance*. Boston: Beacon, 1971.

MacArthur, John R. *The Selling of "Free Trade": NAFTA, Washington, and the Subversion of American Democracy*. New York: Hill and Wang, 2000.

Marable, Manning. *Race, Reform, and Rebellion: The Second Reconstruction in Black America, 1945–1990*. Jackson: University Press of Mississippi, 1991.

Martin, Bradford. *The Other Eighties: A Secret History of America in the Age of Reagan*. New York: Hill and Wang, 2011.

Mayer, Jane. *Dark Money: The Hidden History of the Billionaires behind the Rise of the Right*. New York: Doubleday, 2016.

McCarthy, Timothy Patrick, and John Stauffer, eds. *Prophets of Protest: Reconsidering the History of American Abolitionism*. New York: New Press, 2006.

McGuire, Danielle L. *At the Dark End of the Street: Black Women, Rape, and Resistance—A New History of the Civil Rights Movement from Rosa Parks to the Rise of Black Power*. New York: Vintage, 2011.

McKay, George. *Senseless Acts of Beauty: Cultures of Resistance since the Sixties*. London: Verso, 1996.

McMillen, Neil R. *The Citizens' Council: Organized Resistance to the Second Reconstruction, 1954–1964*. Urbana: University of Illinois Press, 1971.

Meier, Deborah, and George Wood, eds. *Many Children Left Behind: How the No Child Left Behind Act Is Damaging Our Children and Our Schools*. Boston: Beacon, 2004.

Mettler, Suzanne. *Dividing Citizens: Gender and Federalism in New Deal Public Policy*. Ithaca, NY: Cornell University Press, 1998.

Moffitt, Kimberly R., and Duncan A. Campbell, eds. *The 1980s: A Critical and Transitional Decade*. New York: Lexington Books, 2011.

Moghadam, Valentine M., ed. *Democratic Reform and the Position of Women in Transitional Economies*. Oxford, UK: Clarendon, 1993.

Moore, Alan, and Marc Miller, eds. *No Rio Dinero: The Story of a Lower East Side Art Gallery*. New York: ABC No Rio with Collaborative Projects, 1985.

Moore, Ryan. "Friends Don't Let Friends Listen to Corporate Rock: Punk as a Field of Cultural Production." *Journal of Contemporary Ethnography* 36, no. 4 (2007).

Morgan, Edward P. *What Really Happened to the 1960s: How Mass Media Culture Failed American Democracy*. Lawrence: University Press of Kansas, 2010.

Morris, Aldon. *The Origins of the Civil Rights Movement*. New York: Free Press, 1984.

Muñoz, Carlos, Jr. *Youth, Identity, Power: The Chicano Movement*. London: Verso, 1989.

Murolo, Priscilla, and A. B. Chitty. *From the Folks Who Brought You the Weekend: A Short, Illustrated History of Labor in the United States*. New York: New Press, 2003.

Nash, Jere, Andy Taggart, and John Grisham, *Mississippi Politics: The Struggle for Power*. Jackson: University Press of Mississippi, 2009.

Nelson, Jennifer. *Women of Color and the Reproductive Rights Movement*. New York: NYU Press, 2003.

Newton, Huey P. *War against the Panthers: A Study of Repression in America*. New York: Harlem River, 2000.

Nicholls, Walter J. *The DREAMers: How the Undocumented Youth Movement Transformed the Immigrant Rights Debate*. Stanford, CA: Stanford University Press, 2013.

Olmsted, Kathryn S. *Challenging the Secret Government: The Post-Watergate Investigations of the CIA and FBI*. Chapel Hill: University of North Carolina Press, 1996.

Onkst, David. "'First a Negro . . . Incidentally a Veteran': Black World War Two Veterans and the G.I. Bill of Rights in the Deep South, 1944–1948." *Journal of Social History* 31, no. 3 (1998).

Orleck, Annelise. *Rethinking American Women's Activism*. New York: Routledge, 2014.

Oxfam America. *Like Machines in the Field: Workers without Rights in American Agriculture*. Boston: Oxfam America, 2004.

Palmer, Phyllis. "Outside the Law: Agricultural and Domestic Workers under the Fair Labor Standards Act." *Journal of Policy History* 7, no. 4 (1995).

Patterson, Clayton, ed. *Resistance: A Radical Political and Social History of the Lower East Side*. New York: Seven Stories, 2007.

Payne, Charles M. *I've Got the Light of Freedom*. Berkeley: University of California Press, 1995.

Phillips-Fein, Kim. *Invisible Hands: The Making of the Conservative Movement from the New Deal to Reagan*. New York: Norton, 2009.

Piketty, Thomas, and Emmanuel Saez. "Income Inequality in the United States, 1913–1998." *Quarterly Journal of Economics* 118, no. 1 (2003).

Piven, Frances Fox. *Challenging Authority: How Ordinary People Change America*. Lanham, MD: Rowman and Littlefield, 2006.

——. *The War at Home*. New York: New Press, 2004.

Piven, Frances Fox, and Richard Cloward. *Poor People's Movements: Why They Succeed, How They Fail.* New York: Vintage, 1979.

Piven, Frances Fox, Lorraine C. Minnite, and Margaret Groarke. *Keeping Down the Black Vote: Race and the Demobilization of American Voters.* New York: New Press, 2009.

Polletta, Francesca. *Freedom Is an Endless Meeting.* Chicago: University of Chicago Press, 2002.

Portney, Paul R., ed. *Natural Resources and the Environment: The Reagan Approach.* Washington, DC: Urban Institute Press, 1984.

Precious Knowledge. Directed by Ari Luis Palos. Dos Vatos Productions, 2011.

Pring, George William, and Penelope Canan. *SLAPPs: Getting Sued for Speaking Out.* Philadelphia: Temple University Press, 1996.

Profane Existence. *Making Punk a Threat Again: The Best Cuts, 1989–1993.* Minneapolis, MN: Loin Cloth, 1997.

Putnam, Robert. *Bowling Alone: The Collapse and Revival of American Community.* New York: Simon and Schuster, 2001.

Ransby, Barbara. *Ella Baker and the Black Freedom Movement.* Chapel Hill: University of North Carolina Press, 2004.

Raphael, Ray. *A People's History of the American Revolution: How Common People Shaped the Fight for Independence.* New York: New Press, 2001.

Ravitch, Diane. *The Life and Death of the Great American School System.* New York: Basic Books, 2010.

Rose, Tricia. *Black Noise: Rap Music and Black Culture in Contemporary America.* Middletown, CT: Wesleyan University Press, 1994.

Rosen, Ruth. *The World Split Open: How the Modern Women's Movement Changed America.* New York: Viking, 2000.

Rosenow, Michael. *Death and Dying in the Working Class, 1865–1920.* Urbana: University of Illinois Press, 2015.

Rothschild, Joyce P., and J. Allen Whitt. *The Cooperative Workplace: Potentials and Dilemmas of Organizational Democracy and Participation.* Cambridge: Cambridge University Press, 1986.

Sale, Kirkpatrick. *The Green Revolution: The American Environmental Movement, 1962–1992.* New York: Hill and Wang, 1993.

Saloma, John S., III. *Ominous Politics: The New Conservative Labyrinth.* New York: Hill and Wang, 1984.

Santa Ana, Otto, and Celeste González de Bustamante, eds. *Arizona Firestorm: Global Immigration Realities, National Media, and Provincial Politics.* New York: Rowman and Littlefield, 2012.

Scahill, Jeremy. *Blackwater: The Rise of the World's Most Powerful Mercenary Army.* New York: Nation Books, 2008.

———. *Dirty Wars: The World Is a Battlefield.* New York: Nation Books, 2013.

Scarce, Rik. *Eco-Warriors: Understanding the Radical Environmental Movement.* Walnut Creek, CA: Left Coast, 1990.

Schwartz, Joseph M. "Democracy against the Free Market: The Enron Crisis and the Politics of Global Deregulation." *Connecticut Law Review* 35, no. 3 (2003).

Scott, James C. *Weapons of the Weak: Everyday Forms of Peasant Resistance.* New Haven, CT: Yale University Press, 1987.

Shepard, Benjamin, and Ronald Hayduk, eds. *From ACT UP to the WTO: Urban Protest and Community Building in the Era of Globalization.* New York: Verso, 2012.

Shoemaker, Rebecca S. *The White Court.* Santa Barbara, CA: ABC-CLIO, 2004.

69. Directed by Nikolaj Viborg. Hybrid Films, 2008.

Smith, Christian. *Resisting Reagan: The US Central America Peace Movement.* Chicago: University of Chicago Press, 1996.

Smith, Paul Chaat, and Robert Allen Warrior. *Like a Hurricane: The Indian Movement from Alcatraz to Wounded Knee.* New York: New Press, 1996.

Smith, W. Leon, and the staff of the *Lone Star Iconoclast.* *The Vigil: 26 Days in Crawford, Texas.* New York: Disinformation, 2005.

Solnit, David, ed. *Globalize Liberation: How to Uproot the System and Build a Better World.* San Francisco: City Lights Books, 2004.

Solnit, Rebecca. *Hope in the Dark: Untold Histories, Wild Possibilities.* Chicago: Haymarket Books, 2016.

Starhawk. *Webs of Power.* Gabriola Island, BC: New Society, 2002.

Stewart, James Brewer. *Holy Warriors: The Abolitionists and American Slavery.* New York: Hill and Wang, 1976.

Stewart, Shannon. *In Every Town: An All-Ages Music Manualfesto.* Seattle: All-Ages Movement Project, 2010.

Stiglitz, Joseph E. *Globalization and Its Discontents.* New York: Norton, 2002.

———. *The Price of Inequality.* New York: Norton, 2012.

Street, Paul, and Anthony DiMaggio. *Crashing the Tea Party: Mass Media and the Campaign to Remake American Politics.* Boulder, CO: Paradigm, 2011.

Students for a Democratic Society. *Port Huron Statement.* New York: Students for a Democratic Society, 1962.

Sugrue, Thomas. *Sweet Land of Liberty: The Forgotten Struggle for Civil Rights in the North.* New York: Random House, 2008.

Sullivan, Patricia. *Lift Every Voice: The NAACP and the Making of the Civil Rights Movement.* New York: New Press, 2009.

Swerdlow, Amy. *Women Strike for Peace: Traditional Motherhood and Radical Politics in the 1960s.* Chicago: University of Chicago Press, 1993.

Tanielian, Terri, and Lisa H. Jaycox, eds. *Invisible Wounds of War: Psychological and Cognitive Injuries, Their Consequences, and Services to Assist Recovery.* Santa Monica, CA: RAND, 2008.

Taylor, Keeanga-Yamahtta. *From #BlackLivesMatter to Black Liberation.* Chicago: Haymarket Books, 2006.

Thompson, Heather Ann. "Why Mass Incarceration Matters: Rethinking Crisis, Decline, and Transformation in Postwar American History." *Journal of American History* 97, no. 3 (2010).

Tillman Story, The. Directed by Amir Bar-Lev. Passion Pictures, 2010.

Uetricht, Micah. *Strike for America: Chicago Teachers against Austerity.* New York: Verso, 2014.

US Department of Homeland Security. "2004 Budget in Brief." Accessed July 3, 2012, www.dhs.gov.

Vellela, Tony. *New Voices: Student Activism in the '80s and '90s.* Boston: South End, 1988.

Vogel, S. K. *Freer Markets, More Rules: Regulatory Reform in Advanced Countries.* Ithaca, NY: Cornell University Press, 1996.

Von Bertrab, Hermann. *Negotiating NAFTA: A Mexican Envoy's Account.* Westport, CT: Praeger, 1997.

Wacquant, Loïc. "Three Steps to a Historical Anthropology of Actually Existing Neoliberalism," *Social Anthropology* 20, no. 1 (2012).

Wallach, Lori, and Michelle Sforza. *Whose Trade Organization? Corporate Globalization and the Erosion of Democracy.* Washington, DC: Public Citizen, 1999.

Warshall, Peter. "The Biopolitics of the Mt. Graham Red Squirrel (Tamiasciuris hudsonicus grahamensis)." *Conservation Biology* 8, no. 4 (1994).

West, William F. "The Institutionalization of Regulatory Review: Organizational Stability and Responsive Competence at OIRA." *Presidential Studies Quarterly* 35, no.1 (March 2005).

Western, Bruce, and Jake Rosenfeld. "Unions, Norms, and the Rise in US Wage Inequality." *American Sociological Review* 76, no. 4 (2011).

Whittaker, William G. *Child Labor in America: History, Policy, and Legislative Issues.* Washington, DC: Congressional Research Service, 2005.

Wilson, D. Mark, and William Beach. *The Economic Impact of President Bush's Tax Relief Plan.* Washington, DC: Heritage Foundation Center for Data Analysis, 2001.

Winkler, Ernest William, ed. *Journal of the Secession Convention of Texas, 1861.* Austin, TX, 1912.

Wolff, Richard D. *Capitalism's Crisis Deepens.* Chicago: Haymarket Books, 2016.

Wood, Ellen Meiksins. *Empire of Capital.* London: Verso, 2003.

Writers for the 99%. *Occupying Wall Street: The Inside Story of an Action That Changed America.* New York: OR Books, 2012.

Zakin, Susan. *Coyotes and Town Dogs: Earth First! and the Environmental Movement.* Tucson: University of Arizona Press, 1993.

INDEX

ABOUT THE AUTHOR

Dawson Barrett is Assistant Professor of US History at Del Mar College in Corpus Christi, Texas. He is a teacher, recovering punk rocker, and cheerleader for rabble-rousers and troublemakers of all ages. His book *Teenage Rebels: Successful High School Activists from the Little Rock Nine to the Class of Tomorrow* has been featured on a variety of social justice reading lists for young adults.